Henrik Ibsen's Ghosts:
A Dramaturgical Sourcebook

Henrik Ibsen's *Ghosts:*
A Dramaturgical Sourcebook

Edited by Donald Marinelli

Carnegie Mellon University Press
Pittsburgh 1997

Cover: Both works on the cover are from *The Graphic Works of Edvard Munch*, Dover, 1979.
   Front cover: Edvard Munch, *Anxiety*, 1896, Lithograph
   Back cover: Edvard Munch, *Anxiety*, 1896, Woodcut
Every effort has been made to determine ownership of this material. Dover reports " . . . to the best of our knowledge the material is in the public domain."

Text of Henrik Ibsen's *Ghosts* taken from the Smith & Kraus book *Ibsen: Four Major Plays*. Translation copyright (c) 1995 by Rick Davis and Brian Johnston. Reprinted by permission of Smith & Kraus Publishers.

Photograph of Mavourneen Dwyer as Ms. Alving and Dikran Tulaine as Osvald in the Alliance Theatre Company of Atlanta production of *Ghosts* by permission of David Zeiger Photography.

Caricature of Henrik Ibsen receiving Mr. William Archer from the Robert H. Taylor Collection by permission of Princeton University Library.

Fergusson, Francis; *The Idea of a Theater: A Study of Ten Plays, The Art of Drama in Changing Perspective*. Copyright ©1949 by Princeton University Press. Reprinted by permission of Princeton University Press.

"Foreword" by Rolf Fjelde, from *Four Major Plays, Vol. II* by Henrik Ibsen, translated by Rolf Fjelde. Translation copyright (c) 1970 by Rolf Fjelde. Used by permission of Dutton Signet, a division of Penguin Books USA Inc.

Brian Johnston, *The Ibsen Cycle: The Design of Plays from Pillars of Society to When We Dead Awaken*, (University Park: The Pennsylvania State University Press, 1992), 189–236, copyright 1992 by the Pennsylvania State University. Reproduced by permission of the publisher.

Chapter II: Mrs. Alving/*Ghosts*, is from *Lou Salome, Ibsen's Heroines*, edited, translated and with an introduction by Siegfried Mandel, copyright Siegfried Mandel, 1985, published by Black Swan Books, Ltd., Redding Ridge, CT 06876.

Emma Goldman's work is from her book *The Social Significance of Modern Drama*, copyright 1914 by Richard G. Badger and copyright 1987 by Applause Theatre Book Publishers.

Reviews
"An Articulate 'Ghosts'." By Sylvie Drake, March 15, 1993, copyright 1993, *Los Angeles Times*. Reprinted by permission.

"AIT Stages Haunting 'Ghosts'." By Christopher Rawson, June 27, 1985, *The Pittsburgh Post-Gazette*.

"Liv Ullmann Is the Star of 'Ghosts' " by Mel Gussow, August 31, 1982 and "At the Theater" by Brooks Atkinson, February 17, 1948, *The New York Times*. Copyright 1982 by The New York Times Co. Reprinted by Permission.

"A Great Landmark Is Weakly Revived." By Louis Kronenberger, February 18, 1948 *PM Exclusive*.

"At the Theater." By Brooks Atkinson, February 17, 1948, *The New York Times*. Copyright 1948 by The New York Times Co. Reprinted by Permission. Copyright 1948 by The New York Times Co. Reprinted by Permission.

"Outdated Situations Haunt 'Ghosts' Revival." By William Hawkins, February 17, 1948. *New York World-Telegram*.

"Bleak Night at Mrs. Alving's." By Ward Morehouse, February 17, 1948. *The Sun*.

Carnegie Mellon University Press has attempted to obtain, and has specifically received, in most cases permission to use all of the above material. Every effort has been made to ascertain and attribute copyright.

CAUTION: Professionals and amateurs are hereby warned that the Rick Davis/Brian Johnston translation of Henrik Ibsen's *Ghosts* is subject to a royalty. It is fully protected under the copyright laws of the United States of America, and of all countries covered by the International Copyright Union (including the Dominion of Canada and the rest of the British Commonwealth), and of all countries covered by the Pan-American Copyright Convention and the Universal Copyright Convention and of all countries with which the United States has reciprocal copyright relations. All rights, including professional, amateur, motion picture, recitation, lecturing, public reading, radio broadcasting, television, video or sound taping, all other forms of mechanical or electronic reproductions such as information storage and retrieval systems and photocopying, and the rights of translation into foreign languages, are strictly reserved. Particular emphasis is laid upon the question of readings. All permissions must be secured in writing from the author's agent, Helen Merrill, Ltd. 435 West 23rd Street, #1A, New York, NY 10011.

Library of Congress Catalog Number 94-068944
ISBN 0-88748-200-7

Copyright ©1997 by Donald Marinelli
Manufactured in the United States of America
All rights reserved

Contents

Donald Marinelli	*Foreword*	vii
	General Chronology	1
Brian Johnston	*Historical Background*	9
William Archer	*Ghosts*	35
George Bernard Shaw	*The Quintessence of Ibsenism*	43
J. T. Grein	*London Playbill, Friday the 13th, March 1891*	47
Henrik Ibsen	Ghosts: *The Play*	51
William Archer	*Ghosts and Gibberings*	117
Francis Fergusson	Ghosts *and* The Cherry Orchard: *The Theater of Modern Realism*	123
Rolf Fjelde	*Foreword*	135
Brian Johnston	*Archetypal Repetition in* Ghosts	139
Lou Andreas-Salomé	*Ibsen's Heroines*	167
Emma Goldman	*Ghosts*	177
Henrik Ibsen	*Letters*	183
James Joyce	*Selected Letters*	191
James Joyce	*Epilogue to Ibsen's* Ghosts *April 1934*	195

v

George Bernard Shaw	Ghosts *at the Jubilee*	197
	Other Reviews	203
	Contributors	217
	Bibliography	223

Donald Marinelli *Foreword*

The Carnegie Mellon University Dramaturgical Sourcebook series is designed to address the needs of the production dramaturge, as well as the college professor, secondary school teacher, or theatre participant who wants to grasp fully the world from which a distinctive work of dramatic art was born. For dramaturge and teacher alike, the ultimate goal of this scholarly investigation is to understand fully the historical, sociological, and cultural history of a play from a production and/or literary point-of-view.

In detailing further the intent and aspiration of this series, a clarification of the field of dramaturgy and the specific work of the production dramaturge would be helpful. When asked by the theatre newspaper *Backstage* what the role of the theatre dramaturge was, Mark Bly, co-chair of playwriting and dramaturgy and associate artistic director and dramaturge at Yale Rep, gave the following response:

> "The dramaturge is that artist who helps the director to shape the historical, sociological, directing, acting, and designing values of any productions they're working on."[1]

Anne Cataneo, Lincoln Center Theatre dramaturge adds, that the dramaturge is "an informed sounding board on how a play is working."[2]

In providing this extensive compilation of material, including historical timeline, text of the play (here in a dynamic new translation), salient articles, relevant essays, letters and comments from the author, reviews of past productions from the time the play first premiered to the present, the Carnegie Mellon University Dramaturgical Sourcebook series hopefully is saving the dramaturge, teacher, professor, critic, director, designer, actor, and theatre *amateur* (in the purest sense of the word) a great deal of time and energy that would otherwise have been spent (or not spent) searching for the disparate and oftentimes hard to find material contained in this volume. By having all of this valuable information readily available and accessible in one place, we are hoping to allow the theatre practitioner time to weigh the merits and significance of the material gathered and to undertake additional research if so desired and deemed necessary (hence the extensive bibliography included in this book).

The decision to select Henrik Ibsen's *Ghosts* as the second play in the dramaturgical sourcebook series was motivated in large part by the seminal position the play holds in modern theatre history. There is almost universal acknowledgment among scholars and critics alike that *Ghosts* is the 19th-century dramatic equivalent of the cosmic "big bang." *Ghosts* is the play that ignited the shockwave of 'modern' drama; a drama suddenly free to criticize and challenge the social morality (or immorality) of the era.

In fact, the fervent desire and need to stage Henrik Ibsen's *Ghosts* can be considered the inciting incident behind the very creation of serious modern drama. The motivation to perform *Ghosts*, a play that had been denigrated and denounced by the most eminent theatre critics and journalists of the day, was very much behind the founding of the Freie Bühne in Berlin (1889) and the Independent Theatre in London (1891). Andre Antoine's recently inaugurated Théâtre Libre in Paris had performed *Ghosts* in 1891. Sitting in the audience for this production was George Moore. Moore was so overwhelmed by the play that he became a founding member of the Irish Literary Theatre—which later became the Abbey Theatre.

The critic Louis Kronenberger captured the significance of this play as the turning point of nineteenth century drama:

> As the masterly first act begins uncoiling; as Mrs. Alving, having been brutally rebuked by Pastor Manders, turns round and brutally rebukes him, we feel that a whole era, so to speak, has shifted its weight. And while Ibsen with one hand turns a highly respectable dwelling into an all-glass house, with the other hand he is already busy throwing stones. And what stones, thrown at what statues! Half the moral statuary of the age ends by being toppled from its pedestals.[3]

Yet, there are few things as compelling as a 'great' play that has proven over time to be elusive and difficult to stage for modern audiences. The critic Howard Barnes actually said that this was a play "which could not have been composed after the discovery of penicillin."[4] Howard Kissel acknowledged that *Ghosts* " ... can be one of the world's most harrowing, troubling plays ... ," but of the 1982 Broadway production Kissel could only remark that, " ... one might conclude *Ghosts* was a drawing room comedy with occasional serious overtones."[5]

---

[1] Robert Simonson, "The Literary Guy: Defining the Dramaturge," *Backstage*, December 8, 1995, p. 20.

[2] Ibid.

[3] Louis Kronenberger, "A Great Landmark is Weakly Revived." *PM Exclusive*, February 18, 1948 in *New York Theatre Critic's Reviews 1948*, New York: N.Y., p. 341.

[4] Howard Barnes, "LeGallienne's 'Ghosts'." *New York Herald Tribune*, February 17, 1948 in *New York Theatre Critic's Reviews 1948*, New York: N.Y., pp. 343–344.

[5] Howard Kissel, "Ghosts." *Women's Wear Daily*, August 31, 1982 in *New York Theatre Critic's Reviews 1982*, New York: N.Y., pp. 238–239.

Foreword

Don Nelson in his review of Liv Ullman's performance on Broadway in 1982 attempted to explain the problematic nature of the play for today's audiences:

> *Ghosts* explores human behavior so keenly and with such economy that it remains a gripping tale 100 years after it was written; but it also is creaky stylistically and falls easily into melodrama. The trick is to dispense with as much theatricality as possible without lowering the emotional charge engendered by the mystery of the Alving family that Ibsen constantly dangles before us. In this regard, the production is somewhat lacking. Good but scarcely absorbing. Melodramatics, particularly in the final scene, reduces the power.[6]

The question of 'how' *Ghosts* can be performed so that it maintains the explosive power it unleashed upon nineteenth-century audiences is fundamental to the 'art of interpretation' that is so much at the heart of theatre as an art form. For example, Don Nelson's admonition that directors "dispense with as much theatricality as possible without lowering the emotional charge" was wisely ignored by director Travis Preston in his brilliant, highly theatrical production of *Ghosts* mounted by the American Ibsen Theatre in Pittsburgh, Pennsylvania in 1985, a production which stunned and mesmerized audiences (I among them) precisely because of this production's heightened theatricality. Theatre critic Christopher Rawson of the *Pittsburgh Post-Gazette* celebrated the "theatricality" of that production:

> The audience sits on the stage, looking towards the actors on the forestage and beyond them to the bank of empty seats.... On the set are the statues of the five characters—their ghosts, or the externals by which we often judge others? A packed dirt floor provides intimacy, softening sounds and facilitating some carefully planned dramatic moments. The statues' placement implies a great deal about relationships, and soon they seem additional actors as characters move them, assault them and sometimes talk to them in preference to their human counterparts.[7]

The very heightening of the play's latent theatricality resulted here in an astounding production. Whereas realism and naturalism was the radical-

---

[6] Don Nelson, "Liv Ullman in Colloquial 'Ghosts'," *Daily News,* August 31, 1982 in *New York Theatre Critic's Reviews 1982,* New York: N.Y., pp. 240–241.

[7] Chris Rawson, "AIT Stages Haunting 'Ghosts,'" *Pittsburgh Post-Gazette,* June 27, 1985, Sec. A, p. 18.

ism of late nineteenth-century drama, a highly symbolic production of the play carried the day in 1985. Yet this in no way proclaims the triumph of one performance style over any other as being better able to realize the power of Ibsen's *Ghosts*. Such is the on-going challenge and joy of the theatrical art form.

All of the above serves to underscore the fact that *Ghosts* is an extremely difficult play to capture on stage, precisely because of its grand metaphor. Fortunately, the interpretation of plays possessing such metaphorical depth is enriched frequently by in-depth study of the history, sociology, and cultural milieu of their era, as well as the study of previous productions of the play and the impact made by these interpretations upon the society of the time.

The volume begins with a detailed chronology of Henrik Ibsen's life, incorporating those events, thoughts, and personages that shaped his thoughts and point-of-view. This is followed by Brian Johnston's highly informative article placing Henrik Ibsen and *Ghosts* in the historical, philosophical, literary, and cultural milieu of the late nineteenth century. George Bernard Shaw succinctly states Ibsen's importance to modern drama in a brief excerpt from his *Quintessence of Ibsenism* while also providing a beautifully succinct plot outline in his discussion of *Ghosts*. William Archer captures the impact and outrage *Ghosts* caused on the 'contemporary' scene, while his compilation of reviewer outrage at the English premiere of the play serves as a testimony of the degree to which Ibsen's play struck such a nerve with ruling- and middle-class audiences alike. Equally important is the insight Archer provides regarding the very role and mission drama was perceived to have for these English audiences.

Francis Fergusson's famous article credits *Ghosts* as the vanguard play in the development of modern realism, as does Brian Johnston's other contribution to the sourcebook, an article detailing how Ibsen turned that darling of boulevard drama, i.e., the "well-made-play," into something highly subversive. Writings by Lou Andreas-Salomé and Emma Goldman focus upon the protagonist, Helene Alving. Each focuses on the motivational throughline within this complex character, but from very distinct points-of-view. Emma Goldman sees the play as a clarion call for female liberation in the service of an even greater socialist revolution. Lou Andreas-Salomé sees Mrs. Alving's journey as being one of self-discovery, of her coming to understand that she did what she did because of a value system now repudiated. Salomé does this dynamically by comparing the awakening self-awareness of Mrs. Alving with the actions and self-discovery of Nora in Ibsen's *A Doll House*, Mrs. Alving's theatrical predecessor in Ibsen's prose canon.

Important primary source material is provided via letters written by Henrik Ibsen himself, discussing *Ghosts* with such luminaries as Georg

Foreword

Brandes and Björnstern Bjørnson. The depth of Ibsen's impact on younger writers is represented here by the correspondence between Ibsen and a young James Joyce. Reviews of various productions of *Ghosts* are presented so that the reader appreciates the difficulty of achieving a production that truly captures the play's greatness, viewing this hopefully as a challenge to be embraced.

Lastly, this dramaturgical sourcebook features a new translation of *Ghosts* by Brian Johnston and Rick Davis. The motivation in selecting this translation came directly from Henrik Ibsen's own words of advice to his first American translator, Professor Rasmus B. Anderson of the University of Wisconsin. Mr. Ibsen urged Professor Anderson:

> ... to see that the language of the translation be kept as close as possible to ordinary everyday speech; all the turns of phrase and expressions which belong only to books should most carefully be avoided in dramatic works, especially mine, which aim to produce in the ... spectator a feeling that he is witnessing a slice of real life."[8]

In my estimation the Johnston/Davis translation ably achieves Ibsen's exhortation. It is colloquial without incorporating slang yet possesses a natural fluidity and innate humor that indeed seems akin to "ordinary everyday speech."

The editor's hope is that enough salient material has been gathered together here to allow for an informed, intelligent deliberation of what this play means and how to make it work for an audience today. It should provide information, knowledge, and criticism to fuel the individual fires of interpretation. At the very least it should make for intense discussion and appreciation of the impact and role theatre can serve in helping to enlighten and change society.

Donald Marinelli
Associate Professor of Drama & Arts Management
Carnegie Mellon University
Pittsburgh, Pennsylvania
July 1997

---

[8] Henrik Ibsen, letter to Rasmus B. Anderson in *Ibsen: Letters and Speeches,* Evert Sprinchorn, editor (New York: Hill and Wang, 1964), p. 211

Henrik Ibsen's *Ghosts:*
A Dramaturgical Sourcebook

General Chronology

1807 —Hegel's *The Phenomenology of Mind.*

1828 —Ibsen born in Skien, Norway, on March 20.
—Leo Tolstoi born in Russia.

1830–31 —Hegel delivers his lectures on "The Philosophy of History."

1835 —Financial problems force the Ibsen family to move out of town to a smaller house for eight years.

1843 —Ibsen leaves home, at age 14, to earn his living as an apothecary's apprentice in the seacoast town of Grimstad. Except for one brief visit he never returns to his hometown.

1846 —A maid in the house, considerably older than Ibsen, bears him an illegitimate son. Ibsen was to financially support this son for many years despite his own straightened circumstances.

1848 —Revolutions throughout Europe. Ibsen writes sonnets in support of these revolutions which are one by one suppressed.
—Karl Marx and Friedrich Engels publish *Manifesto of the Communist Party.*

1848–50 —Ibsen writes his first play, *Catiline*, which is submitted to the Christiania Theatre and rejected.

1849 —Charles Dickens, *David Copperfield.*
—August Strindberg born in Sweden.

1850 —Ibsen writes his second play, *The Burial Mound*, which is performed at the Christiania Theatre.

1851 —Arrives in Bergen to take up an appointment, as playwright in residence and stage manager of the new Norwegian Theatre established by Ole Bull. He was to spend six years there, learning every aspect of dramatic and theatrical craft.
—Herman Melville, *Moby Dick.*

1852 —Dumas Fils play *La Dame aux Camélias.* The novel had been written 1848.

1853 —Herbert Spencer coins the term *evolution.*
—Comte de Gobineau, "Essay on the Inequality of Human Races" insisting on the superiority of the "Arians" in history.

1

1855 —*Lady Inger of Østråt*, a five-act historical tragedy, performed, unsuccessfully in the Norwegian Theatre.
—Reads a paper on Shakespeare and his influence upon Scandinavian literature to a Bergen literary society.
—Walt Whitman publishes *The Leaves of Grass*.
—Sören Kierkegaard, Danish philosopher dies.

1856 —*The Feast at Solhoug* successfully performed in Bergen, then in Christiania.
—Ibsen meets Suzannah Thoreson, his future wife.

1857 —*Olaf Liliekrans* performed in Bergen. Takes up a new post of artistic director at the Norwegian Theatre in Christiania (now Olso).
—Charles Baudelaire's *Les Fleurs du mal* published.

1858 —Gustav Flaubert's *Madame Bovary* published.
—Marries Suzannah Thoreson, June 18.
—*The Vikings at Helgeland* performed at the Christiania Norwegian Theatre.
—Apparition of the Virgin Mary reputed to have appeared to Bernadette Soubirous at Lourdes, France.

1859 —Ibsen's son, Sigurd (named after the pagan Viking hero) born.
—Darwin writes *The Origin of Species*, sparking the major controversy of the age. Darwin's work was quickly translated into Scandinavian and its ideas avidly discussed. Ibsen seems to have had no trouble accepting Darwinism. His later plays will blend Hegelian ideas of cultural/spiritual heredity and evolution with their biological counterparts. This is particularly evident in *Ghosts*.
—Charles Dickens writes *A Tale of Two Cities*.
—Eleanora Duse, Italian actress, born in Pavia.
—John Stuart Mill writes *Essay on Liberty*.
—Karl Marx writes his *Critique of Political Economy*.

1860 —Unification of Italy by Garibaldi and Victor Emmanuel II.
—Anton Chekhov, Russian author, born.

1861 —Outbreak of American Civil War.

1862 —The Norwegian Theatre in Christiania goes bankrupt and Ibsen loses his job. He travels widely in Norway on a university grant gathering folk songs and folk legends. He has no regular income for the next two years.
—*Love's Comedy*, Ibsen's first major play, published in a supplement to a journal. This play was subjected to harsh attacks as "an offence against human decency...." Ibsen himself becomes the object of much critical abuse. The Christiania Theatre dared not perform the play.
—Sarah Bernhardt's debut at the Comédie Française in Racine's *Iphigénie en Aulide*.

General Chronology

1863 —Appointed literary advisor to the Christiania Theatre.
—Publishes *The Pretenders*, a historical tragedy. This play is performed in Christiania, produced by Ibsen.
—Manet's exhibition at Martinet Gallery, Paris.
—Constantin Stavislavsky, Russian theatrical producer, born.
—Edvard Munch, Norwegian painter, born.
—T. H. Huxley writes "Evidence as to Man's Place in Nature."
—Denmark's king, Frederick VII dies; succeeded by Christian IX.
—Schleswig incorporated into Denmark.

1864 —Ibsen begins his long self-exile from Norway which will last until 1891. He and his family settle in Rome.
—Dano-Prussian war. Denmark cedes Schleswig, Holstein, and Lavenberg to Austria and Prussia. Austria and Prussia send ultimatum to Denmark; Danish forces defeated; Denmark invaded.
—Ibsen enraged at the failure of the other Scandinavian nations to come to the aid of Denmark against Bismark's Prussia. Begins writing *Brand* in response.
—Leo Tolstoi commences work on *War and Peace*.

1866 —*Brand*, a play in verse, published and creates a sensation.
—Ibsen now the most famous poet in Scandinavia.
—Fyodor Dostoevsky's *Crime and Punishment.*

1867 —Publishes *Peer Gynt*, another verse play, somewhat less favorably received, but later to become his most popular work.
—Karl Marx's *Das Kapital* published.
—Zola writes *Thérèse Raquin*, first naturalist novel.
—Garibaldi defeated in his third march on Rome; taken prisoner by French and papal forces. Ibsen, in Rome, comments favorably on Garibaldi's followers and compares their heroism with the pusillanimity of the Scandinavians over the Dano-Prussian War.

1868 —After staying in Florence, Bologna, and Venice, Ibsen settles in Germany, first Munich and then Dresden.

1869 —*The League of Youth*, a comedy, published, Ibsen's first realistic modern prose work.
—Ibsen travels widely in Egypt, Nubia, and the Red Sea and is invited by the Khedive of Egypt for the opening of the Suez Canal.
—Ibsen starts his lifelong intellectual friendship with the young Danish critic, Georg Brandes, although Brandes had written unfavorably about *Brand*. Brandes himself was under attack from the arbiters of Danish cultural life for his own onslaughts on religious orthodoxy. He, too, would go into exile but would later become one of the major critics of Europe.
—Wyoming establishes woman suffrage.
—John Stuart Mill writes *On the Subjection of Women.*

1870 —Franco-Prussian War: France declares war on Prussia and is defeated at Weissenburg, Worth, Mars-la-Tour, Gravelotte, and finally Napoleon III capitulates at Sedan.
—Revolt in Paris, proclamation of the Third Republic.
—Schliemann begins excavations at Troy.
—Charles Dickens dies.

1871 —Election of socialists to the Paris Commune, upon which troops led by Thiers on behalf of the French bourgeoisie massacred over 25,000 Communards—men, women, and children in one week. Thousands more were later executed or deported to tropical penal colonies. Ibsen commented to Brandes on these events.
—Georg Brandes' inaugural lecture to what will become his monumental six-volume *Main Currents of Nineteenth Century Literature*. Ibsen declares these lectures "disturbed my sleep ... No more dangerous book could fall into the hands of a pregnant writer. It is one of those works which place a yawning gap between yesterday and today." (Letter, April 4, 1872.)
—William I, King of Prussia, proclaimed German Emperor at Versailles.

1872 —Friedrich Nietzsche, *The Birth of Tragedy*.
—Jules Verne writes *Around the World in 80 Days*.

1873 —*Emperor and Galilean* published. Ibsen's ten act "world-historic drama," in prose, takes up the story of Julian the Apostate who attempted to restore Hellenic paganism to the Christian empire. Ibsen insisted to the end of his life that this was his major work. Its themes and imagery which depict our humanity as tragically divided between two antithetical natures, Hellenic self-fulfillment and Christian self-renunciation, will permeate the twelve-play Realist Cycle.

1874 —First Impressionist exhibition in Paris.

1875 —Leo Tolstoi's *Anna Karenina*.
—Hans Christian Anderson, Danish author, born.

1876 —First performance of *Peer Gynt*, with Grieg's music, at the Christiania Theater.
—Ibsen attends a performance of *The Pretenders* by the Duke of Saxe-Meiningen's players in Berlin.
—Opening of Bayreuth for first complete performance of Richard Wagner's Cycle *Der Ring des Nibelungen*.

1877 —*Pillars of Society* inaugurating Ibsen's Cycle of twelve realist prose plays. (Ibsen is living close to Bayreuth, in Munich.)
—Russo-Turkish War.

General Chronology

1879 —Publishes *A Doll House* in December. The play quickly becomes notorious in Europe, and Ibsen is soon to be the most written about man of letters, internationally, until his death in 1906.
1880 —Emile Zola's *Nana*.
—Fyodor Dostoevsky's *The Brothers Karamazov*.
—Rodin sculpts "The Thinker."
1881 —Publication of *Ghosts* causes a major scandal internationally; the play frequently is banned from public performance. In Scandinavia, bookshops returned copies of the play to the publisher, and it was over ten years before the first edition sold out. No established theater in Scandinavia would perform the play.
—Fyodor Dostoevsky dies.
1882 —*An Enemy of the People* published.
—World premiere of *Ghosts* in Chicago, in Norwegian, by Danish and Norwegian amateurs before an audience of Scandinavian immigrants. This production toured other American cities including Minneapolis and other cities of the Middle West. No notices of this production are recorded.
—James Joyce, Irish novelist, born.
1883 —First European performance of *Ghosts* by August Lindberg in Hälsingborg, Sweden. Lindberg was regularly to direct and act in Ibsen's plays.
—Friedrich Nietzsche writes *Also Sprach Zarathustra*.
—Björnstjerne Björnson writes *Beyond Human Endurance*.
1884 —*The Wild Duck* published.
—Herbert Spencer writes *The Man versus the State*.
1886 —*Rosmersholm* published. Ibsen the guest of the Duke of Saxe-Meiningen, for a production of *Ghosts*.
—Karl Marx's daughter, Eleanor, takes part in a dramatized reading of *A Doll House*, in London. Other participants included her husband, the socialist leader Edward Aveling; William Morris's daughter May; and George Bernard Shaw.
—Nietzsche writes *Beyond Good and Evil*.
1887 —Andre Antoine establishes his Théâtre Libre, the first of the noncommercial theaters that will take up the cause of Ibsen.
—Strindberg writes *The Father*.
—Sir Arthur Conan Doyle writes the first Sherlock Holmes story.
1888 —*The Lady from the Sea* published.
1889 —Otto Brahm and Paul Schlenther open the independent theater, Freie Bühne, in Berlin, to evade censorship and perform *Ghosts*. The *Freie Bühne* was to become a pioneer of the new drama in Germany.
—In Paris, the opening of the Eiffel Tower.

Ibsen's Ghosts: A Dramaturgical Sourcebook

1890 —*Hedda Gabler* published.
—Antoine produces *Ghosts* at the Théâtre Libre. Lugné Poë, later to stage a number of Ibsen plays in a non-realist, Symbolist style, called this production "a thunderbolt in French theatrical history."
—Oscar Wilde writes *The Picture of Dorian Gray.*

1891 —Friday, March 13, J. T. Grein's Independent Theatre opens with *Ghosts*, causing the greatest controversy in British theatrical history. Banned by the Lord Chamberlain from public performance, the Independent Theatre had to operate as a private club.
—*Ghosts* continued to be banned from public performance anywhere in Britain for the next twenty-three years.
—Bernard Shaw's *The Quintessence of Ibsenism.*
—The Independent Theatre movement in Europe now is underway.
—Young Turk Movement, hoping to secure liberal reforms, is formed in Geneva.

1892 —*The Master Builder* published.
—Oscar Wilde's first fashionable play, *Lady Windermere's Fan.*
—Wilde's *Salomé* banned from public performance by Lord Chancellor.
—Bernard Shaw's first play, *Widowers' Houses*, performed by the Independent Theatre.
—Gerhart Hauptmann's *The Weavers* published.
—Walt Whitman and Alfred Lord Tennyson die.
—Maurice Maeterlinck writes *Pelléas et Mélisande.*

1894 —*Little Eyolf* published.
—George Bernard Shaw writes *Arms and the Man.*

1896 —*John Gabriel Borkman* published.
—Chekhov's *The Seagull.*

1897 —Queen Victoria's Diamond Jubilee.
—The Independent Theatre restages *Ghosts.*
—Gerhart Hauptmann's naturalist play, *The Weavers.*
—Edmond Rostand writes *Cyrano de Bergerac.*
—Strindberg writes *The Inferno.*

1898 —The Dreyfus Affair unfolds in France.
—Spanish-American War.

1899 —*When We Dead Awaken* published, closing the Cycle.
—H. G. Wells's *When the Sleeper Wakes.*
—Tolstoi writes *Resurrection.*
—Oscar Wilde's *The Importance of Being Earnest.*

General Chronology

1900 —Ibsen suffers his first stroke and has to stop writing. His second stroke comes in the following year.
—Sigmund Freud publishes *The Interpretation of Dreams.*
—Friedrich Nietzsche dies.
—Oscar Wilde dies.

1901 —Queen Victoria dies, succeeded by her son Edward VII.
—Social Revolutionary Party founded in Russia.
—Strindberg writes *The Dance of Death.*

1902 —Chekhov writes *Three Sisters.*
—Emile Zola dies.

1903 —Shaw writes *Man and Superman.*

1904 —Chekhov writes *The Cherry Orchard.*
—Chekhov dies.
—Freud writes *The Psychopathology of Everday Life.*
—New York policeman arrests woman for smoking cigarette in public.
—Russo-Japanese war begins.

1905 —Norwegian Parliament decides on separation from Sweden; Prince Charles of Denmark elected King Haakon VII of Norway.
—Shaw's *Mrs. Warren's Profession* opens in New York; police censor closes it after one performance.

1906 —Samuel Beckett born Good Friday, April 13 (or on May 13).
—Ibsen dies on May 23 and is buried as a national and international figure.
—Richard Mansfield stars in the first professional production in the United States of *Peer Gynt.*
—Russian actress Nazimova makes her American debut in *Hedda Gabler.*

1914 —The censor lifts the ban on *Ghosts* in England for a performance in London under the patronage of the King and Queen of Norway.
—Outbreak of First World War.

1915 —*Ghosts*, filmed by D. W. Griffith, is the first film in the United States based on an Ibsen play.

1979 —Ibsen Society of America founded in New York.

1983 —The American Ibsen Theater founded in Pittsburgh, Pennsylvania. It will survive until 1986.

Brian Johnston

Historical Background

European Background

In 1828, Ibsen was born into a Europe drastically agitated by competing ideologies that were to erupt into the major oppositions, left and right, of our contemporary world. The earlier conflicts of Rationalism and Belief, Neo-classicism and Romanticism, Revolution and Reaction were being profoundly modified by social changes brought about by the industrial revolution and the consequent growth of the modern megalopolis, of class conflict and of the urban sensibility—with the artist and intellectual class at its center. The bourgeoisie, the social class that Ibsen was to make his subject matter, found its very existence called into question from the beginning. For many, this bourgeoisie forever condemned itself with the execution of up to 25,000 communards in Paris in one week in May 1871, when, in defense of a class that felt threatened by the election of socialists to office, Louis Adolphe Thiers led the troops of the French army against its own citizens. Flaubert, who had no sympathy for the communards, wrote to George Sand: "We are floundering in the afterbirth of the Revolution, which was a miscarriage, a failure, a gross blunder, no matter what may be said about it. And the reason is that it had its origin in the spirit of the Middle Ages and Christianity, an antisocial religion."[1] Ibsen, more sympathetic to the communards, complained to Georg Brandes how the events of the commune had spoiled his anarchist "state theory—or rather nonstate theory. The idea is now ruined for a long time to come."[2] Both writers turned from these horrendous contemporary events and immersed themselves in the classical past, Flaubert with *Salammbô*, set in pagan Carthage, Ibsen with *Emperor and Galilean*, a drama that depicts the final victory of Christianity over the Hellenic pagan world. Two of the most famous creators of modern realism, therefore, turned away from modernity to remote antiquity. This was not a desperate escapism. It was as if the modern world could be understood only by investigating its remote past, by a psychoanalysis of the world soul—a theme Ibsen was to insist upon more than once, and which helps explain much of his method in *Ghosts*.

From the Left, from the radicals, socialists, and anarchists, the middle class found itself attacked for the grim social injustices the industrial revolution had brought about; for the squalor of the cities and the suffering of the proletariat. From the Right, it was attacked for its crass, despiritualized materialism, its betrayal of the cultural past, and its moral cowardice. Writers such as Baudelaire, Flaubert, Nietzsche, the young men known as the Dandies, and many others shared this contempt for bourgeois attitudes and mores. Ibsen, in his dramas, seems to have combined the attacks of both Left and Right. As William Archer observed, "while intellectually an ultraradical he was temperamentally an aristocrat."[3]

The bourgeois identity, in fact, was a potentially tragic—or tragicomic—subject, as much so as the identity of the democratic citizen of fifth century B.C.E. Athens who also explored beyond the confines of an earlier aristocracy-centered social structure and replaced an earlier system of faith with a dynamic rationalism. The post-Darwinian individual of nineteenth-century capitalist culture was uncertain as to his or her identity or destiny and deeply uncertain of the validity of the world now brought into being. If the ideal of heroic literature had been Integrity, and that of the seventeenth and eighteenth centuries, Sincerity (cf. Moliere's *The Misanthrope*), the ideal of the unhappy bourgeoisie of the nineteenth century could be called that of Authenticity. The quest for authenticity is the driving force of *Ghosts*, as it is of all Ibsen's dramas following *Brand* (1866).

The immensely influential philosopher of the age was G. W. F. Hegel, who launched human identity itself into an existential quest for authenticity of being, for the attainment of genuine truth and freedom in an 'alienated' world that denied this possibility—the agonized quest of so many Ibsen characters. The impact of Darwinism was even more shattering, ending once and for all the idea of the world, and our place in it, of the older Christian-derived worldview, already severely damaged by the work of eighteenth-century Enlightenment.

Nationalism, nowadays mostly reactionary and begetting horrendous ethnic hatreds, in the nineteenth century often was a progressive force, as nation after nation, from Eastern Europe to Ireland, from the Mediterranean to the Baltics, struggled for independence from repressive foreign rule. Yet this was the age, also, of a cynical and exploitative European colonial imperialism in the Middle East, Africa, and the Far East and of the annihilation of the native inhabitants of North America. Modern bourgeois man was markedly more rapacious and violent than allowed

---

[1] Francis Steegmuller, editor and translater, *The Letters of Gustave Flaubert 1857–1880* (London: Faber & Faber, 1982), p. 180.
[2] *Ibsen: Letters and Speeches*, ed. Evert Sprinchorn (New York: Hill & Wang, 1964), p. 112
[3] Thomas Postlewait, ed. *William Archer on Ibsen* (Westport, Conn.: Greenwood Press 1984), p. 106.

for by the outmoded moral and religious creeds he still piously affected. This discrepancy between the Christian moral pretensions of society and the ruthless practices of the bourgeoisie is a theme of many of Ibsen's dramas (as it is of George Bernard Shaw's comedies), a theme that decidedly makes him our contemporary. And the hysteria and outrage that greeted *Ghosts* was to a great extent due to the very uneasy consciences of those who professed the orthodox morality. Europe, and especially England, in the late nineteenth century closely resembled the United States today, where, similarly, an amoral capitalism cloaks itself in the piety of an ineffectual and therefore "safe" Christianity. And, for a society given over to the worship of Mammon, nothing is more convenient than, like the pious public depicted in *Ghosts,* to deflect one's moral censure from capitalist to sexual and hedonist practices. Hence the propensity of the Anglo-Saxon world in particular, as Henry James noted apropos Ibsen, again and again to erupt into howls of moral outrage, especially in the realm of art.

Europe was divided violently between the new politics of the Left and the Right: on one side, the heirs to the Holy Alliance of the Church and the European monarchies set up in 1815 to undo the work of the French Revolution, and, on the other, the evolving International Socialist Movement with its alliance of intellectuals and the working class, seeking to fulfill the aims of the revolution. In the realm of literature, this conflict is magisterially set out by Ibsen's lifelong friend, Georg Brandes, in his six-volume *Main Currents of Nineteenth Century Literature.* The radical alliance was a totally new phenomenon in the world, and it coincided, indeed depended upon, the new status accorded to the artist and intellectual in society—the result of the displacement of the traditional authorities of church and monarchy.

Ibsen saw his work, together with that of such allies as Georg Brandes, as furthering the radical cause against the forces of reaction. We miss much of the intention of a drama like *Ghosts* if we fail to see the larger cultural forces behind the metaphors of domestic drama. Pastor Manders is the voice of the discredited Church; the "law and order" against which Helene Alving rebels is the whole weight of traditional culture going back centuries; Osvald Alving is the quest for "joy of life" (*livsgleden*) through Art. Ibsen came of age in 1848, the year of revolutions throughout Europe, and, from the obscurity of Grimstad, wrote youthful poems in support of the Hungarian revolutionaries. He was to follow the massacre of the Communards in 1871, see Garibaldi's defeat in Rome, and, when he died in 1906, it was only eight years before the outbreak of the First World War. The century he lived in, therefore, was almost as turbulent and terrible as our own and Ibsen, perhaps better than anyone, saw the fragility of the seemingly solid bourgeois culture he so reluctantly inhabited. Ibsen might well have shared Flaubert's patron saint, St. Polycarp, who lamented "Oh God, oh God, in what a century hast Thou made me live!"

Ibsen's work is never partisan nor didactic, though often misunderstood to be so. Like William Blake, he sought to "open the doors of perception"; to get his audience, in his own words, "to think greatly" (to think great thoughts.)[4] Where Blake, in his *Prophetic Books*, created a vast amorphous cosmos inhabited by shadowy and exotically named forces and powers undergoing baffling transformations and repetitions, Ibsen, after the three great dramas *Brand, Peer Gynt,* and *Emperor and Galilean* disciplined his huge subject matter into the requirements of a stringent, modern, realistic drama. His art served not to "attack" his society but spiritually to liberate it. In this act of liberation he made the modern world reveal the presence of its total cultural past, its total identity within the fabric of modernity.

Ibsen insisted that an extensive study of history and culture was essential for a modern writer to describe his own age.[5] *Emperor and Galilean* reveals a wide knowledge of Hellenic, Hellenistic, and Christian cults, myths, doctrines. Set in the fourth century, it is in many ways Ibsen's most modern work and certainly intellectually his most audacious. In this play Ibsen explores what he believes is the source of the modern world's malaise: a huge cultural failure to integrate opposing yet complementary aspects of our cultural identity into what he termed a "third kingdom/empire"—a term then innocent of the sinister meanings it later was to acquire.

The findings of archaeology, especially the famous discoveries of Schliemann at Troy, added richly to the modern European sense of its cultural identity, just at the time when the theories of Darwin removed from humanity any privileged place in the cosmos and unnervingly expanded the nature and scale of our biological identity. The result was that Ibsen saw his contemporaries as ephemera, as ghosts, carrying the cargo of previous cultural identities and launched on a questionable and dubious destiny as a species. The past, as in *Ghosts,* is always ambiguously present in Ibsen's work: as "the corpse in the cargo" holding us back, imprisoning our souls, and encouraging the horrifying atavisms that still plague us, but also as a realm of neglected or tabooed and banished powers that, recovered, could liberate us from the despotic and despiritualized reality of modernity.

So radical and complex a view of our human condition could only be baffling to the larger public. Ibsen, wrote Henry James, was asking "the

---

[4]*Ibsen: Letters and Speeches,* p. 57.
[5]Ibid., p. 181.

Brian Johnston: Historical Background

average moral man to see too many things at once. It will never help Ibsen with the multitude that the multitude shall feel that the more they look the more intentions they shall see, for of such seeing of many intentions the multitude is but scantily desirous. It keeps indeed a positively alarmed and jealous watch in that direction; it smugly insists that intentions shall be rigidly limited."[6] Or, as Shaw put it: "When any person objects to an Ibsen play because it does not hold the mirror up to his own mind, I can only remind him that a horse might make exactly the same objection."[7]

For independent and exploring intellects, a radical new idea of the world emerged from the unsettling discoveries of biology (our long evolutionary history), of geology (the great age of the earth), of astronomy (the great spaces surrounding us), and of physics. Just as the social world we inhabited was unstable and controversial, so too was the world of Nature, which no longer supplied the confident spiritual comforts of Romantic nature worship. One might say that "Ibsenian humanity" is a huge subjective enigma (evolved consciousness) surrounded by a huge objective enigma (the evolving cosmos). The dawning sun and glaciers of the end of *Ghosts* do not "comment on" the preceding action as suddenly supply a completely different perspective, that of the indifferent cosmos, onto the human drama. One should see that the scale of the Ibsen drama is as immense as Greek or Shakespearean drama though radically different in its terms. Change, evolution, dialectical conflict are seen as the natural and healthy disquietude of the questing spirit and not as the alarming "Chaos is come again" of the Shakespearean vision. Order, the static, the hierarchical, all that the Shakespearean vision sets up as the desired norm is, for the Ibsen drama, the unnatural and constraining. It is this that made him the quintessential dramatist of his turbulent culture.

In the realm of the intellect and the arts, the period was particularly fruitful and dynamic: in philosophy, Hegel, Schopenhauer, Kierkegaard, Nietzsche, Darwin, and Marx decisively set up the central "dialogue" of modern culture that continues to the present day. (Sigmund Freud was to emerge from this culture a little later.) It was an age that saw traditional beliefs in retreat, and the idea of humanity and its place in the cosmos entirely refashioned, often unnervingly. To be human was to be part of a dynamic evolution of spirit (Hegel) or of mechanistic chance (Darwin) but also to be thrust into the Absurd, either into the need for agonizing individual choice (Kierkegaard), into an individual life and a cosmos equally without meaning (Schopenhauer), or into an absolute perspectivism in

---

[6] Henry James, *The Scenic Art* (New Brunswick: Rutgers University Press, 1948), pp. 252–53.

[7] Bernard Shaw, *Dramatic Opinions Vol. II* (New York: Brentano's, 1928), p. 159.

which the concept of Truth, of a knowable reality, was a delusion (Nietzsche). For the thinker, including the playwright as thinker, the ultimately comforting Christian worldview was smashed forever.

The decline of religion led to the exaltation of the artist, who now took the place of the priest, prophet, or hierophant, as seer and as spiritual explorer whose work was an agonizing existential quest. The title of Thomas Mann's essay, "The Sufferings and Greatness of Richard Wagner," reveals to what an extent the modern artist had replaced the traditional prophet, martyr, or saint. The artist became not only the mediator between abstract philosophy and the 'ordinary' sensibility, as Friedrich Schiller predicted, but also the hierophant of new mysteries, the intrepid explorer of the human condition, even at the risk of despair, madness, and death. At no other time did the artist take on so "mantic" a role nor was the artist's vocation ever before accorded so high a status.

Of all the art forms of the nineteenth century, the drama was the one most resistant to these developments. It remained resolutely committed to a popular, conventional, undisturbing, and, when successful, highly profitable existence, free of the controversies that surrounded Baudelaire, Flaubert, Zola, the Impressionist exhibition, or the "music of the future" of Richard Wagner. But Ibsen was to demonstrate the possibilities for a new, minority theater serving a non-popular sensibility. After a number of short runs of Ibsen's plays in London, George Bernard Shaw noted the conditions that ensured a drama such as Ibsen's would not reach the commercial stage:

> A fashionable run of one of Ibsen's studies of modern society is about as feasible as a fashionable run of Beethoven's posthumous quartets. A late Ibsen play will not bring in twenty thousand pounds: it will bring in fifteen hundred or two thousand. On the other hand, the play which *may* bring in twenty thousand pounds also may, and in nine cases out of ten does, bring in less than its very heavy expenses; whereas the expenses of an Ibsen play, including a rate of profit which would be considered handsome in any ordinary non-speculative business, can be kept well within its practically certain returns, not to mention a high degree of artistic credit and satisfaction to all concerned. Under these circumstances it can hardly be contended that Ibsen's plays are not worth producing. In legitimate theatrical business Ibsen is as safe and profitable as Beethoven and Wagner in legitimate musical business.[8]

---

[8] Ibid., pp. 156–57.

Ibsen is not taken up by the commercial theater, Shaw goes on, because the latter is run by syndicates interested only in the speculatively hazardous bonanzas of popular success. "The formation of a wealthy syndicate to produce a 'Little Eyolf' would be like the promotion of a joint stock company to sweep a crossing."[9] Yet, as Shaw goes on to demonstrate, the production of Ibsen's plays was a financially sound, even if modest, proposition. Shaw, in effect, is describing the conditions out of which his own drama and that of other serious minority dramatists, now would emerge. William Archer, refuting critics who claimed that the British public "would not have Ibsen at any price," set out the record of the profits from Ibsen productions in London up to 1893 and concluded: "Does it not rather seem that there is a public, and not a very small one, which will have Ibsen at any price, despite such a chorus of critical anathema as was never heard before in the history of the English stage?"[10]

Another feature of Ibsen's introduction to Britain was the successful publication of his plays as they appeared. It was almost unheard of at the time to publish plays in Britain, for contemporary English drama, for good reason, was not considered a branch of literature. Yet, as Archer showed, the publication of Ibsen's plays had proved spectacularly successful:

> About four years ago *The Pillars of Society, Ghosts,* and *An Enemy of the People* were published in a shilling volume.... Of that volume, up to the end of 1892, Mr. Walter Scott had sold 14,367 copies. In 1890 and 1891 the same publisher issued an authorised uniform edition of Ibsen's prose drama in five volumes, at three and sixpence each. Of these volumes, up to the end of 1892, 16,834 copies had been sold. Thus Mr. Walter Scott alone has issued (in round numbers) thirty-one thousand volumes of the works of a man for whom nobody "outside a silly clique" cares a brass farthing."[11]

Archer relates that when he first approached publishers with the project of publishing his translations, he was told that "no modern plays could ever 'sell' in England"; and he adds, "except in the one case of Ibsen, experience justified this assertion."[12]

This breakthrough into publishing the plays was to be as significant as the establishing of the Independent Theatre movement: it enabled George Bernard Shaw to find a public, through publishing his plays, when

---

[9] Ibid.
[10] Postelwait, *Archer on Ibsen,* 500–511.
[11] Ibid., p. 48.
[12] Ibid.

the commercial theaters shunned him. We now take the publishing of contemporary drama for granted: but until the Ibsen years, this was considered a radical and even foolhardy undertaking.

Ibsen was the first dramatist to create a modern drama adequate to the intellect of the age. The result was that he was excoriated and attacked more virulently than any artist of the time—probably of any time. With the most meager financial rewards (he probably earned less from his lifework than a popular dramatist earned from one commercial success), he single-handedly lifted dramatic art to the highest levels of the consciousness of his age. By 1897, with the appearance of William Archer's translation of *John Gabriel Borkman*, Shaw could declare:

> Already Ibsen is a European power: this new play has been awaited for two years, and is now being discussed and assimilated into the consciousness of the age with an interest which no political or pontifical utterance can command.... Ibsen is translated promptly enough nowadays; yet no matter how rapidly the translation comes on the heel of the original, newspapers cannot wait for it: detailed accounts based on the Norwegian text, and even on stolen glimpses of the proof-sheets, fly through the world from column to column as if the play were an Anglo-American arbitration treaty.[13]

It was the three productions of *Ghosts*, in Berlin (1889), Paris (1890), and London (1891), and the scandals and uproar they occasioned, that more than anything brought this about. These were the three seismic shocks that forever altered the modern cultural landscape.

Scandinavia and Europe

Ibsen is the first world-dramatist; that is, the first dramatist conscious of addressing a world audience rather than a national one, whose plays, as soon as they appeared, more than any other dramatist's, were to be major cultural events fervently discussed by and performed before an international audience. "It may be questioned," wrote James Joyce in 1900, "whether any man has held so firm an empire over the thinking world in modern times."[14] Joyce noted that Ibsen "has provoked more discussion and criticism than that of any other living man."[15]

---

[13] Shaw, *Dramatic Opinions*, II, p. 158.
[14] James McFarlane, ed. *Henrik Ibsen*, Penguin Critical Anthologies (Harmandsworth, Middlesex: Penguin Books, 1970), p. 173.
[15] Ibid.

Brian Johnston: Historical Background

The odds against Ibsen becoming this world figure were enormous: he was born in a little nation whose language was spoken by only a tiny population on the fringes of European culture. As William Archer noted of Ibsen's astonishing European success: "his Dano-Norwegian language is spoken by some four and a half million people in all, and the number of foreigners who learn it is infinitesimal. The sheer force of his genius has broken this barrier of language...."[16] Moreover, Norway was a nation that had no theatrical tradition, and indeed hardly any literary tradition at all since the Middle Ages.

And even in Norway Ibsen was more than usually disadvantaged. He was born in the little provincial town of Skien into a family in which the father became bankrupt early in Ibsen's childhood. He left Skien and his home at the age of sixteen, never to return (except for a single fleeting visit), to earn his living as an apothecary's apprentice in the even smaller town of Grimstad. He never graduated from university and his first play, *Catiline*, written when he was eighteen in his scant spare hours from work, was rejected by the theater to which it was submitted. When Ibsen left Grimstad for Christiania (now Oslo) to seek his calling as poet or painter (he was uncertain which art mainly to pursue), his prospects for success, to any impartial observer of the aspirations of the human inhabitants of this planet, must have seemed remote in the extreme. And for years, failure and poverty were to pursue him like dismal and relentless furies.

The Scandinavian countries, and Norway in particular, though by no means "backward" nations, were outside the mainstreams of European culture. Georg Brandes' account of the Scandinavian intellectual climate, after all, could apply at least equally to Britain or the United States in the nineteenth century:

> Not only are there periods in which we do not know how our people thought and felt, but there are periods in which our thoughts and feelings were more dull and feeble than those of other nations. Consequently, some important European movements reached us while others did not. Indeed it sometimes happened that, without having participated at all in the main action, whose broad waves were flat and spent before they reached our sandy shores, we found ourselves participating in the reaction.[17]

---

[16] Postlewait, *William Archer on Ibsen*, p. 55.
[17] Eric Bentley, ed. *The Theory of the Modern Stage* (Harmondsworth, Middlesex: Penguin Books, 1968), p. 385.

Yet Brandes' complaint suggests that Scandinavia was standing at an odd angle toward Europe rather than dwelling in outer darkness, getting its ideas late and often second-hand, but nevertheless getting them:

> ... at this time, the imported ideas in philosophy lose ground here, the newly started Hegelian schools suspend their activities, Heiberg gives way to Kierkegaard, and the passion for thought to the passion for faith. The philosophical movement ceases temporarily without having produced a single work, even a short work, while the ethical, religious movement that now begins does find a parallel and a continuation in literature.[18]

Norway generally was the most provincial of the Scandinavian nations (excluding Finland and Iceland). Politically, it was more or less benignly dominated by Sweden, and culturally, by Denmark. In the theater, Denmark was the dominant force; Danish actors and Danish taste predominated. When Ole Bull asked Ibsen to help establish a Norwegian theater company, they had to start from scratch, recruiting men and women who had never worked in a theater before. The predominant Danish taste favored either the *vaudeville*, practiced by Hans Christian Anderson among others, or, like that of most of Europe, the well-made-play formula practiced in Paris by Eugène Scribe and his followers.

The secret of the well-made-play was to offer the public the maximum of theatrical excitement with the minimum of conceptual risk, basically the role of mainstream theater today. A *technically* complicated situation was subjected to the pressure of artificial theatrical time, the wished for or feared event teasingly delayed or excruciatingly approached, with stunning reversals in each act, until the coup-de-théâtre of the final scene. The trick was to ensure that the play never strayed into the dangerous area of ideas or ideology, for this would be unwelcome to the well-heeled patrons of the theater in Paris and throughout Europe. It would have been even more unwelcome to the omnipresent European censorship which was vigilant against the kind of expression that once abetted a revolution in France and threatened revolution elsewhere.

The well-made-play, therefore, for all its appearance of innocuous entertainment, entirely free of politics or ideology, actually was political. Like the entertainments of Hollywood and the television networks today, it was created to direct public attention away from a dangerous interest in social/political realities. The government in France, for example, gladly permitted the performance of the safely "scandalous" *La Dame aux*

---

[18]Ibid.

Camélias because it would distract public attention from its own controversial policies. The political function of "the media" then, as today, was apparent from the furore that occured any time a serious issue intruded into the conventional format.

In the well-made-play, *things* took the place of ideas: to reverse *Hamlet's* motto, "the thing's the play." A concealed letter, a locked cabinet, a goblet of poison, an incriminating bracelet, a glass of water, a loaded pistol, all were made to transfix the audience's attention with the suspense of delayed revelation and approaching crisis. It was the suspense of the stock exchange, itself subject to dramatic reversals and triumphs, completely appropriate for a *belle époque* Paris that was the playground of South American rubber barons and the *nouveaux riches* of industrial capitalism. Chance, accident, not tragic necessity, dictated the action. Scribe's very deft *The Glass of Water* in which the destinies of two nations revolve around the rivalries of two powerful women over a pretty guardsman, the intrigue manipulated by a cynical Bolingbroke who denies the role of any serious ideas or issues in history, is a good example of the political purposes of the genre.

The well-made-play was the cleverly constructed entertainment of a middle class eager to avoid all confrontation with political or ethical reality. It had supplanted the earlier melodrama—a popular art form which did present a simplistic but powerful moral universe. As Peter Brook has shown in *The Melodramatic Imagination*, the melodramas of Pixérécourt, and the novels of Balzac, Dickens, and even Henry James, were concerned to create an art of the "moral occult" where human actions took on metaphysical configuration, and where a moral cosmos was responsive to human actions. The product of post-revolutionary France, melodrama provided the mostly illiterate populace with the equivalent of the older, hierarchical, metaphysically sanctioned worldview, which Shakespeare, for example, had employed. Shakespeare's plays revealed a world centred on the monarchy and aristocracy and contested by powers of light and darkness, as in *Macbeth*. The perfidy of melodrama's villains, and the sufferings of its victims, similarly extended into the world of active Nature where, in a dramaturgy of astonishing "signs," flood, fire, storm and earthquakes act as a cosmic commentary on the human action. This metaphysical or occult dimension was renounced by the more cynical writers of the well-made-play who mostly confined their actions to smart living rooms, smart characters and dialogue, and the complications of upper middle-class adultery and murder. Ibsen, whose years with the Norwegian Theatre in Bergen required supervising hundreds of productions of well-made-plays, dismissed them contemptuously as "Scribe & Co.'s sugar candy confections." Early in his career, therefore, he sought for an alternative to the superficial cosmopolitanism of the well-made-play. It is one of his major achievements in the modern theater to have restored the historical, natural, and metaphysical dimensions of reality to the vocabulary of modern drama.

In Norway, as in many nations in Europe at that time, writers urged the creation of an authentic national drama which could "enjoy its own language and its own poetry on its own stage,"[19] arguing for "the deep national significance of theaters, the necessity of a truly national theater as part of the self-revelation and development of nationality."[20] Ibsen took up this program, and his early plays are explorations by the poet of the historical past of Norway, attempts to recover for the present the submerged layers of Norwegian cultural consciousness. He contrasted the mind-set of fashionable theater-goers, patrons of the well-made-play, who "visit the theater only when offered the opportunity of being titillated by some novel situation or excited by some novel intrigue," with the actual needs of the Norwegian people:

> If the new is to appeal to the people it must also in a certain sense be old; it must not be invented but rediscovered; it must not appear as something strange and incongruous in the conceptual range inherited by the people from their ancestors and in which our national strength mainly resides.[21]

In his early plays, therefore, Ibsen attempted to re-create the past, to bring onto the stage its myths and legends and history, much as his contemporary, Richard Wagner, was doing. The belief that the past was a rich repository of spiritual reality neglected by the present was to remain long after Ibsen abandoned historical costume drama. Later, disillusioned with his culture, with modernity, Ibsen reversed his earlier process of leaving the present world to return to the past. Instead, in his twelve-play Realist Cycle, he brought the past into the present, revealed its subversive presence under the surface of modernity. He re-created modern Norway as an occult space where the ghosts, or "gengangere" ("they that walk again," the more accurate translation of *Gengangere*) occupy and take over the contemporary scene.[22] Ibsen's seemingly contemporary stage, from the moment the play commences, begins to reveal mythopoeic and archety-

---

[19] Laurence Selenick, ed. *National Theater in Northern and Eastern Europe, 1746–1900* (Cambridge: Cambridge University Press, 1991), p. 151. The quotation is from Bjørnstjerne Bjørnson.
[20] Ibid., p. 165. (Quotation from M. J. Monrad.)
[21] James McFarlane, ed. and translator, *The Oxford Ibsen, I* (London: Oxford Universtiy Press, 1960), p. 672.
[22] For a full account of the scale of Ibsen's realist cycle cf. Brian Johnston, *The Ibsen Cycle*, Revised Edition (University Park: Pennsylvania State University Press, 1992), *passim*.

pal content. Ibsen's task, as an artist, was to find a stage language to express this idea, and it was here that his "other art," that of painting, of visual symbolism, came to his aid.

It was his genius to see that the well-made-play's obsession with things, with objects, could be made the vehicle of a new theatrical poetry, a poetry of the theater, if it was linked to the metaphysical dimensions of the earlier melodrama. The action of *Ghosts*, for example, is thousands of years old and extends into a cosmos whose agents are this planet and the finally emergent sun. The human species shown onstage is racked and divided by such historical forces as Paganism and Christianity, and the ghosts of Greek tragedy haunt the modern scene, characters, actions, and dialogue. Humanity's larger biological history and destiny is figured in the repression of Eros—the Alving heritage tainted by cultural conflict as much as by medically identifiable misfortune. A whole cluster of images and objects—*things*—amplify this conflict: the sun vs. the rain, the wine and champagne, the freethinking books on Helene Alving's table vs. Manders' confident Pauline orthodoxy, the plants and flowers, the deeds of the new children's home, the lamp whose light streams over Regina as she brings it into the darkened room; the references to duty vs. joy of life, Osvald's art, the priestly identity of Manders—all these and more create a visual "supertext" that carries the play's argument from verbal language into a universal world that can be seen and touched.

We have to see that the meticulous realism Ibsen creates is not just to simulate everyday reality, but to create a new metaphysical vocabulary, where objects, things, acquire and accumulate "mana"—symbolic power, as extensions of the conflicting characters. Characters, actions, objects, dialogue earn their place on Ibsen's stage insofar as they are able to embody archetypal meaning or identity. Consider, to take only one example, how that centrally placed table, in *Ghosts*, by the end of the play has accumulated its history of Helene's freethinking books, the deeds of the hypocritical Captain Alving's children's home (or asylum), the champagne with its connotations of "joy-of-life" brought up from the cellar by Regina, and the lamp, Helene's little ray of Reason soon to be extinguished in the merciless light of the sun. Each of these objects, as well as others, has had its moment of "epiphany" (showing forth). In the two-hours-or-so history of the table the whole argument of the play is reflected. By these deft means, Ibsen invents a new form of the 'moral occult'; converting his contemporary Norway into a metaphysical space where the ghosts of the past awaken on his stage as in a séance. The characters onstage are unaware of these ghostly dimensions to their drama, but the vigilant among the audience can detect them. Ibsen does not write "symbolic" drama in the manner of Strindberg and the Symbolist and Expressionist dramatists, in which the symbolic signifiers are unrooted in everyday reality.

In Ibsen, the symbolic is always everyday reality looked at from another perspective—a perspective often evaded by the characters onstage. It is this symbolism rooted in reality that gives Ibsen's method its power. And this is why to perform Ibsen in the style one would perform strictly naturalist drama is finally a disservice to his art, wiping away half of the plays' power and scale: they attain levels of almost hallucinatory intensity, like ritualist art, and performance terms need to be devised to accommodate this.

Ibsen's drama returns to the scale of Greek and Shakespearean drama by making his metaphors, his imagery, into vehicles of universal forces, even if the dialectics of Ibsen's plays are the opposite of, for example, Shakespeare's. For Shakespeare, dis-order, change, and conflict are the feared, unnatural, and tragic (or comic) disturbers of a desired harmony; for Ibsen they are the desired, natural, and healthy disquietude of spirit essential for growth into authentic human identity, i.e., self-realization; the "self" is always a project, not a given. The self-assured, self-justifying Helene Alving of the opening of *Ghosts* is living in delusion, unaware of the horror-struck, self-condemning, and anguished identity that is lying in wait for her at the play's close. This dialectical nature of Ibsen's art means that it is always irrevocably evolving: there is no going back to the world-view of Act One in Act Two of *Ghosts*, nor to this Act when we have reached Act Three. And this is true of the whole Cycle: each play is such an evolving structure, each play destroys its terms of existence and cannot be returned to.

Ibsen's own career is one of the most impressive examples of self-realization known. From the impoverished apothecary's apprentice in a small provincial town in Norway, he became an arbiter of modern European and Western consciousness, making us what we are, as Ezra Pound noted. For most of his career he lived outside Norway but, with the exception of *Emperor and Galilean*, he fashioned his dramatic metaphors only in images of contemporary Norwegian reality. But this restriction of his dramatic *milieu* was only the starting point for the most wide-ranging artistry. When we discover the dimensions of Ibsen's art, we discover, at the same time, the possible dimensions of our own modern identity. That is, his plays open up a "great argument," as his lifelong disciple James Joyce (who also restricted his art to a confined time and space—modern Dublin) perceived:

> To begin an account of a play of Ibsen's is surely no easy matter. The subject is, in one way, so confined and in another way, so vast. . . . Ibsen's plays do not depend for their interest on the action, or on the incidents. Even the characters, faultlessly drawn though

they be, are not the first thing in his plays. But the naked drama—either the perception of a great truth, or the opening up of a great question, or a great conflict which is almost independent of the conflicting actors and has been and is of far-reaching importance—this is what primarily rivets our attention."[23]

The nineteenth-century Norway Ibsen reluctantly inhabited has passed away. But the Norway he reimagined in his drama has become an indispensable terrain of the human spirit.

The Appearance of *Ghosts*

Ibsen, then living in Rome, sent the manuscript of *Ghosts* to his publisher Hegel in Copenhagen in the fall of 1881 so that it could appear in time for the Christmas sales in December. One can imagine no more dismaying an apparition for that pious and festive season in Scandinavia. He remarked to Hegel, "*Ghosts* will probably cause alarm in certain circles; but that cannot be helped. If it did not, it would not have been necessary to write it."[24] William Archer recounts that at a Christmas eve festival at the Scandinavian Club in Rome, Ibsen remarked that "Christmas was usually regarded as a season of peace, but that for him it was very often much the reverse, since his books generally appeared a little before Christmas. But he did not believe that peace was the most desirable condition; on the contrary, he held warfare to be more wholesome for human nature."[25]

Even Ibsen, however, could not have anticipated the "fury" of the warfare that broke out, first in Scandinavia, then throughout Europe, at the appearance of *Ghosts*. Both the published play and the very few courageous performances occasioned perhaps the greatest scandal in the history of the theater. The previous play, *A Doll House*,[26] had made Ibsen controversial in Europe; *Ghosts* made him infamous. As is usual with the publication of a play by Ibsen, there was at first a great deal of excitement. But then came the horrified reaction. August Lindberg, later to be one of the courageous few to put on the play, records how *Ghosts* "was contraband, something

---

[23] McFarlane, *Henrik Ibsen*, p. 174.
[24] *Ibsen: Letters and Speeches*, pp. 196–97.
[25] *William Archer on Ibsen*, p. 109.
[26] *A Doll Home* is the accurate but unusable translation of *Et dukkehjem*. Most earlier translations believing Nora was the only "doll," translated *A Doll's House* and when referring to these translations or productions based on them, that's the title that appears in citations. But *A Doll House* is the title used by me and Rick Davis, and is the title of the Rolf Fjelde translation of the play, too. It is a more accurate compromise.

that could not be discussed."[27] The bookstores all over Scandinavia were forced by scandalized patrons to return a large portion of the first edition to the publisher; in fact this edition did not sell out for many years. Even former supporters of Ibsen turned against him. One, Ludvig Josephson, termed the play "one of the filthiest things ever written in Scandinavia."[28]

This, in fact, was the almost universal response by critics in Scandinavia, both conservative and liberal. One left-wing paper pronounced, "complete silence would, in our opinion, be the most fitting reception for such a work."[29] Another remarked, "The book has no place on the Christmas table of any Christian home."[30] A reviewer in the *Berlingske Tidende* proclaimed that Ibsen had made good his promise, in an earlier poem, of placing "a torpedo under the Ark,"[31] a comment that at least shows an awareness of the *scale* of Ibsen's devastation. The commercial and established theaters of Scandinavia, of course, refused to stage it. Against this almost universal hostility, Ibsen maintained a dogged resolve. He had been used to this throughout his career. When *Peer Gynt* was first attacked as not being poetry, he replied, "My book is poetry, and if it isn't, then it shall be. The conception of poetry in our country, in Norway, shall be made to conform to my book."[32] In March 1882, after the storm of horrified criticism throughout Scandinavia, the disastrous sales of the book, and the refusal of the theaters to stage his play, he wrote to Hegel: "As regards *Ghosts* I feel certain that in due time, and not very long at that, the real meaning of the play will penetrate the minds of the good people at home.... My book belongs to the future."[33]

And Ibsen did have defenders; from the feminists, Amalie Skram and Camilla Collett, to his most famous literary rival in Norway, Bjørnstjerne Bjørnson, who praised the play as "free, brave and courageous."[34] Ibsen's friend, Georg Brandes, said the play was "the noblest deed in his literary career," while a professor of Greek at Christiania (Oslo) University, P. O. Schjøtt, declared:

> "... of all the modern dramas we have read, *Ghosts* comes closest to classical tragedy.... When the dust of ignorant criticism has subsided, which we trust will happen soon, this play of Ibsen's,

---

[27] Michael Meyer, *Ibsen: A Biography* (New York: Doubleday & Co., 1971), p. 484.
[28] Ibid.
[29] Ibid.
[30] Ibid.
[31] *William Archer on Ibsen*, p. 110.
[32] *Ibsen: Letters and Speeches*, p. 67.
[33] Ibid., p. 206.
[34] Meyer, p. 485.

with its pure bold contours, will stand not only as his noblest deed but as the greatest work of art which he, or indeed our whole dramatic literature, has produced.[35]

Given the Greek elements Ibsen incorporated into *Ghosts*, this last commendation must particularly have pleased him.

Above all, he found his defenders where he most wanted to find them, among the young; not only in Scandinavia but throughout Europe, thus justifying his claim that his play belonged to the future. The truly subversive aspects of *Ghosts* are not the implications of syphilis (today it would be AIDS, as critics have noted),[36] the seeming endorsement of incest, the attack on religious orthodoxy, and the possibility of euthanasia at the close, but far more unsettling, a total denial of any certain basis for human identity or human belief beyond the unceasing and agonized struggle for authenticity of being: that as humans we are an unrealized project, journeying experimentally through phases of biological and cultural evolution we cannot comprehend. We therefore need to devise fictions of faiths, moralities, identities, sciences, forms of "knowledge"—what a later Ibsen character, in *The Wild Duck*, will call creating the "life-lie." Ibsen wrote in a note to the play, "The whole of mankind [is] on the wrong track."[37] The house of Alving and its devastation thus stands for "all humanity."

Far more consoling would have been the stance of the rebel, who would at least represent some "positive" alternative to alienated reality. But, like Sophocles' *Oedipus Tyrannos*, *Ghosts* seems to render humanity itself as the victim of some horrible cosmic joke, possibly a joke we have unwittingly committed against ourselves. This is not the story of a particular aberrant family, but as the *archetypal* identities of the characters insist, humanity itself. Not only the sources of biological generation, but of spiritual generation, also, are polluted, fundamentally diseased, and Helene Alving's questing and suffering intellect explores a world in which all her values, even her intellect itself, is brought abruptly in confrontation with an indifferent cosmos (the sun and the glaciers) which is as implacable as the Apollo of *Oedipus Tyrannos*. Such a tough-minded view philosophically was stated by Ibsen's contemporary, Friedrich Nietzsche, but Ibsen's drama, by forcing the audience into an unbearably close confrontation with a human experience of the idea is far more unsettling than Nietzsche. Thus there are not "ideas in" Ibsen: each play is itself

---

[35] Ibid.
[36] Cf. Sylvia Drake, *Los Angeles Times*, March 15, 1993.
[37] James McFarlane, ed. *Henrik Ibsen* (Oxford: Oxford University Press, 1961), p. 468.

a multilayered Idea, a Concept, explored to its limits, here to the limits of desolation. The hysteria with which the play almost universally was greeted might well have been due to the critics' detecting the enormity of the desolation Ibsen is exploring, the completeness of his denial of the human spirit's pretensions.

It was outside Scandinavia that the most eventful reception of *Ghosts* was to occur. Its rejection by the "official" theaters everywhere led to the most important development of modern drama: the creation of the alternative or "little" theater movement: the point where the history of the theater and the history of the drama separate. The great technical breakthroughs in the history of the mainstream modern theater have little to do with the most important events in the history of the modern drama. One could teach the evolution of the modern theater without mentioning one masterpiece. The plays of Ibsen, Strindberg, Wedekind, Hauptmann, Shaw, Brecht, Pirandello, Beckett, and so on, all could be and were performed on modest and traditional stages, requiring none of the technological wizardry that drew the crowds to the boulevard melodramas and draws them to "spectaculars" on Broadway today. And more than any other play, *Ghosts* reveals this cultural divide (which already existed in the other arts) coming into being. For a long time the theaters successfully had resisted recognizing this division of modern culture, creating, instead, a bland fiction of cultural and social cohesion. The appearance of *Ghosts* and its reception, destroyed this fiction of public unity forever.

By some very strange decision on the part of the *Zeitgeist*, the world premiere of the play took place in Chicago on May 20, 1882, in a United States completely out of touch with events in the avant-garde theater in Europe, and where the record-breaking attraction of the period for over fifty years after its first production in 1852 was an adaptation of *Uncle Tom's Cabin*.[38] Staged in the Aurora Turner Hall in Chicago, *Ghosts* starred Helga Bluhme, daughter of a Danish theater manager, as Mrs. Alving. There seem to have been no reviews or reports of the event, no doubt because the play was performed in Dano-Norwegian before an audience of Scandinavian immigrants. The company then took the play on tour to other Scandinavian communities in the Middle West. The performances seemed to have taken place unruffled by incident, protest—or result—in marked contrast to what was about to happen in Europe. One can only speculate the company received the Christmas edition copy and decided to stage it before news of its scandal reached America. In fact, the Ibsen controversy in America had to wait until the Richard Mansfield produc-

---

[38] Robert A. Schanke, *Ibsen in America* (Metuchen, N.J.: The Scarecrow Press, 1988), p. 5.

Brian Johnston: Historical Background

tion of *A Doll House* in 1889, when it flared up with all its European virulence.

The young Swedish actor, August Lindberg, who played Osvald, produced *Ghosts* in Sweden on August 22, 1883. Opening at Hälsingborg on the west coast, it prefigured the later career of *Ghosts*; its rejection by the official theaters and its performance by a dedicated team of young actors in a little theater before enthusiastic young audiences and a hostile establishment press. (An unfortunate reporter for a Danish newspaper who recorded his enthusiasm for the performance was sacked by his editor in consequence.) *Ghosts* became an "underground" play surviving, despite press hostility, by word of mouth. It became the pathbreaker of the modern minority theater movement.

In Germany, the intrepidly independent Duke of Saxe-Meiningen staged one performance of the play by his famous company on December 22, 1886, and invited Ibsen to stay with him as a guest. While being vilified by the popular and establishment press of Europe, Ibsen had the gratifying experience of being fêted not only by the duke and his son Prince Ernst, but also by the Crown Prince and Princess of Meiningen, the last two traveling from Rome to see the play. The performance was a success with the invited audience, like the same company's performance of Ibsen's historical play, *The Pretenders*, over a decade earlier. Writing joyfully to his publisher over the magnificent reception (and coveted ducal medal) he received Ibsen added, "Please do not think that it is vanity that makes me tell you this. But I do not deny that the honor gives me a certain pleasure when I think back to the stupid denunciations hurled at the play for such a long time in Scandinavia."[39]

Then, in annual succession in Berlin (1889), Paris (1890), and London (1891), there took place the events that would forever change the nature of drama in Europe. In Berlin, two young enthusiasts, Otto Brahm and Paul Schlenther, taking their cue from André Antoine's Théâtre Libre in Paris (recently founded to put on plays banned from the established theaters), and determined to get around the censorship against public performances of *Ghosts* (regularly suppressed by the police), created a private theater club limited to its members in order to perform the play. The pair had been in the audience at the earlier Meiningen players performance and were overwhelmed. Brahm wrote:

> If the aim in the development of literature is to absorb more and more of nature into art, to wrest new poetic fields from life, as Faust obtained land from the sea, then no recent dramatist has

---

[39] *Ibsen: Letters and Speeches*, p. 263.

gone forward more boldly and more magnificently than the author of *Ghosts*.[40]

Another member of the audience was the young Gerhart Hauptmann whose future drama was to continue, in its own way, the new path opened up by Ibsen. Ibsen seems to have been somewhat less enthralled either by a rehearsal or even by the performance itself. According to Paul Schlenther, "He sat with a friend in the stalls, and throughout the performance kept on pinching his companion and ejaculating, 'Oh! oh!' in apparent agony, varying the exclamation at some points—as when Regina made her entrance in a peasant costume—with an emphatic 'Oh, nein!'"[41]

Brahm and Schlechter sought to create a "free" theater, Freie Bühne, which they opened on September 29, 1889. *Ghosts* thus inaugurated the alternative theater movement in Germany and this was to have a major effect on modern German drama. In the ensuing Ibsen controversy in Germany, especially in Berlin, "a certain set of critics had taken to exalting him to the skies and flinging him at the head of their own poets."[42] One might say that out of this production of *Ghosts* would emerge the plays not only of his follower, Hauptmann, but (even if in post-Strindbergian reaction) of Wedekind (an ambivalent admirer of Ibsen) much Expressionist drama, as well as the plays of Brecht. All these dramatists, whatever their attitude to Ibsen, could count on the new intellectual climate in the theater, and the new audiences hitherto absent, brought about by Ibsen and by the eager debate his plays gave rise to. For the first time, the theater became the vehicle in which the intellect of the modern age found its most potent expression. In the years that followed, Ibsen was the most performed dramatist in Germany.

It could not be long before André Antoine, in Paris, also would want to stage *Ghosts*, for this was precisely the kind of play, feared by the authorities and in the forefront of the new literature of the age, for which he created his Théâtre Libre. On May 29 and 30, 1890, *Ghosts* was performed at Antoine's theater. It was typical of any staging of *Ghosts* at the time in that it required only two performances to serve as a landmark in the history of any nation's drama. George Moore, the Irish novelist and resident of Paris, was galvanized enough by the performance to write of the final scene of *Ghosts*, "Most assuredly nothing finer was ever written by man or god. Its blank simplicity strikes upon the brain, until the brain reels, even as poor Osvald's brain is reeling."[43] As a result, Moore soon was to be

---

[40] Meyer, p. 575.
[41] *William Archer on Ibsen*, p. 122.
[42] Ibid., p. 117.
[43] Justin Huntley McCarthey, *Impressions and Opinions* (London, 1914), pp. 162–67.

a founding member of the Irish Literary Theatre (later the Abbey Theatre), composed of those fiercely for the Ibsen revolution in drama (Moore and Edward Martyn) and those fiercely against (W. B. Yeats and J. M. Synge). Aurelian Lugné Poë, a young man destined to become a major force in French theater, including "Symbolist" productions of Ibsen of which Ibsen highly approved, claimed that the play was "a thunderbolt in French theatrical history. It can never be described how stunned and shaken we were that day."[44]

It was in London, however, that the appearance of *Ghosts* in 1891 drew from the establishment of both theater critics and leaders of society a response that only can be described as reactionary mass hysteria. The earlier appearance of *A Doll House* had identified the opponents in the cultural war. A private reading of *A Doll House*, for example, was held in 1886 in a Bloomsbury drawing room in which Karl Marx's daughter Eleanor played her namesake, Nora; her common law husband, the socialist leader Edward Aveling, played Helmer; William Morris' daughter May, played Mrs. Linde; and a bright young critic and socialist named George Bernard Shaw played Krogstad. Those who were attracted to the Norwegian playwright, it seems, were of a decidedly radical cast of mind and strongly at variance with the political, literary, and cultural establishment. Indeed, as we will see, the rage of the newspapers was to be directed as much at the audience of the performance as at the performance itself.

It was with *Ghosts* that the cultural war in England commenced in earnest. The man behind the scheme of setting up in England a free theater on the lines of Antoine's Théâtre Libre or the Freie Bühne was J. T. Grein, a young Dutch shipping clerk of very modest means (like Antoine) who famished for serious theater in London. The influential critic and later translator of Ibsen, William Archer, had prepared the ground with his criticisms of the state of London theater and its dramatists when contrasted with Ibsen. Following the Bloomsbury reading, a notable production of *A Doll House* managed to sustain a comparitively long run. It had become apparent, therefore, that there was an audience "out there" hungry for an authentic modern drama. Armed with eighty pounds—a reward for his work introducing British dramatists to the Netherlands—Grein decided to launch his project which was, in effect, a direct affront to the theatrical establishment.

His choice of *Ghosts* to open his theater ensured that the scale of the affront would be immense, though he probably was unaware of the extent of this until the day after the performance. Even so, for a young

---

[44] Meyer, p. 634.

man foreign to the culture he was confronting, Grein must have possessed considerable courage. As the Lord Chamberlain had banned the play from public performance, it could only be staged privately.

The censorship in England was probably the most obtuse in Europe. As 'Michael Orme' writes in her biography of her husband, Grein, the purpose of the censor in Britain was to make sure that no subject could be treated with real seriousness. Infidelity, for instance, was indulgently permitted only so long as it was treated as farce. Treated as serious drama, it would at once be banned.[45] But the censor had no jurisdiction over private performances to which the general public was not admitted and no money was taken at the door. In 1886, for example, Shelley's *The Cenci*, banned from public performance, was privately presented by the Shelley Society. This was the model Grein decided to adopt.

He named his venture The Independent Theatre Society, whose members included, among many luminaries, Thomas Hardy, Henry James, George Meredith, as well as George Bernard Shaw and William Archer. One can see that the desire for authentic drama was not restricted to radical members of society but included all who wanted to see the theater attain the same distinction as the best literature of the time. It is a startling fact that in England there had been no serious new drama since Sheridan in the late eighteenth century—a period of over one hundred years. At a time when the British literary genius in Romantic poetry and in the novel was the equal of any in the world, the serious drama was non-existent— well below even the level of the French well-made-play that it pillaged. Charles Dickens, who delighted in the theater, performed only in melodramas. Even Shakespeare was revived in just a handful of plays, and these in such hopelessly garbled texts that George Bernard Shaw once remarked that if Sir Henry Irving were to present himself onstage in as mutilated a condition as he presented Shakespeare's text, a shriek of horror would go up from the entire audience. Of an Irving production of *Cymbeline* Shaw warned: "In a true republic of art Sir Henry Irving would ere this have expiated his acting versions on the scaffold. He does not merely cut plays: he disembowels them."[46]

When Grein announced the first offering of his theater would be *Ghosts*, there was a shriek of horror of another sort—the hysterical reaction commencing even before the rehearsals. Defying augury, Grein decided to open on Friday, March 13, and had invited so many people to attend that he had to convert a dress rehearsal into virtually a prior performance. The critic, "Spectator," of *The Star* prophetically announced:

---

[45] Michael Orme, *J. T. Grein* (London: John Murray, 1936), p. 73.
[46] Bernard Shaw, *Dramatic Opinions, I*, p. 55.

"Yesterday I received an invitation, innocent enough on the face of it, yet possibly to be valuable one of these days as an epoch-making document in connection with the history of the English stage."[47] The results the following morning were astonishing, not only for their hysteria and virulence against Ibsen, Grein, the players, and the audience: they were all the more astonishing for representing, in England, any intense interest at all on the part of the public, in matters of art. George Bernard Shaw was to recollect the event some years later:

> There was one crowded moment when, after the first performance of "Ghosts," the atmosphere of London was black with vituperation, with threats, with clamor for suppression and extinction, with everything that makes life worth living in modern society.[48]

William Archer wrote of the reception by the British press of this private performance of *Ghosts:* "The shriek of execration with which this performance was received by the newspapers of the day has scarcely its counterpart in the history of criticism."[49]

As Shaw noted, "Fortunately, the newspaper press went to such bedlamite lengths on this occasion that Mr. William Archer ... was able to put the whole body of hostile criticism out of court by simply quoting its excesses in an article entitled 'Ghosts and Gibberings.' "[50] As this note of moral hysteria is a recurring one in Anglo-American culture (as recent reactions from the far right on the grants of the National Endowment for the Arts will show), it is worth inspecting, as under a microscope, this mentality when it is worked into the extreme moral agitation William Archer's article [reprinted elsewhere in this source book] reveals.

As Archer complained, " ... who can carry on a rational discussion with men whose first argument is a howl for the police?"[51] Henry James, at the time actually involved in a production of *Hedda Gabler* with his friend, the actress Elizabeth Robins, observed of Archer's article:

> This catalogue is a precious document, one of those things that the attentive spirit would not willingly let die. It is a thing, at any rate, to be kept long under one's hand, as a mine of suggestion and reference; for it illuminates, in this matter of the study of Ibsen, the second characteristic of our emotion (the first ... being

---

[47] Orme, *J. T. Grein*, p. 78.
[48] Bernard Shaw, *Dramatic Opinions*, I, p. 49.
[49] Meyer, p. 657.
[50] Bernard Shaw, *The Quintessence of Ibsenism* (New York: Hill & Wang, 1957), p. 91.
[51] *William Archer on Ibsen*, p. 27.

its peculiar intensity): the fact that that emotion is conspicuously and exclusively moral, one of those cries of outraged purity which have so often and so pathetically resounded through the Anglo-Saxon world.[52]

Ghosts remained banned from public performance in Britain until 1914, when for a performance under the patronage of the King and Queen of Norway, the ban was lifted. In a way, then, the press hysteria had succeeded in its object: of frightening the censor into keeping *Ghosts* off the public stage for twenty-three years.

But it was a Pyrrhic victory, for this same hysteria alerted a section of the public to Ibsen's existence, and the young and the rebellious in particular were bound to be attracted to an author who so horrified their elders. An Ibsen cult was started in Britain that continues to this day. "By the end of 1891," wrote Miriam Franc, "Ibsen was a name known to every reader of a London newspaper,"[53] and, in The *Fortnightly Review* in November, William Archer observed, "If we may measure fame by mileage of newspaper comment, Henrik Ibsen has for the past month been the most famous man in the English literary world."[54] One of Ibsen's early defenders, Justin Huntley McCarthy, observed, less than a year after the performance of *Ghosts*, "To contest the influence of Ibsen upon this country would be needless.... It may be said of Ibsen's influence, as Napoleon said of the French Republic, that it is as obvious as the Sun in Heaven, and asks for no recognition."[55]

As late as 1897, when Ibsen still was the subject of fierce newspaper commentary and obloquy, Henry James remarked of the controversy:

> ... let me pay it, for what it has been and what it still may be, the mere superficial tribute of saying that it constitutes one of the very few cases of contagious discussion of a matter not political, a question not of mere practice, of which I remember to have felt, in a heavy air, the engaging titillation. In London, generally, I think, the wandering breath of criticism is the stray guest at the big party—the shy young man whom nobody knows. In this remarkable instance the shy young man has ventured to pause and hover, has lighted on a topic, introduced himself and, after a gasp of consternation in the company, seen a little circle gather round

---

[52] Henry James, *The Scenic Art* (New Brunswick, Mass.: Rutgers University Press, 1948), p. 245.
[53] Meyer, p. 659.
[54] *William Archer on Ibsen*, p. 13.
[55] *Gentleman's Magazine*, January, 1892.

him. I can only speak as one of the little circle, testifying to my individual glee.⁵⁶

That same year (1897) was Queen Victoria's Jubilee, and in June *Ghosts* was revived in private performance by the Independent Theatre, prompting Shaw to make a playful contrast: "On the one hand the Queen and the Archbishop of Canterbury: on the other Mrs. Alving and Pastor Manders. Stupendous contrast!"⁵⁷

Shaw speculated, over a number of paragraphs, how life might have "brought to the Queen the lessons it brought to Mrs. Alving."⁵⁸ This actually has led to the wildly preposterous myth, in the standard Norwegian biography of Ibsen and in a number of later works, that the Queen and the Archbishop actually did attend the performance!⁵⁹

It was to take longer before James McFarlane could remark that Ibsen now has become "naturalized by syllabus" in England and is a major topic in universities of the study of *English* literature. In contrast to the situation in the United States, Ibsen is a regular feature of the British stage and not, as in the United States, as the author of only two supposedly "feminist" plays, *A Doll's House* and *Hedda Gabler*. *Ghosts* is the most performed of the plays in Britain; but all the plays of the Cycle have established their place as part of the repertoire of the British theater. When a British playwright recently was described as the "English Ibsen," another critic protested that we already have an English Ibsen—Henrik Ibsen!

The example of Ibsen emboldened others to write an adult drama in which the modern world could honestly be depicted. No other writer of his time dared go as far as *Ghosts*, and Ibsen himself, in his other plays, developed other aspects of his dramatic art, often more puzzling to hostile critics, but less scandalous. Without Ibsen's example, in which the performances by the Independent Theatre of *Ghosts* were pivotal events, it is doubtful if George Bernard Shaw's career would have been launched or that of Harley Granville Barker. In Germany, we saw, Hauptmann, Wedekind, and Brecht, all benefited from the intellectual climate in the theater created by Ibsen. In the United States, Eugene O'Neill, Clifford Odets, Arthur Miller, Tennessee Williams, and Edward Albee are his heirs, even if sometimes indirect ones. O'Neill's greatest play, *Long Day's Journey Into Night*, an agonizing family drama resurrecting the painful past

---

⁵⁶James, *The Scenic Art*, p. 299.
⁵⁷Shaw, *Dramatic Opinions*, II, p. 299.
⁵⁸Ibid.
⁵⁹The myth is perpetuated in Halvdan Koht's biography, *Henrik Ibsen*, Oslo 1954, in Ronald Gray's lively polemic against Ibsen, *Ibsen: A Dissenting View* (Cambridge: Cambridge University Press, 1977), p. 205, and in the latest collection of essays on Ibsen, *The Cambridge Companion to Ibsen* (Cambridge: Cambridge University Press, 1994), p. 168.

within a drawing room in a single day, is closer to *Ghosts* than to any other drama.

Yet the label attached to Ibsen, "the father of modern drama," is far too limiting, for no modern drama has yet approached the immensity, richness, and complexity of his twelve-play Realist Cycle. *Ghosts*, for all its power, is only one stage of this huge dramatic odyssey, and we cannot really know *Ghosts* until we know the whole Cycle, just as no one Book of *The Iliad, The Odyssey,* or *Paradise Lost,* nor any one Canto of Dante's *Commedia* can be understood until we see where it stands in the structure of the whole. That is the scale upon which Ibsen's realist art is working.

Ibsen, perhaps, did not so much *cause* the new drama to come into being in Europe, nor dictate the paths it was to take, so much as to give drama once again a central place in modern culture and provide a demonstration that even the most controversial minority drama could gain an enthusiastic international following. Rainer Maria Rilke, who hailed Ibsen as a fellow visionary poet (as did Thomas Mann, Hugo von Hoffmansthal, James Joyce, Ezra Pound, and others), after seeing a performance at Antoine's theater of *The Wild Duck*, recorded, "But the poetry! . . . There was something great, deep, essential. Last Judgement. A finality. And suddenly the hour was there when Ibsen's majesty deigned to look at me for the first time. A new poet, whom we shall approach by many roads now that I know one of them. And again someone misunderstood in the midst of fame. Someone quite different from what one hears."[60]

Wrote William Archer: "Poetry,—poetry: that is the first word and the last of any true appreciation of Ibsen. It is largely because he has applied to purposes of poetry a vehicle hitherto used only for prosaic ends that he has been so strangely misunderstood."[61]

So he still needs to be discovered by us. Behind the Ibsen many of his interpreters claim to know is a vaster, unknown one who one day may come to be discovered by those younger generations in whom Ibsen put so much faith.

---

[60] Rainer Maria Rilke, *Selected Letters, 1902–1926* (London: Quartet Books, 1988), p. 95
[61] *William Archer on Ibsen*, p. 67.

William Archer *Ghosts*

The winter of 1879–80 Ibsen spent in Munich, and the greater part of the summer of 1880 at Berchtesgaden. November 1880 saw him back in Rome, and he passed the summer of 1881 at Sorrento. There, fourteen years earlier, he had written the last acts of *Peer Gynt*: there he now wrote, or at any rate completed, *Gengangere*.

The surviving "foreworks" for this play are very scanty. Of the dialogue only two or three brief fragments remain. The longest is a sketch of the passage in which Oswald shocks Pastor Manders by his account of artist life in Paris. We possess, however, some scattered memoranda relating to the play, some of them written on the back of an envelope addressed to "Madame Ibsen, 75 via Capo le Case, Citta" (that is to say, Rome). They run as follows:

> The piece will be like an image of life. Faith undermined. But it does not do to say so. "The Asylum"—for the sake of others. They shall be happy—but this also is only an appearance—it is all ghosts.
>
> One main point. She has been believing and romantic—this is not wholly obliterated by the stand-point afterwards attained—"It is all ghosts."
>
> It brings a Nemesis on the offspring to marry for external reasons, even if they be religious or moral.
>
> She, the illegitimate child, may be saved by being married to—the son—but then——

> He was in his youth dissipated and worn out; then she, the religiously awakened, appeared; she saved him; she was rich. He had wanted to marry a girl who was thought unworthy. He had a son in his marriage; then he returned to the girl; a daughter——

> These women of to-day, ill-treated as daughters, as sisters, as wives, not educated according to their gifts, withheld from their vocation, deprived of their heritage, embittered in mind—these it is who furnish the mothers of a new generation. What will be the consequence?

> The fundamental note shall be the richly flourishing spiritual life among us in literature, art, etc.; and then, as a contrast, all humanity astray on wrong paths.

The complete human being is no longer a natural product, but a product of art, as corn is, and fruit-trees, and the creole race, and the higher breeds of horses and dogs, the vine, etc.

The fault lies in the fact that all humanity has miscarried. When man demands to live and develop humanly, it is megalomania. All humanity, and most of all the Christians, suffer from megalomania.

Among us we place monuments over the dead, for we recognise duties towards them; we allow people only fit for the hospital [literally, lepers] to marry: but their offspring—? The unborn——

The fourth and fifth of these six sections seem to have as much bearing on other plays—for instance, *An Enemy of the People,* and *The Lady from the Sea*—as on *Ghosts.* I should take them rather for general memoranda than for notes specially referring to this play.

Gengangere was published in December 1881, after he had returned to Rome. On December 22 he wrote to Ludwig Passarge, one of his German translators, "My new play has now appeared, and has occasioned a terrible uproar in the Scandinavian press; every day I receive letters and newspaper articles decrying or praising it.... I consider it utterly impossible that any German theater should accept the play at present. I hardly believe that they will dare to play it in the Scandinavian countries for some time to come." How rightly he judged we shall see anon.

In the newspapers there was far more obloquy than praise. Two men, however, stood by him from the first: Björnson, from whom he had been practically estranged ever since *The League of Youth,* and George Brandes. The latter published an article in which he declared (I quote from memory) that the play might or might not be Ibsen's greatest work, but that it was certainly his noblest deed. It was, doubtless, in acknowledgment of this article that Ibsen wrote to Brandes on January 3, 1882:

"Yesterday I had the great pleasure of receiving your brilliantly clear and so warmly appreciative review of *Ghosts.* . . . All who read your article must, it seems to me, have their eyes opened to what I meant by my new book—assuming, that is, that they have any *wish* to see. For I cannot get rid of the impression that a very large number of the false interpretations which have appeared in the newspapers are the work of people who know better. In Norway, however, I am willing to believe that the stultification has in most cases been unintentional; and the reason is not far to seek. In that country a great many of the critics are theologians, more or less disguised; and these gentlemen are, as a rule, quite unable to write rationally about creative literature. That enfeeblement of judgment which, at least in the case of the average man, is an inevitable consequence of prolonged occupation with theological studies, betrays itself more especially in the judging of human character, human actions, and human motives. Practical business judgment, on the other hand, does not suffer so much from studies of this order. Therefore the reverend gentlemen are very often excellent members of local boards; but they are unquestionably our worst critics." This passage is interesting as showing clearly the point of view from which Ibsen conceived the character of Manders. In the next paragraph of the same letter he discusses the attitude of "the so-called Liberal press"; but as the paragraph contains the germ of *An Enemy of the People,* it may most fittingly be quoted in the Introduction to that play.

Three days later (January 6) Ibsen wrote to Schandorph, the Danish novelist: "I was quite prepared for the hubbub. If certain of our Scandinavian reviewers have no talent for anything else, they have an unquestionable talent for thoroughly misunderstanding and misinterpreting those authors whose books they undertake to judge.... They endeavour to make me responsible for the opinions which certain of the personages of my drama express. And yet there is not in the whole book a single opinion, a single utterance, which can be laid to the account of the author. I took good care to avoid this. The very method, the order of technique which imposes its form upon the play, forbids the author to appear in the speeches of his characters. My object was to make the reader feel that he was going through a piece of real experience, and nothing could more effectually prevent such an impression than the intrusion of the author's private opinions into the dialogue. Do they imagine at home that I am so inexpert in the theory of drama as not to know this? Of course I know it, and act accordingly. In no other play that I have written is the author so external to the action, so entirely absent from it, as in this last one."

"They say," he continued, "that the book preaches Nihilism. Not at all. It is not concerned to preach anything whatsoever. It merely points to the ferment of Nihilism going on under the surface, at home as elsewhere. A Pastor Manders will always goad one or other Mrs. Alving to revolt. And just because she is a woman, she will, when once she has begun, go to the utmost extremes."

Towards the end of January Ibsen wrote from Rome to Olaf Skavlan: "These last weeks have brought me a wealth of experiences, lessons, and discoveries. I of course foresaw that my new play would call forth a howl from the camp of the stagnationists; and for this I care no more than for the barking of a pack of chained dogs. But the pusillanimity which I have observed among the so-called Liberals has given me cause for reflection. The very day after my play was published, the *Dagblad* rushed out a hurriedly-written article, evidently designed to purge itself of all suspicion of complicity in my work. This was entirely unnecessary. I myself am responsible for what I write, I, and no one else. I cannot possibly embarrass any party, for to no party do I belong. I stand like a solitary franc-tireur at the outposts, and fight for my own hand. The only man in Norway who has stood up freely, frankly, and courageously for me is Björnson. It is just like him. He has in truth a great, kingly soul, and I shall never forget his action in this matter."

One more quotation completes the history of these stirring January days, as written by Ibsen himself. It occurs in a letter to a Danish journalist, Otto Borchsenius. "It may well be," the poet writes, "that the play is in several respects rather daring. But it seems to me that the time had come for moving some boundary-posts. And this was an undertaking for which a man of the older generation, like myself, was better fitted than the many younger authors who might desire to do something of the kind. I was prepared for a storm; but such storms one must not shrink from encountering. That would be cowardice."

It happened that, just in these days, the present writer had frequent opportunities of conversing with Ibsen, and of hearing from his own lips almost all the views expressed in the above extracts. He was especially emphatic, I remember, in protesting against the notion that the opinions expressed by Mrs. Alving of Oswald were to be attributed to himself. He insisted, on the contrary, that Mrs. Alving's views were merely typical of the moral chaos inevitably produced by reaction from the narrow conventionalism represented by Manders.

With one consent, the leading theaters of the three Scandinavian capitals declined to have anything to do with the play. It was more than eighteen months old before it found its way to the stage at all. In August 1883 it was acted for the first time at Helsingborg, Sweden, by a travelling company under the direction of an eminent Swedish actor, August Lindberg, who himself played Oswald. He took it on tour round the principal cities of Scandinavia, playing it, among the rest, at a minor theater in Christiania. It happened that the boards of the Christiania Theatre were at the same time occupied by a French farce; and public demonstrations of protest were made against the managerial policy which gave *Tête de Linotte* the preference over *Gengangere*. Gradually the prejudice against the play broke down. Already in the autumn of 1883 it was produced at the Royal (Dramatiska) Theatre in Stockholm. When the new National Theatre was opened in Christiania in 1899, *Gengangere* found an early place in its repertory; and even the Royal Theatre in Copenhagen has since opened its doors to the tragedy.

Not until April 1886 was *Gespenster* acted in Germany, and then only at a private performance, at the Stadt-theater, Augsburg, the poet himself being present. In the following winter it was acted at the famous Court Theatre at Meiningen, again in the presence of the poet. The first (private) performance in Berlin took place on January 9, 1887, at the Residen Theatre; and when the Freie Bühne, founded on the model of the Paris Théâtre-Libre, began its operations two years later (September 29, 1889), *Gespenster* was the first play that it produced. The Freie Bühne gave the initial impulse to the whole modern movement which has given Germany a new dramatic literature; and the leaders of the movement, whether authors or critics, were one and all ardent disciples of Ibsen, regarding *Gespenster* as his typical masterpiece. In Germany, then, the play certainly did, in Ibsen's own words, "move some boundary-posts." The Prussian censorship presently withdrew its veto, and on November 27, 1894, the two leading literary theaters of Berlin, the Deutsches Theater and the Lessing Theater, gave simultaneous performances of the tragedy. Everywhere in Germany and Austria it is now freely performed; but it is naturally one of the least popular of Ibsen's plays.

It was with *Les Revenants* that Ibsen made his first appearance on the French stage. The play was produced by the Théâtre-Libre (at the Théâtre des Menus-Plaisirs) on May 29, 1890. Here, again, it became the watchword of the new school of authors and critics, and aroused a good deal of opposition among the old school. But the most hostile French criticisms were moderation itself compared with the torrents of abuse which were poured upon *Ghosts* by the journalists of London when, on March 13, 1891, the Independent Theatre, under the direction of Mr. J. T. Grein, gave a private performance of the play at the Royalty Theatre, Soho. I have elsewhere placed upon record some of the amazing feats of vituperation achieved of the critics, and will not here recall them. It is sufficient to say that if the play had been a tenth part as nauseous as the epithets hurled at it and its author, the Censor's veto would have been amply justified. That veto is still (1911) in force. England enjoys the proud distinction of being the one country in the world where *Ghosts* may not be publicly acted.

In the United States, the first performance of the play in English took place at the Berkeley Lyceum, New York City, on January 5, 1894. The production was described by Mr. W. D. Howells as "a great theatrical event—the very greatest I have ever known." Other leading men of letters were equally impressed by it. Five years later, a second production took place at the Carnegie Lyceum; and an adventurous manager has even taken the play on tour in the United States. The Italian version of the tragedy, *Gli Spettri*, has ever since 1892 held a prominent place in the repertory of the great actors Zaccone and Novelli, who have acted it, not only throughout Italy, but in Austria, Germany, Russia, Spain, and South America.

In an interview, published immediately after Ibsen's death, Björnstjerne Björnson, questioned as to what he held to be his brother-poet's greatest work, replied, without a moment's hesitation, *Gengangere*. This dictum can scarcely, I think, be accepted without some qualification. Even confining our attention to the modern plays, and leaving out of comparison *The Pretenders, Brand,* and *Peer Gynt,* we can scarcely call *Ghosts* Ibsen's richest or most human play, and certainly not his profoundest or most poetical. If some omnipotent Censorship decreed the annihilation of all his works save one, few people, I imagine, would vote that that one should be *Ghosts.* Even if half a dozen works were to be saved from the wreck, I doubt whether I, for my part, would include *Ghosts* in the list. It is, in my judgment, a little bare, hard, austere. It is the first work in which Ibsen applies his new technical method—evolved, as I have suggested, during the composition of *A Doll's House*—and he applies it with something of fanaticism. He is under the sway of a prosaic ideal—confessed in the phrase, "My object was to make the reader feel that he was going through a piece of real experience"—and he is putting some constraint upon the poet within him. The action moves a little stiffly, and all in one rhythm. It lacks variety and suppleness. Moreover, the play affords some slight excuse for the criticism which persists in regarding Ibsen as a preacher rather than as a creator—an author who cares more for ideas and doctrines than for human beings. Though Mrs. Alving, Engstrand and Regina are rounded and breathing characters, it cannot be denied that Manders strikes one as a clerical type rather than an individual, while even Oswald might not quite unfairly be described as simply and solely his father's son, an object-lesson in heredity. We cannot be said to know him, individually and intimately, as we know Helmer or Stockmann, Hialmar Ekdal or Gregers Werle. Then, again, there are one or two curious flaws in the play. The question whether Oswald's "case" is one which actually presents itself in the medical books seems to me of very trifling moment. It is typically true, even if it be not true in detail. The suddenness of the catastrophe may possibly be exaggerated, its premonitions, and even its essential nature, may be misdescribed. On the other hand, I conceive it probable that the poet had documents to found upon, which may be unknown to his critics. I have never taken any pains to satisfy myself upon the point, which seems to me quite immaterial. There is not the slightest doubt that the life-history of a Captain Alving may, and often does, entail upon posterity consequences quite as tragic as those which ensue in Oswald's case, and far more wide-spreading. That being so, the artistic justification of the poet's presentment of the case is certainly not dependent on its absolute scientific accuracy. The flaws above alluded to are of another nature. One of them is the prominence given to the fact that the Asylum is uninsured. No doubt there is some symbolical purport in the circumstance; but I cannot think that it is either sufficiently clear or sufficiently important to justify the emphasis thrown upon it at the end of the second act. Another dubious point is Oswald's argument in the first act as to the expensiveness of marriage as compared with free union. Since the parties to free union, as he describes it, accept all the responsibilities of marriage, and only pretermit the ceremony, the difference of expense, one would suppose, must be neither more nor less than the actual marriage fee. I have never seen this remark of Oswald's adequately explained, either as a matter of economic fact, or as a trait of character. Another blemish, of somewhat greater moment, is the inconceivable facility with which, in the third act, Manders suffers himself to be victimized by Engstrand. All these little things, taken together, detract, as it seems to me, from the artistic completeness of the play, and impair its claim to rank as the poet's masterpiece. Even in prose drama, his greatest and most consummate achievements were yet to come.

Must we, then, wholly dissent from Björnson's judgment? I think not. In a historical, if not in an aesthetic, sense, *Ghosts* may well rank as Ibsen's greatest work. It was the play which first gave the full measure of his technical and spiritual originality and daring. It has done far more than any other of his plays to "move boundary-posts." It has advanced the frontiers of dramatic art and implanted new ideals, both technical and intellectual, in the minds of a whole generation of playwrights. It ranks with *Hernani* and *La Dame aux Camélias* among the epoch-making plays of the nineteenth century, while in point of essential originality it towers above them. We cannot, I think, get nearer to the truth than George Brandes did in the above-quoted phrase from his first notice of the play, describing it as not, perhaps, the poet's greatest work, but certainly his noblest deed. In another essay, Brandes has pointed to it, with equal justice, as marking Ibsen's final breach with his early—one might almost say his hereditary—romanticism. He here becomes, at last, "the most modern of the moderns." "This, I am convinced," says the Danish critic, "is his imperishable glory, and will give lasting life to his works."

George Bernard Shaw

The Quintessence of Ibsenism

These pieces are from *The Quintessence of Ibsenism* published in 1891.

It is a striking and melancholy example of the preoccupation of critics with phrases and formulas to which they have given life by taking them into the tissue of their own living minds, and which therefore seem and feel vital and important to them whilst they are to everybody else the deadest and dreariest rubbish (this is the great secret of academic dryasdust), that to this day they remain blind to a new technical factor in the art of popular stage-play making which every considerable playwright has been thrusting under their noses night after night for a whole generation. This technical factor in the play is the discussion. Formerly you had in what was called a well-made play an exposition in the first act, a situation in the second, an unravelling in the third. Now you have exposition, situation and discussion; and the discussion is the test of the playwright. The critics protest in vain. They declare the discussions are not dramatic, and that art should not be didactic. Neither the playwrights nor the public take the smallest notice of them. The discussion conquered Europe in Ibsen's *Doll's House*; and now the serious playwright recognizes in the discussion not only the main test of his highest powers, but also the real centre of his play's interest....

Up to a certain point in the last act, *A Doll's House* is a play that might be turned into a very ordinary French drama by the excision of a few lines and the substitution of a sentimental happy ending for the famous last scene: indeed the very first thing the theatrical wiseacres did with it was to effect exactly this transformation, with the result that the play thus pithed had no success and attracted no notice worth mentioning. But at just that point in the last act, the heroine very unexpectedly (by the wiseacres) stops her emotional acting and says: 'We must sit down and discuss all this that has been happening between us.' And it was by this new technical feature: this addition of a new movement, as musicians would say, to the dramatic form, that *A Doll's House* conquered Europe and founded a new school of dramatic art....

The drama was born of old from the union of two desires: the desire to have a dance and the desire to hear a story. The dance became a rant: the story became a situation. When Ibsen began to make plays, the art of the dramatist had shrunk into the art of contriving a situation. And it was held that the stranger the situation, the better the play. Ibsen saw that, on the contrary, the more familiar the situation, the more interesting the play. Shakespeare had put ourselves on the stage but not our situations. Our uncles seldom murder our fathers, and cannot legally marry our mothers; we do not meet witches; our kings are not as a rule stabbed and succeeded by their stabbers; and when we raise money by bills we do not promise to pay pounds of our flesh. Ibsen supplies the want left by Shakespeare. He gives us not only ourselves, but ourselves in our own situations. The things that happen to his stage figures are things that happen to us. One consequence is that his plays are much more important to us than Shakespeare's. Another is that they are capable both of hurting us cruelly and of filling us with excited hopes of escape from idealistic tyrannies, and with visions of intenser life in the future....

The technical novelties of the Ibsen and post-Ibsen plays are, then: first, the introduction of the discussion and its development until it so overspreads and interpenetrates the action that it finally assimilates it, making play and discussion practically identical; and, second, as a consequence of making the spectators themselves the persons of the drama, and the incidents of their own lives its incidents, the disuse of the old stage tricks by which audiences had to be induced to take an interest in unreal people and improbable circumstances, and the substitution of a forensic technique of recrimination, disillusion, and penetration through ideals to the truth, with a free use of all the rhetorical and lyrical arts of the orator, the preacher, the pleader, and the rhapsodist.
(187–205)

Ghosts—1881

In his next play, Ibsen returned to the charge with such an uncompromising and outspoken attack on marriage as a useless sacrifice of human beings to an ideal, that his meaning was obscured by its very obviousness. *Ghosts,* as it is called, is the story of a woman who has faithfully acted as a model wife and mother, sacrificing herself at every point with selfless thoroughness. Her husband is a man with a huge capacity and appetite for sensuous enjoyment. Society, prescribing ideal duties and not enjoyment for him, drives him to enjoy himself in underhand and illicit ways. When he marries his model wife, her devotion to duty only makes life harder for him; and he at last takes refuge in the caresses of an undutiful but pleasure-loving housemaid, and leaves his wife to satisfy her conscience by managing his business affairs whilst he satisfies his cravings as best he can by reading novels, drinking, and flirting, as aforesaid, with the servants. At this point even those who are most indignant with Nora Helmer for walking out of the doll's house, must admit that Mrs. Alving would be justified in walking out of *her house*. But Ibsen is determined to shew you what comes of the scrupulous line of conduct you were so angry with Nora for not pursuing. Mrs. Alving feels that her place is by her husband for better for worse, and by *her child*. Now the ideal of wifely and womanly duty which demands this from her also demands that she shall regard herself as an outraged wife, and her husband as a scoundrel. And the family ideal calls upon her to suffer in silence lest she shatter her innocent son's faith in the purity of home life by letting him know the disreputable truth about his father. It is her duty to conceal that truth from the world and from him. In this she falters for one moment only. Her marriage has not been a love match: she has, in pursuance of her duty as a daughter, contracted it for the sake of her family, although her heart inclined to a highly respectable clergyman, a professor of her own idealism, named Manders. In the humiliation of her first discovery of her husband's infidelity, she leaves the house and takes refuge with Manders; but he at once leads her back to the path of duty, from which she does not again swerve. With the utmost devotion she now carries out an elaborate scheme of lying and imposture. She so manages her husband's affairs and so shields his good name that everybody believes him to be a public-spirited citizen of the strictest conformity to current ideals of respectability and family life. She sits up of nights listening to his lewd and silly conversation, and even drinking with him, to keep him from going into the streets and being detected by the neighbors in what she considers his vices. She provides for the servant he has seduced, and brings up his illegitimate daughter as a maid in her own household. And, as a crowning sacrifice, she sends her son away to Paris to be educated there, knowing that if he stays at home the shattering of his ideals must come sooner or later.

Her work is crowned with success. She gains the esteem of her old love the clergyman, who is never tired of holding up her household as a beautiful realization of the Christian ideal of marriage. Her own martyrdom is brought to an end at last by the death of her husband in the odor of a most sanctified reputation, leaving her free to recall her son from Paris and enjoy his society, and his love and gratitude, in the flower of his early manhood.

But when her son comes home, the facts refuse as obstinately as ever to correspond to her ideals. Oswald has inherited his father's love of enjoyment; and when, in dull rainy weather, he returns from Paris to the solemn strictly ordered house where virtue and duty have had their temple for so many years, his mother sees him shew the unmistakable signs of boredom with which she is so miserably familiar from of old;

then, sit after dinner killing time over the bottle; and finally—the climax of anguish—begin to flirt with the maid who, as his mother alone knows, is his own father's daughter. But there is this worldwide difference in her insight to the cases of the father and the son. She did not love the father: She loves the son with the intensity of a heart-starved woman who has nothing else left to love. Instead of recoiling from him with pious disgust and Pharisaical consciousness of moral superiority, she sees at once that he has a right to be happy in his own way, and that she has no right to force him to be dutiful and wretched in hers. She sees, too, her injustice to the unfortunate father, and the cowardice of the monstrous fabric of lies and false appearances she has wasted her life in manufacturing. She resolves that the son's life shall not be sacrificed to ideals which are to him joyless and unnatural. But she finds that the work of the ideals is not to be undone quite so easily. In driving the father to steal his pleasures in secrecy and squalor, they had brought upon him the diseases bred by such conditions; and her son now tells her that those diseases have left their mark on him, and that he carries poison in his pocket against the time, foretold to him by a Parisian surgeon, when general paralysis of the insane may destroy his faculties. In desperation she undertakes to rescue him from his horrible apprehension by making his life happy. The house shall be made as bright as Paris for him: he shall have as much champagne as he wishes until he is no longer driven to that dangerous resource by the dulness of his life with her: if he loves the girl he shall marry her if she were fifty times his half-sister. But the half-sister, on learning the state of his health, leaves the house; for she, too, is her father's daughter, and is not going to sacrifice her life in devotion to an invalid. When the mother and son are left alone in their dreary home, with the rain still falling outside, all she can do for him is to promise that if his doom overtakes him before he can poison himself, she will make a final sacrifice of her natural feelings by performing that dreadful duty, the first of all her duties that has any real basis. Then the weather clear up at last; and the sun, which the young man has so longed to see, appears. He asks her to give it to him to play with; and a glance at him shews her that the ideals have claimed their victim, and that the time has come for her to save him from a real horror by sending him from her out of the world, just as she saved him from an imaginary one years before by sending him out of Norway.

This last scene of Ghosts is so appallingly tragic that the emotions it excites prevent the meaning of the play from being seized and discussed like that of *A Doll's House*.

London Playbill, Friday the 13th, March 1891

The Independent Theatre of London,

(THÉÂTRE LIBRE).

Founder and Literary Manager - - - J. T. GREIN.

'The object of the Independent Theatre is to give special performances of plays which have a **LITERARY** and **ARTISTIC,** rather than a commercial value.

The **INDEPENDENT THEATRE** will start its career on Friday, March 13th, 1891, when

AN INVITATION PERFORMANCE OF

"GHOSTS."

BY HENRIK IBSEN, TRANSLATED BY W. ARCHER.

will be produced at the

ROYALTY.

The following Plays will form the Repertoire:

ORIGINAL plays have been promised by Messrs. Geo. Moore, W. Wilde, Cecil Raleigh, J. Zangwill, C. W. Jarvis.

TRANSLATIONS.

"DON JUAN," from the French by MOLIERE.   "EMILIA GALOTTI," from the German by LESSING.
"THE DOMINION OF DARKNESS," from the Russian by TOLSTOI.
"THE WILD DUCK," from the Norwegian by H. IBSEN.   "THE FATHER," from the Swedish by A. STRINDBERG.
"THE GAUNTLET." from the Norwegian by BJORNSTERNE-BJORNSON.
"SISTER PHILOMENE," from the French by DE GONCOURT, (Dramatised by ARTHUR BYL & JULES VIDAL).
"THE KISS," from the French by TH. DE BANVILLE.
'HONOUR," from the Dutch by W. G. VAN NOUHOUYS.   "NAPOLEON," from the German by K. BLEIBTREU.

MEMBERSHIP.

For **TERMS OF MEMBERSHIP** (including admission to the performances) to the Independent Theatre, apply to:

Mr. FRANK LINDO, 108, Elgin Avenue, Maida Vale.

The Independent Theatre is to be maintained by **voluntary Contributions** only, Which will be gladly received by:

MR. J. T. GREIN,
84, Warwick Street,
Belgrave Road, S.W.

None but *Members* or invited *Guests* can be admitted to the performances of the Independent Theatre.

The five performances will take place in the following order:

March 13th,   April 24th,   May 29th,   June 26th,   September 11th, 1891.

Alterations will be duly notified to all Members and Donors.

[P.T.O.

The Independent Theatre of London.
(THÉÂTRE LIBRE).

The first performance will take place at the

ROYALTY THEATRE,

ON

FRIDAY, MARCH 13TH, 1891,

AT 8 P.M.,

WHEN IBSEN'S

"GHOSTS,"

will be played by special permission of the Author and Translator,

MR. WILLIAM ARCHER.

CHARACTERS:

Mrs. Alving	MRS. THEODORE WRIGHT.
Oswald Alving ... . (her son) ...	MR. FRANK LINDO.
Pastor Manders	MR. LEONARD OUTRAM.
Jacob Engstrand	MR. SYDNEY HOWARD.
Regina	MISS EDITH KENWARD.

BUSINESS MANAGER: MR. FRANK LINDO, 103, Elgin Avenue, Maida Vale.

J. T. GREIN 84, Warwick Street, S.W.

Henrik Ibsen

Ghosts:
The Play

This play was translated by Brian Johnston and Rick Davis.

Text of Henrik Ibsen's *Ghosts* taken from the Smith & Kraus book *Ibsen: Four Major Plays*. Translation copyright (c) 1995 by Rick Davis and Brian Johnston. Reprinted by permission of Smith & Kraus Publishers.

Characters

MRS. HELENE ALVING, widow of Captain,
    later Chamberlain, Alving.
OSVALD ALVING, her son, a painter.
PASTOR MANDERS.
JAKOB ENGSTRAND, a carpenter.
REGINA ENGSTRAND, in service to Mrs. Alving.

The action takes place on Mrs. Alving's country estate by a large fjord in West Norway.

Act One

(A spacious garden room, with a door in the left wall and two doors in the wall on the right. In the middle of the room a round table surrounded by chairs; on the table lie books, magazines and newspapers. In the foreground to the left, a window, near it a little sofa with a sewing table in front of it. In the background, the room is continued in an open and somewhat smaller garden room or conservatory, which ends in a wall of large glass panes. In the right wall of the garden room is a door that leads down into the garden. Through the glass wall can be glimpsed a gloomy fjord landscape, veiled by steady rain. Engstrand is standing by the garden door. His left leg is somewhat deformed; under the sole of his boot he has a wooden block. Regina, with an empty flower-sprayer in her hands, prevents him from coming any nearer.)

REGINA: *(In a low voice.)* What do you want? Stay right where you are. You're soaking wet.

ENGSTRAND: It's Our Lord's rain, my child.

REGINA: It's the devil's rain, that's what it is.

ENGSTRAND: For Christ's sake, Regina—the things you say! *(He limps a couple of steps into the room.)* But here's what I wanted to tell you.

REGINA: Don't stomp around with that foot of yours! The young master is upstairs sleeping.

ENGSTRAND: Sleeping now? In broad daylight?

REGINA: None of your business.

ENGSTRAND: I went out on a binge last night...

REGINA: I can believe that.

ENGSTRAND: Yes, for we humans are weak, my child.

REGINA: We certainly are.

ENGSTRAND: And this world's full of temptations, you see—but by God, I made it to work at five-thirty this morning just the same.

REGINA: Yes, yes, but now you have to get out of here. I won't stay here rendezvousing with you.

ENGSTRAND: What aren't you doing?

REGINA: I don't want anyone to find you here. So—get going.

ENGSTRAND: I'm damned if I'll go before I get to talk to you. This afternoon I'll finish up at the schoolhouse, and then I'll scoot back to town on the night boat.

REGINA: *(Mutters.)* Nice trip.

ENGSTRAND: Thanks for that, my child. Tomorrow they'll be dedicating the orphan asylum, and you know they'll throw a huge party with—you know—lots of drinking: and no one will be able to say that Jakob Engstrand can't keep himself clear of temptation.

REGINA: Ha!

ENGSTRAND: Yes, because, there'll be a lot of important people here tomorrow. Pastor Manders is expected from town.

REGINA: He's coming today.

ENGSTRAND: There, you see? I'll be damned if I'll give him any reason to say a word against me. You understand?

REGINA: Aha! So that's it!

ENGSTRAND: What do you mean, that's it?

REGINA: What are you trying to trick the Pastor into this time?

ENGSTRAND: Shh, you're crazy. Would I trick the Pastor into anything? No, no: Pastor Manders is much too good to me. But that's what I wanted to talk to you about, see—I'm going home tonight.

REGINA: The sooner the better, as far as I'm concerned.

ENGSTRAND: Yes, but I want you with me, Regina.

REGINA: *(Her mouth open.)* You want me with you? What are you saying?

ENGSTRAND: I'm saying I want you back home with me.

REGINA: *(Scornfully.)* You'll never get me back there. Not in this life.

ENGSTRAND: We'll soon see about that.

REGINA: You bet we'll see. Me, who's been brought up by a lady like Mrs. Alving; a chamberlain's wife? Who's been treated almost like part of the family? I should run home to you? To a house like that? Uch!

ENGSTRAND: What the hell is this? Talking back to your own father, you little bitch?

REGINA: *(Muttering, without looking at him.)* You've said often enough that I'm no concern of yours.

ENGSTRAND: Puh! You're not going to worry about that—

REGINA: Haven't you often cursed me. Called me a—*fi donc!*

ENGSTRAND: No, God help me, I've never used such an ugly word.

REGINA: I remember perfectly well what word you used.

ENGSTRAND: Yes, well, only when I was a little—this world is full of temptations, Regina.

REGINA: Uch!

ENGSTRAND: When your mother nagged me like she did I had to find a way to get back at her. The way she played the fine lady! *(Imitating her.)* "Let me go, Engstrand! Leave me alone! I've served three years in the household of Chamberlain Alving of Rosenvold!" Jesus, God, she never could shut up about the fact that the captain was made a chamberlain while she was in service there.

REGINA: Poor Mother. You drove her to her death quick enough.

ENGSTRAND: Oh yes, oh yes. I'm guilty of everything.

REGINA: Uff! And then that leg of yours!

ENGSTRAND: What's that you're saying, my child?

REGINA: *Pied de mouton.*

ENGSTRAND: Is that English?

REGINA: Yes.

ENGSTRAND: It's good you've learned a few things; that'll come in handy now, Regina.

REGINA: *(After a short silence.)* What did you want with me in town?

ENGSTRAND: Can you even ask what a Father might want with his only child? Aren't I a lonely, deserted widower?

REGINA: Don't give me that crap. Why do you want me there?

ENGSTRAND: All right. I'll tell you. I'm thinking of trying something new.

REGINA: *(Cynically.)* Again? It never amounts to anything.

ENGSTRAND: Ah, but this time you'll see, Regina—may the devil have me for dinner if—

REGINA: *(Stamps her foot.)* Stop swearing!

ENGSTRAND: Shhh, shhh! You're absolutely right, my child. Let me just say this: I've saved quite a bit of money from this orphanage job.

REGINA: Really? That'll be nice for you.

ENGSTRAND: And after all, what can you spend it on out here in the country?

REGINA: So. What about it?

ENGSTRAND: So, I got the idea to put that money into something that will pay. Some sort of establishment for seamen.

REGINA: Oh God.

ENGSTRAND: A really classy establishment, you understand. Not some flea-bag hotel for sailors. No, damn it. This place will be for ship's captains and mates—the best people, you see?

REGINA: And I'm supposed to—?

ENGSTRAND: You get to help out, you know what I mean? As you can imagine, it would do wonders for appearances. You wouldn't have a hell of a lot to do, my girl. In fact you could do exactly as you pleased.

REGINA: Oh come on!

ENGSTRAND: Because you have to have women around the place, that's clear as day. You want some entertainment in the evenings, some singing and dancing and so on. See, these are wayfaring seamen who range the world's oceans. *(Coming closer.)* Don't be stupid now and get in your own way, Regina. What'll become of you out here? What good will all that education do you? Helping with the children in the new orphanage—is that really right for you? Do you really want to work yourself to death for those god-awful little brats?

REGINA: No: if what I really wanted—it could happen. It could happen.

ENGSTRAND: What could happen?

REGINA: Never mind. So you've saved a lot of money?

ENGSTRAND: Altogether, probably about seven, eight hundred kroner.

REGINA: Not bad.

ENGSTRAND: It's enough to get started, my girl.

REGINA: What about giving me a little of that money?

ENGSTRAND: No, by God, that's out of the question.

REGINA: Not even enough to buy material for a stupid dress?

ENGSTRAND: Just come into town with me and you'll have plenty of dresses.

REGINA: Ffft. I could manage that on my own if I wanted to.

ENGSTRAND: Ah, but it's much better with a father's guiding hand, Regina. Right now I can get a nice house on Little Harbor Street. They don't want too much of a deposit, and it could make a perfect seamen's establishment, you see.

REGINA: But I don't want to live with you! I don't want anything to do with you! Now go!

ENGSTRAND: You sure as hell wouldn't have to stay with me very long, my girl. Especially if you knew how to market yourself—as good-looking a thing as you've turned into these last couple of years.

REGINA: Me—?

ENGSTRAND: It wouldn't be long before a mate—maybe even a captain—

REGINA: Forget that. Sailors have no *savoir vivre*.

ENGSTRAND: What don't they have?

REGINA: I know all about sailors, thank you. I'm not marrying one.

ENGSTRAND: So forget about marrying them. The other way can pay off just as well. *(More confidentially.)* Him—the Englishman—the one with the yacht—he paid three hundred dollars, and she was no prettier than you.

REGINA: *(Going for him.)* Get out of here!

ENGSTRAND: *(Retreating.)* Hey, hey—you aren't going to hit me now, are you?

REGINA: Aren't I? Talk that way about Mother, and you bet I'll hit you! Get out of here! *(Drives him toward the garden door.)* And don't slam the door—young Mr. Alving—

ENGSTRAND: Is sleeping, I know. It's amazing how much you worry about young Mr. Alving—*(Lowering his voice.)* Ah ha! It wouldn't happen to be him that's—?

REGINA: Out, out, out! You're crazy, I tell you! No, don't go that way. Pastor Manders is coming. Go down the kitchen stairs.

ENGSTRAND: *(Towards the right.)* Yes, yes, I'm going. But you have a talk with the one coming there. He's the man to tell you what a child owes her father. And I am your father, all the same. I can prove it in the parish register.
(He goes out through the door that Regina has opened for him and closes it after himself. Regina quickly looks at herself in the mirror, fans herself with a handkerchief and straightens her collar, then busies herself with flowers. Pastor Manders, in an overcoat, carrying an umbrella and with a small traveling bag on a strap over his shoulder, enters through the garden door into the conservatory.)

PASTOR MANDERS: Good day, Miss Engstrand.

REGINA: *(Turning in happy surprise.)* Well, good day, Pastor! Is the steamer here already?

PASTOR MANDERS: It's just in. *(Comes into the room.)* The weather's been terrible lately.

REGINA: *(Following him.)* It's a blessing for the farmers, Pastor.

PASTOR MANDERS: Yes, of course. You're right. We townspeople don't remember that often enough. *(He begins to take off his overcoat.)*

REGINA: Oh, can't I help you? There we go. You're all wet! I'll just hang this in the hall. Now your umbrella—I'll set it so it can dry.
(She goes out with the things through the other door on the right. Pastor Manders sets his traveling bag and hat down on a chair. Meanwhile Regina returns.)

PASTOR MANDERS: It is really good to be indoors. So—everything's in readiness here?

REGINA: Yes, thank you.

PASTOR MANDERS: I imagine you're awfully busy getting ready for tomorrow.

REGINA: Oh, yes. There's a lot to do.

PASTOR MANDERS: And Mrs. Alving's at home, I trust?

REGINA: Heavens, yes. She's upstairs right now giving the young master some hot cocoa.

PASTOR MANDERS: I heard down at the pier that Osvald's home.

REGINA: Yes, he came the day before yesterday. We didn't expect him 'til today.

PASTOR MANDERS: And in fine fettle, I hope.

REGINA: Yes, thanks, he certainly is. Of course, he's awfully tired after his trip. He came all the way from Paris without a break—I mean, he made the whole trip on the same train. I think he's sleeping now, so we should be just a little quieter.

PASTOR MANDERS: Shhh, we'll be so, so quiet.

REGINA: *(Moving an armchair up to the table.)* And please sit down, Pastor, make yourself at home.
(He sits. She slips a footstool under his feet.)

REGINA: There! Is the Pastor comfortable now?

PASTOR MANDERS: Thanks, thanks. I'm perfectly comfortable. *(Looking at her.)* You know, Miss Engstrand, I really think you've grown since I saw you last.

REGINA: You think so, Pastor? The mistress says I've filled out too.

PASTOR MANDERS: Filled out? Well, perhaps a bit. Quite appropriately. *(A short silence.)*

Henrik Ibsen: GHOSTS—*Act One*

REGINA: Should I tell the mistress—?

PASTOR MANDERS: Thank you, there's no hurry. Now tell me, my dear Regina, how are things with your father out here?

REGINA: He's doing very well, thank you, Pastor.

PASTOR MANDERS: He came to see me last time he was in town.

REGINA: Did he really? He's always so pleased when he can speak with the Pastor.

PASTOR MANDERS: And you make sure to see him every day?

REGINA: Me? Oh, of course, whenever I get the time to—

PASTOR MANDERS: Your father does not have a very strong personality, Miss Engstrand. He really needs a guiding hand—

REGINA: Yes. That's probably true.

PASTOR MANDERS: Someone around him he can turn to, whose judgment he can count on. He confessed that to me quite openly last time he came to see me.

REGINA: Yes, he said something like that to me too. But I don't know if Mrs. Alving could do without me—especially now, when we've got to take care of the new orphanage. And I owe her so much, she's always been so kind to me.

PASTOR MANDERS: Remember a daughter's duty, my dear girl. Naturally, we would have to get Mrs. Alving's consent—

REGINA: But I'm not sure it would be exactly right for me, at my age, to keep house for a single man.

PASTOR MANDERS: What? Miss Engstrand, we're talking about your own father!

REGINA: Yes, maybe, but all the same. If only it was a good house, and a really respectable man—

PASTOR MANDERS: But, my dear Regina—

REGINA: One that I could feel affection for, and look up to as if I were his daughter—

PASTOR MANDERS: Yes, but my dear, good child—

REGINA: In that case, I'd gladly go back to town. It's so lonely out here—and you yourself know, Pastor, what it's like to be all alone in the world. I think I can say that I'm ready, willing, and able. Doesn't the Pastor know of anyplace for me?

PASTOR MANDERS: I? I certainly do not know ...

REGINA: But dear, dear Pastor—please think of me, anyway, if there ever—

PASTOR MANDERS: *(Getting up.)* I certainly will, Miss Engstrand.

REGINA: Yes, because if—

PASTOR MANDERS: Would you perhaps be so kind as to get Mrs. Alving?

REGINA: Right away, Pastor.

(She goes out to the left. Pastor Manders walks up and down the room a few times, stands for a while at the back of the room with his hands behind his back and looks out at the garden. Soon, he approaches the table, takes a book, looks at the title page, and begins inspecting others.)

PASTOR MANDERS: Hm. Well, well!

(Mrs. Alving comes in through the door at left. She is followed by Regina, who immediately goes out through the door right.)

MRS. ALVING: *(Holding out her hand.)* Welcome, Pastor.

PASTOR MANDERS: Good day to you, Mrs. Alving. Here I am, as promised.

MRS. ALVING: Punctual as ever.

PASTOR MANDERS: But you can imagine I was hard pressed to get away. All these blessed committees and councils I sit on—

MRS. ALVING: All the kinder of you to come so promptly. Now we can get through our business before lunch. But where's your bag?

PASTOR MANDERS: *(Hastily.)* My things are down at the general store. I'm staying there tonight.

MRS. ALVING: *(Suppressing a smile.)* You really can't be persuaded to spend the night in my house?

PASTOR MANDERS: No, no, thanks just the same. I'll stay down there like I usually do. It's so convenient for the return trip.

MRS. ALVING: Well, you'll do what you want. But I really think that a pair of old folks like us—

PASTOR MANDERS: Good heavens, how you joke! But of course you're overflowing with joy today. There's the celebration tomorrow, and you've got Osvald home.

MRS. ALVING: Yes, imagine how lucky I am! He hasn't been home in more than two years. And he's promised to stay with me all winter.

PASTOR MANDERS: Has he really? That's a gracious son you have there—I can imagine that life in Rome or Paris offers other sorts of attractions.

MRS. ALVING: Yes, but here at home, you see, he has his mother. Ah, my dear, blessed boy—still a place in his heart for his mother.

Henrik Ibsen: GHOSTS—*Act One*

PASTOR MANDERS: It would be a great sadness if separation and the pursuit of a thing like art could dull his natural feelings.

MRS. ALVING: Yes, you could say that. But there's no fear of that with him. I can't wait to see if you'll recognize him. He'll be down shortly. Right now he's resting a little on the sofa upstairs. But sit down, my dear Pastor.

PASTOR MANDERS: Thanks. So it's a good time, then, to—?

MRS. ALVING: Yes, absolutely. *(She sits at the table.)*

PASTOR MANDERS: Good. Let me show you—*(He goes over to the chair where his traveling bag is lying, takes a sheaf of papers out of it, sits on the opposite side of the table and searches for a clear space for the papers.)* Now—first we have—*(Breaking off.)* Tell me, Mrs. Alving, how did these books get here?

MRS. ALVING: These books? I'm reading them.

PASTOR MANDERS: You read this kind of thing?

MRS. ALVING: Of course I do.

PASTOR MANDERS: Do you think this kind of reading makes you any happier or better?

MRS. ALVING: I think I've become more confident, yes.

PASTOR MANDERS: That's extraordinary. In what way?

MRS. ALVING: Well, I find that I'm much clearer and surer about so many of the things I've been working out on my own. That's what's so odd, Pastor Manders, there's nothing really new in these books. Nothing but what most people already think and believe. But most people aren't ready to confront these things, or even acknowledge them.

PASTOR MANDERS: But my God! Do you seriously believe that most people—?

MRS. ALVING: Yes, I truly believe that.

PASTOR MANDERS: But not here in this country—among us?

MRS. ALVING: Oh, yes—among us as well.

PASTOR MANDERS: Well—I must say I—

MRS. ALVING: What do you have against these books anyway?

PASTOR MANDERS: I hope you don't think I spend my time researching these kinds of publications.

MRS. ALVING: Then I guess you don't really know what you're condemning.

PASTOR MANDERS: I have read more than enough about these writings to condemn them.

MRS. ALVING: What about your own judgment?

PASTOR MANDERS: Dear lady, there are innumerable instances in life when you must rely on others for your judgments. That's the way this world works, and it's for the best. How else would society function?

MRS. ALVING: Well, well. Maybe you're right.

PASTOR MANDERS: Otherwise, I couldn't deny that there can be a considerable fascination in these writings. And I can't really blame you for wanting to get acquainted with the intellectual currents which we hear about as they spread through the wider world—where you've let your son wander for so long. But—

MRS. ALVING: But—?

PASTOR MANDERS: *(Lowering his voice.)* But you don't have to talk about it, Mrs. Alving. You're not obliged to offer everyone who wanders in a catalog of your library—or a summary of your private thoughts.

MRS. ALVING: No, of course not—I think that's true.

PASTOR MANDERS: Just consider your obligations to this children's home, which you decided to build at a time when your thinking about spiritual matters was profoundly different from what it is now—as I understand it, in any case.

MRS. ALVING: Yes, yes. I admit that completely—but about the children's home—

PASTOR MANDERS: That's what we're here to talk about, yes. All the same—prudence, dear lady. Now let's get down to business. *(Opens folder and takes out some papers.)* You see these?

MRS. ALVING: The deeds?

PASTOR MANDERS: All of them, in perfect order. You can't imagine how hard it's been to get them ready in time. I actually had to press for them—the authorities are almost painfully scrupulous when they have a decision to make. Anyway, here they are. *(Leafing through the papers.)* Here is the deed of conveyance for the property known as Solvik, within the Rosenvold estate, along with the new buildings: the schoolhouse, teacher's dormitory and chapel. And here is the authorization for the bequest, and for the by-laws of the asylum. Would you like to see?—*(He reads.)* "By-Laws of the Children's Home to be known as the 'Captain Alving Memorial.'"

Henrik Ibsen: GHOSTS—*Act One*

MRS. ALVING: *(Looks at the papers for a long time.)* So there it is.

PASTOR MANDERS: I chose "Captain" instead of "Chamberlain." "Captain" seemed less pretentious.

MRS. ALVING: Whatever you think.

PASTOR MANDERS: And here's the bankbook showing the interest on the capital endowment set aside for operating expenses.

MRS. ALVING: Thank you—but would you mind holding on to it?

PASTOR MANDERS: I'd be happy to. I think we should leave the money in the bank for now, even though the interest isn't very attractive—four percent with six months notice for withdrawal. If we came across a good mortgage investment—naturally it would have to be a first mortgage and absolutely secure—then we could get together and discuss it in more detail.

MRS. ALVING: Yes, yes, Pastor Manders, you're the expert on all that.

PASTOR MANDERS: In any case, I'll keep my eyes open. There's just one thing, though, that I've been meaning to ask you several times.

MRS. ALVING: And what might that be?

PASTOR MANDERS: Should the Memorial buildings be insured or not?

MRS. ALVING: Of course they should be insured.

PASTOR MANDERS: Wait a moment, Mrs. Alving. Let's examine the matter a little more closely.

MRS. ALVING: I have insurance for everything—the buildings, their contents, my crops and livestock—

PASTOR MANDERS: Obviously. On your own possessions. I do the same thing, of course. But here, you see, it's a different matter. The Memorial is, as it were, to be consecrated to a high purpose.

MRS. ALVING: Yes, but what if—

PASTOR MANDERS: Speaking for myself, I can't honestly think of the slightest objection to insuring ourselves fully.

MRS. ALVING: No, that's what I think, too.

PASTOR MANDERS: But how would that sit with public opinion around here? You're a better judge of that than I.

MRS. ALVING: Hmm. Public opinion ...

PASTOR MANDERS: Is there a significant body of important opinion—I mean really important opinion—that might object?

MRS. ALVING: What do you mean by really important opinion?

PASTOR MANDERS: I was thinking mostly of people whose influence—whose position—make it hard to avoid giving their opinions a certain weight.

MRS. ALVING: You could find quite a few like that who might object to this—

PASTOR MANDERS: There, you see! In town we have any number of them. Just think of my colleagues and their flocks. It would be terribly easy for them to infer that neither you nor I had sufficient faith in Divine Providence.

MRS. ALVING: But you know for yourself that you're—

PASTOR MANDERS: Yes, yes, I know, I know—I have a clear conscience, true enough. But even so we might not be able to avoid a damaging appearance, and that could easily interfere with the work of the Memorial.

MRS. ALVING: If that were to happen, then—

PASTOR MANDERS: Nor can I quite set aside the difficult—I think I can even say painful position I would probably be put in. There's a lot of interest in this institution in the town's leading circles. It benefits the town as well, of course, and there's hope that it will lead to a major reduction in our community welfare taxes. Since I've been your adviser on the business side of things, I'm afraid those fanatics would turn on me first and foremost.

MRS. ALVING: You shouldn't be subjected to that.

PASTOR MANDERS: Not to mention the attacks in the press—

MRS. ALVING: Enough, Pastor—the matter is settled.

PASTOR MANDERS: Then you don't want any insurance?

MRS. ALVING: No, we'll do without.

PASTOR MANDERS: *(Leaning back in his chair.)* But if an accident were to happen—one never knows. Would you be able to guarantee—?

MRS. ALVING: No, absolutely not—I can tell you that right now.

PASTOR MANDERS: Well then, Mrs. Alving. This really is a grave responsibility we're taking upon ourselves.

MRS. ALVING: But do you think we have any other choice?

PASTOR MANDERS: No, that's just it. We can't do anything else. We shouldn't leave ourselves open to censure—and we have no right to stir up indignation in the community.

MRS. ALVING: You certainly shouldn't, anyway, in your position.

PASTOR MANDERS: I think we really can count on having luck on our side in this project—even a kind of special dispensation.

MRS. ALVING: Let's hope so, Pastor Manders.

PASTOR MANDERS: So, we'll leave things as they are?

MRS. ALVING: Certainly.

PASTOR MANDERS: Good. As you wish. *(Makes a note.)* And so—no insurance.

MRS. ALVING: You know, it's odd that you happened to bring this up today of all days—

PASTOR MANDERS: I've often intended to—

MRS. ALVING: Because yesterday we almost had a fire down there.

PASTOR MANDERS: What?

MRS. ALVING: Well, it didn't amount to much. Some wood shavings in the carpenter's shop caught fire.

PASTOR MANDERS: Where Engstrand works?

MRS. ALVING: Yes—they say he's pretty careless with matches.

PASTOR MANDERS: He has so much on his mind, that man—so many tribulations. But God be praised, I hear he's making an effort now to lead an irreproachable life.

MRS. ALVING: Really? Who told you that?

PASTOR MANDERS: He himself. And he's a good worker, too.

MRS. ALVING: As long as he's sober.

PASTOR MANDERS: Ah, that unfortunate weakness! But he tells me he's driven to it because of his leg. The last time he was in town—it was very moving—he came up to me and thanked me so sincerely for getting him this job here, so he could be with Regina.

MRS. ALVING: He doesn't see that much of her.

PASTOR MANDERS: Oh yes—he speaks with her every day. He told me so himself.

MRS. ALVING: Well, maybe so.

PASTOR MANDERS: He's convinced that he needs someone to hold him back when temptation looms. That's what's so lovable about Jakob Engstrand—the way he comes to you, helpless, reproaching himself and confessing his trespasses. The last time he saw me—listen, Mrs. Alving, if it were absolutely necessary for him to have Regina home with him again—

MRS. ALVING: *(Rising quickly.)* Regina!

PASTOR MANDERS: Then you mustn't stand against the idea.
MRS. ALVING: But I am against it—completely against it! And besides, Regina will have a position with the Memorial.
PASTOR MANDERS: Remember that he is her father, no matter what.
MRS. ALVING: And I know just exactly the kind of father he's been to her. No, she'll never get my consent to go back with him.
PASTOR MANDERS: *(Rising.)* My dear lady, don't take it so violently. I'm sorry to see you misjudge Jakob Engstrand so completely. It's almost as if you were frightened—
MRS. ALVING: *(More calmly.)* Never mind. I have taken Regina into my house, and she'll stay in my house. *(Listens.)* Shh, Pastor Manders, let's not talk about this any more. *(Joy lights up her face.)* Listen! Osvald's coming downstairs. Now we'll concentrate on him. *(Osvald Alving, in a light overcoat, hat in hand and smoking a large meerschaum pipe, enters through the door, left.)*
OSVALD: *(Remains standing in the doorway.)* Oh, excuse me, I thought you were in the study. *(Comes forward.)* Good morning.
PASTOR MANDERS: *(Staring.)* That's extraordinary!
MRS. ALVING: Yes, what do you have to say about him now, Pastor Manders?
PASTOR MANDERS: I'd say—I'd say—but is it really—?
OSVALD: Yes, it really is the Prodigal Son, Pastor.
PASTOR MANDERS: My dear young friend—
OSVALD: Well, the homecoming son, then.
MRS. ALVING: Osvald remembers when you had so much against his becoming a painter.
PASTOR MANDERS: To mortal eyes, many a step can well seem perilous that later—ah, welcome, welcome home! Really, my dear Osvald—I suppose I may still use your first name?
OSVALD: Of course, what else would you call me?
PASTOR MANDERS: Good. What I meant was—my dear Osvald—you mustn't think that I condemn everything artists stand for. I assume there must be quite a few who can preserve their inner selves unstained in that way of life.
OSVALD: Let's hope so.
MRS. ALVING: *(Beaming with pleasure.)* I know one who has preserved an unstained self both inside and out. All you have to do is look at him, Pastor.

OSVALD: *(Pacing up and down.)* Yes, yes, Mother—that's enough.

PASTOR MANDERS: Without a doubt, there's no denying it. And you've already begun to make a name for yourself. The papers have mentioned you quite a bit, and always in glowing terms. Although I have to say that lately there hasn't been as much.

OSVALD: *(Near the conservatory.)* I haven't been painting much recently.

MRS. ALVING: A painter needs to rest now and then, like everyone else.

PASTOR MANDERS: Yes, I understand—to prepare himself, to gather strength for some really big project.

OSVALD: Yes. Mother, are we eating soon?

MRS. ALVING: In half an hour. He's got a good appetite, thank God.

PASTOR MANDERS: And a taste for tobacco, too.

OSVALD: I found Father's pipe upstairs in the bedroom, so—

PASTOR MANDERS: Aha! That's it then.

MRS. ALVING: What?

PASTOR MANDERS: When Osvald came through that door there with the pipe in his mouth, it was as if I saw his father alive again.

OSVALD: Really?

MRS. ALVING: How can you say that? Osvald takes after me.

PASTOR MANDERS: Yes, but there's a line there, around the corners of the mouth, something about the lips, that brings Alving back to mind—at least when he's smoking.

MRS. ALVING: No, absolutely not. I think Osvald's mouth reminds me more of a priest's.

PASTOR MANDERS: Yes, yes, many of my colleagues have a similar expression.

MRS. ALVING: Put the pipe down now—I don't want smoking in here.

OSVALD: *(Does so.)* Gladly. I just wanted to try it—because I smoked it once before, as a child.

MRS. ALVING: You did?

OSVALD: Yes. I was very small at the time. And I remember I came up to Father's room one evening when he was feeling happy and good.

MRS. ALVING: Oh, you don't remember anything from those years.

OSVALD: Oh yes—I remember it clearly. He took me and sat me on his knee and let me smoke his pipe. "Smoke it, boy," he said—"smoke it down deep, boy." And I smoked as much as I could, until I felt myself going pale and my forehead broke out in huge drops of sweat. Then he laughed so uproariously—

PASTOR MANDERS: Extraordinary.

MRS. ALVING: It's just something he dreamt.

OSVALD: No, Mother, I definitely didn't dream it. Don't you remember? You came in then and carried me to the nursery. I got sick, and I saw you were crying. Did Father often play jokes like that?

PASTOR MANDERS: As a young man he was so full of the joy of life.

OSVALD: And yet he was able to accomplish so much in the world—so much that was good and useful, even dying as young as he did.

PASTOR MANDERS: Yes, it's a fact that you've inherited the name of an energetic and worthy man, Osvald Alving. Let's hope it will be an inspiration to you—

OSVALD: It ought to be.

PASTOR MANDERS: It was nice of you to come home for these celebrations in his honor.

OSVALD: It's the least I can do for Father.

MRS. ALVING: And the nicest thing of all is how long I'll get to keep him.

PASTOR MANDERS: Yes, I hear you'll be staying all winter.

OSVALD: I'll be staying indefinitely, Pastor. Oh, it's wonderful to come home again.

MRS. ALVING: *(Beaming.)* Yes, isn't that true?

PASTOR MANDERS: *(Looking at him sympathetically.)* You went out into the world very early, Osvald.

OSVALD: Yes, I did. I wonder sometimes if it wasn't too early.

MRS. ALVING: Not at all. It's good for a bright boy. Especially when he's an only child. He shouldn't be kept at home to be spoiled by his mother and father.

PASTOR MANDERS: That's a highly debatable point, Mrs. Alving. The ancestral home is and always will remain a child's rightful place.

OSVALD: Now I'm in total agreement with the Pastor.

PASTOR MANDERS: Just look at your own son. Yes, we can talk about this in front of him. What has the result been for him? He's twenty-six or twenty-seven and he's never had the chance to see what a respectable home is like.

OSVALD: I beg your pardon, Pastor, but you're quite mistaken about that.

PASTOR MANDERS: Really? I thought you lived almost exclusively among artists.

OSVALD: I did, yes.

PASTOR MANDERS: Mostly among younger artists.

OSVALD: Yes, that's right.

PASTOR MANDERS: But I thought most of those people didn't have the means to support a home and family.

OSVALD: Many of them lack the means to get married, Pastor.

PASTOR MANDERS: That's what I'm saying.

OSVALD: But they can still have a home. And one or two do—very respectable, very pleasant homes.
(Mrs. Alving, following closely, nods but says nothing.)

PASTOR MANDERS: I'm not talking about bachelor's houses. When I say home, I mean a real family home where a man lives with his wife and his children.

OSVALD: Yes, or with his children and their mother.

PASTOR MANDERS: *(Startled, claps his hands.)* But merciful—!

OSVALD: Well?

PASTOR MANDERS: Lives with—his children's mother?

OSVALD: Yes. What should he do—abandon her?

PASTOR MANDERS: So you're talking about illicit relationships! About those irresponsible, so-called "free marriages!"

OSVALD: I've never noticed anything especially irresponsible about the way these people live together.

PASTOR MANDERS: But how is it possible that young men and women of even moderately decent upbringing can bring themselves to live like that—in the public eye.

OSVALD: What should they do instead? A poor young artist—a poor young girl—getting married costs money. What should they do?

PASTOR MANDERS: What should they do? Well, Mr. Alving, I'll tell you what they should do. They should stay away from each other from the beginning, that's what they should do.

OSVALD: That kind of advice wouldn't get you very far with young, warm-blooded people in love.

MRS. ALVING: No, not too far.

PASTOR MANDERS: *(Persisting.)* And the authorities tolerate such things! It goes on openly, no one stops it! *(Facing Mrs. Alving.)* Didn't I have good reason to be worried about your son? Moving in circles where blatant immorality is the custom—where it's even claimed as a right?

OSVALD: Let me tell you something, Pastor. I've been a regular Sunday guest in some of these unconventional homes—

PASTOR MANDERS: On Sundays, no less!

OSVALD: Yes, when people should be enjoying themselves. And never once have I heard an offensive word, much less witnessed anything that could be called immoral. But do you know where I have encountered immorality among the artists?

PASTOR MANDERS: No, praise God!

OSVALD: Then I think I should enlighten you: I run into it whenever one of our exemplary husbands and fathers comes down there to get a close look at the other side of life—so they do us artists the honor of paying a visit to our humble cafés. What an education we're treated to then! Those gentlemen can teach us about places and things we never even dreamed of.

PASTOR MANDERS: What? You're claiming that respectable men from here at home would—?

OSVALD: Haven't you ever—when these respectable men come home again—haven't you heard them screaming about the rampant epidemic of immorality abroad?

PASTOR MANDERS: Naturally, of course—

MRS. ALVING: I've heard it too.

OSVALD: Well, they know what they're talking about. There are connoisseurs among them. *(Clutching his head.)* Ah!—this beautiful, glorious, free life out there—polluted like that!

MRS. ALVING: You mustn't excite yourself, Osvald, it's not good for you.

OSVALD: No, Mother, you're right. It's not healthy. It's this damn fatigue. I'll go for a little walk before we eat. I'm sorry, Pastor—I know you can't bring yourself to see that. But it just suddenly came over me and I had to say it. *(He goes out through the second door, right.)*

MRS. ALVING: My poor boy.

PASTOR MANDERS: Yes, you might well say that. So this is what's become of him. *(Mrs. Alving looks at him silently. Manders walks up and down.)* He called himself the Prodigal Son. Alas, how true—how true. So what do you think of all this?

MRS. ALVING: I think every word Osvald said was right.

PASTOR MANDERS: *(Stops short.)* Right? Right! With those principles?

MRS. ALVING: Here—all by myself—I've come to think exactly the same way. But I've never dared to talk about it. All right, now my boy will speak for me.

PASTOR MANDERS: You are a pitiable woman, Mrs. Alving. Now I must speak to you seriously; no longer as your business adviser and executor, nor as the life-long friend of your husband and yourself. I stand before you as your priest: exactly the same one who stood before you in your life's most desperate hour.

MRS. ALVING: And what does the priest have to say to me?

PASTOR MANDERS: First, I will rouse your memory a little, Mrs. Alving. The moment is right for it. Tomorrow is the tenth anniversary of your husband's death; tomorrow a memorial will be unveiled in commemoration of that event; tomorrow I will speak to the whole assembled company—but today I want to speak to you alone.

MRS. ALVING: All right, Pastor. Speak!

PASTOR MANDERS: Do you remember how, after being married barely a year, you came to the outer edge of the abyss? How you left your house and home, fled your husband—yes, Mrs. Alving, fled—fled him and refused to go back to him, no matter how much he pleaded and begged you to?

MRS. ALVING: Have you forgotten how unbelievably miserable I was that first year?

PASTOR MANDERS: The spirit of rebellion makes us seek happiness here in this life; that's precisely its aim. But what claim have we human beings to happiness? No, Mrs. Alving, we must do our duty! And your duty was to stand by the man you had chosen, and to whom you were bound by sacred ties.

Mrs. Alving: You know very well what kind of life Alving was leading in those days—the debaucheries he was guilty of.

Pastor Manders: I am all too aware of the rumors about him that were making the rounds. And I am the last person to condone his behavior then, insofar as the rumors had any truth to them. But a wife is not her husband's judge; your job was to bear, with a humble spirit, the cross that a higher will destined for you. Instead you rebelliously cast away the cross, abandoned the weak and faltering, whom you should have supported—went off and put your good name and reputation at risk—and nearly dragged other reputations into it as well.

Mrs. Alving: Others? I think you mean one other.

Pastor Manders: It was exceedingly reckless of you to seek refuge with me.

Mrs. Alving: With our pastor—in the home of a good friend?

Pastor Manders: For that reason especially. Thank the Lord your God that I found the necessary firmness—that I was able to turn you away from your hysterical intentions, and that it was granted me to lead you back to your duty, home to your lawful husband.

Mrs. Alving: Yes, Pastor Manders, that was certainly your work.

Pastor Manders: I was but a humble instrument in the hand of a higher power. And from this moment—when I bent you to the yoke of duty and obedience—didn't there grow a great blessing which filled all the days of your life? Didn't I foretell all this? Didn't Alving turn away from his errors, exactly as a man must do, and live with you lovingly and blamelessly for the rest of his life? Didn't he become a benefactor to this district, lifting you up alongside him until you became a colleague in everything he did? And a true colleague you were, Mrs. Alving—that I'll give you. But now I come to the next great failure in your life.

Mrs. Alving: What do you mean by that?

Pastor Manders: Just as you once shirked the duties of a wife, you've shirked those of a Mother in the same way.

Mrs. Alving: Ah—

Henrik Ibsen: GHOSTS—*Act One*

PASTOR MANDERS: All your life you've been ruled by a disastrously rebellious spirit. Your longings have drawn you toward everything undisciplined and lawless. You would never tolerate the slightest restraint. You've recklessly and irresponsibly tossed aside every inconvenience in your life, like some package you could just put down at will. It didn't please you to be a wife any longer, and so you left your husband. Being a mother was too much trouble, and so you turned your child loose with strangers.

MRS. ALVING: Yes, that's true. That's what I did.

PASTOR MANDERS: And in so doing, you've become a stranger to him.

MRS. ALVING: No, no. That I am not!

PASTOR MANDERS: You are. You must be! And look at the state in which you got him back! Consider well, Mrs. Alving. You trespassed against your husband; this memorial you're raising to him shows you admit this in your heart. Now admit, as well, that you have trespassed against your son; there might still be time to turn him away from his errors. Turn away yourself—and save what can still be saved in him. For truly *(With raised forefinger.)*—truly, Mrs. Alving, you are a profoundly guilty woman. I've considered it my duty to tell you this.
(Silence.)

MRS. ALVING: *(Slowly and deliberately.)* Now you've spoken, Pastor; and tomorrow you'll speak publicly, in my husband's memory. I won't be speaking tomorrow. But I'll speak a bit to you today just as you have spoken to me.

PASTOR MANDERS: Of course, you want to make excuses for your conduct—

MRS. ALVING: No, I'll just tell you something.

PASTOR MANDERS: Well?

MRS. ALVING: Everything you've just been saying about my husband and me and our life together after—as you put it—you led me back to the path of duty—none of that is based on even the slightest observation on your part. From that moment on, you—our everyday best friend—never again set foot in our house.

PASTOR MANDERS: You and your husband moved away from town—

MRS. ALVING: Yes, and you never came out here to see us while my husband was alive. Business finally forced you to visit me, since you had gotten involved with the Memorial.

PASTOR MANDERS: *(Softly and uncertainly.)* Helene—if this is meant as a reproach, I'd ask you to consider—

MRS. ALVING: The sensitivities of your calling, yes. And of course I was a runaway wife—you can't be too careful with senseless creatures like that.

PASTOR MANDERS: Dear—Mrs. Alving, that is a gross exaggeration.

MRS. ALVING: Yes, yes, yes, let it go. I just want to say this: when you pass judgment on my married life, you are basing it on nothing more than the common gossip of the time.

PASTOR MANDERS: What if that's true? What then?

MRS. ALVING: Now, Pastor Manders—now I'm going to tell you the truth. I swore to myself that you—and only you—would know it someday.

PASTOR MANDERS: And what is this truth?

MRS. ALVING: The truth is that my husband died just as debauched as he lived his whole life.

PASTOR MANDERS: *(Fumbling for a chair.)* What did you say?

MRS. ALVING: Just as debauched, after nineteen years of marriage—in his proclivities, anyway—as he was before you married us.

PASTOR MANDERS: But these youthful errors—these improprieties, dissipations if you will—you call these a debauched life?

MRS. ALVING: Those are the words our family doctor used.

PASTOR MANDERS: I don't understand you.

MRS. ALVING: You don't have to.

PASTOR MANDERS: I feel dizzy. Your entire marriage—all those years of life with your husband—were nothing more than wallpaper over an abyss!

MRS. ALVING: Nothing more. Now you know.

PASTOR MANDERS: This—I find I can't comprehend it. I cannot understand—can't grasp—how was it possible? How could something like that be kept quiet?

MRS. ALVING: That has been my struggle, day after day. When we had Osvald, I thought Alving was getting better—but that didn't last long. Now the struggle had to be redoubled, a life-and-death struggle to guarantee that no one would find out what kind of man my child's father was. And you know how charming Alving was. People couldn't help thinking well of him. He was one of those people whose real lives never get in the way of their reputations. But then, Manders—you have to know this too—then came the most disgusting thing of all.

PASTOR MANDERS: More disgusting than all this?

MRS. ALVING: I put up with everything as long as it was done in secret, away from the house. But when the sickness came right within our own four walls—

PASTOR MANDERS: What are you saying? Here!

MRS. ALVING: Yes, right here in our home. *(Points toward the first door on the right.)* In there in the dining room was where I first discovered it. I needed something inside, and the door was ajar. I heard our maid come up from the garden to water the plants in here—

PASTOR MANDERS: Then—?

MRS. ALVING: I heard Alving come in. I heard him saying something to her very softly. And then I heard *(With a short laugh.)*—oh, I can still hear it, so devastating and at the same time so ludicrous—I heard my own maid whisper: "Let go of me. Chamberlain Alving! Leave me alone!"

PASTOR MANDERS: That was terribly indiscreet of him! Oh, but it wasn't anything more than a momentary lapse, I'm sure, Mrs. Alving. Please, believe me.

MRS. ALVING: I soon found out what to believe. Chamberlain Alving had his way with the girl—and that affair had its consequences, Pastor Manders.

PASTOR MANDERS: *(As if turned to stone.)* And all that in this house! In this house!

MRS. ALVING: I've had to endure a lot in this house. To keep him home evenings—and nights—I had to join him over a bottle up in his room. I had to sit alone with him, toasting and drinking with him, listening to his obscene, nonsensical talk, had to drag him into bed with my bare hands—

PASTOR MANDERS: *(Shaken.)* That you could endure that!

MRS. ALVING: I endured it for my little boy. But when that last humiliation occurred—my own maid—then I swore to myself that this would be the end! And so I took power in this house—absolute power over him and everything else. Now I had a weapon against him, you see; he didn't dare object. Then I sent Osvald away. He was almost seven—he'd begun to notice things, and ask questions the way children do. And I couldn't bear that, Manders. I thought the child would be poisoned just by breathing the air in this polluted house. And now you can see why he never set foot

MRS. ALVING: here as long as his father lived. No one can possibly know what that has cost me.
PASTOR MANDERS: Your life has certainly tested you to the limit.
MRS. ALVING: I couldn't have survived without my work. Yes, I have worked—all these additions to the estate, all the improvements, all the innovations that Alving got credit for—do you think those were his? He, who'd lie on the sofa all day reading old government papers! No; now I'll tell you this too: I was the one who steered him in the right direction whenever he had a lucid moment, and I had to carry the whole weight when he went back to his "errors" or just collapsed in a spineless, miserable heap.
PASTOR MANDERS: And you are raising a memorial to such a man.
MRS. ALVING: You see the power of a bad conscience.
PASTOR MANDERS: A bad—? What do you mean?
MRS. ALVING: I was always haunted by the idea that the truth would someday come out and be believed. So the memorial was meant to kill all the rumors and rule out every doubt.
PASTOR MANDERS: That you've certainly done, Mrs. Alving.
MRS. ALVING: And there was one other reason. I was determined that Osvald, my own son, wouldn't get anything at all from his father's inheritance.
PASTOR MANDERS: Then it's Alving's fortune that—
MRS. ALVING: Yes. The amount I've contributed to this institution every year comes to the exact total that made lieutenant Alving such a good match at the time.
PASTOR MANDERS: Then—I understand—
MRS. ALVING: It was the market price. I don't want that money to touch Osvald's hands. My son will get everything from me, and me alone.
(Osvald Alving comes through the second door, right. He has left his hat and coat outside.)
MRS. ALVING: You're back again, dear? My dear, dear boy!
OSVALD: Yes, you can't do anything in this interminable rain! But we're eating soon, I hear—that's good news!
REGINA: *(With a package from the dining room.)* A package has just come for Mrs. Alving.
MRS. ALVING: *(With a glance at Pastor Manders.)* The choral parts for tomorrow, probably.

PASTOR MANDERS: Hmm.

REGINA: And the meal is served.

MRS. ALVING: Good. We'll be there in a moment. I'll just—*(Begins to open package.)*.

REGINA: *(To Osvald.)* Will Mr. Alving have red or white wine?

OSVALD: Both, Miss Engstrand.

REGINA: *Bien*. Very well, Mr. Alving. *(She goes into the dining room.)*

OSVALD: I'll help her uncork the bottles. *(He also goes in, the door half-closing behind him.)*

MRS. ALVING: *(Having opened the package.)* Yes, that's right—the choir music, Pastor Manders.

PASTOR MANDERS: *(With folded hands.)* How I'll ever be able to give my speech tomorrow with a clear conscience, I don't—

MRS. ALVING: Oh, you'll find a way.

PASTOR MANDERS: *(Softly, so as not to be heard in the dining room.)* Yes, above all we can't risk any scandal—

MRS. ALVING: *(Quietly but firmly.)* No. And then this long, horrible farce will come to an end. From tomorrow on, it will be as if the dead had never lived in this house. There'll be no one here but my boy and his Mother.
(In the dining room, the sound of a chair being overturned. At the same time, Regina's voice in a sharp whisper.)

REGINA: Osvald! Are you crazy? Let me go!

MRS. ALVING: *(Starting in terror.)* Ah—

PASTOR MANDERS: *(Agitated.)* What's happening? What is it, Mrs. Alving?

MRS. ALVING: *(Hoarsely.)* Ghosts. Those two from the greenhouse—are walking again.

PASTOR MANDERS: What are you saying? Regina—is she—?

MRS. ALVING: Yes. Come on. Not a word.
(She grips Manders' arm and goes shakily towards the dining room.)

End of Act One

Act Two

(The same room. A mist still lies heavily over the landscape. Pastor Manders and Mrs. Alving enter from the dining room.)

MRS. ALVING: *(Still in the doorway.)* You're very welcome, Pastor. *(Calling into the dining room.)* Aren't you joining us, Osvald?

OSVALD: *(Within.)* No thanks. I think I'll go out for a while.

MRS. ALVING: Yes, why don't you do that, now that the rain's let up. *(Closes the dining room door, goes to the hall door and calls.)* Regina!

REGINA: *(Outside.)* Yes, ma'am?

MRS. ALVING: Go down to the laundry and help with the decorations.

REGINA: Yes, ma'am. *(Mrs. Alving makes sure that Regina has gone; then she closes the door.)*

PASTOR MANDERS: Are you sure he can't hear anything in there?

MRS. ALVING: Not with the door closed. Besides, he's going out.

PASTOR MANDERS: I'm still in shock. I don't know how I managed to eat a bite of that heavenly meal.

MRS. ALVING: *(Controlling her agitation. Pacing up and down.)* I feel the same. But what can we do?

PASTOR MANDERS: Yes, what can we do? Believe me, I don't know—I've got no experience in things like this.

MRS. ALVING: I don't think anything bad has happened yet.

PASTOR MANDERS: No, heaven forbid! But it's a tricky situation all the same.

MRS. ALVING: It's just a whim of Osvald's, you can be sure of that.

PASTOR MANDERS: Well, like I said, I'm not really up on these things, but I definitely think that—

MRS. ALVING: She has to leave the house, without a doubt. Right away. That's as clear as day.

PASTOR MANDERS: Yes, that's understood.

MRS. ALVING: But where should she go? We can't very well—

PASTOR MANDERS: Where? Home to her father, naturally.

MRS. ALVING: To whom did you say?

PASTOR MANDERS: To her—aha—Engstrand's not—of course. But Good Lord, Mrs. Alving, how can this be? You're mistaken, I'm sure.

MRS. ALVING: Unfortunately not—about any of it. Johanna had to come to me and confess everything, and Alving couldn't deny it. The only thing to do was cover up the whole affair.

PASTOR MANDERS: Yes, that's right—that was all you could do.

MRS. ALVING: The girl left right away, with a pretty good sum of money in her pocket to keep quiet. She took care of everything else when she got to town. She revived an old relationship with Engstrand—I'd imagine she let it be known that she had some money—and came up with some story about a foreigner who had docked his yacht here that summer. So she and Engstrand got married in a hurry. Oh, of course—you married them.

PASTOR MANDERS: How am I supposed to make sense of all this—? I distinctly remember when Engstrand came to me to set up his wedding. He was so completely repentant—he did nothing but criticize himself for his own irresponsibility.

MRS. ALVING: Of course he took the blame himself.

PASTOR MANDERS: But the hypocrisy of the man! And against me! I would never have believed that of Jakob Engstrand. Well, I'll certainly prepare a rather serious sermon for him—he can look forward to that. And the immorality of that kind of marriage—for money! How much did the girl get?

MRS. ALVING: Three hundred.

PASTOR MANDERS: Think about it—to let yourself get dragged into marrying a fallen woman for a miserable three hundred dollars!

MRS. ALVING: Well, what do you have to say to me—I let myself get dragged into marrying a fallen man.

PASTOR MANDERS: Good God, what are you talking about? A fallen man!

MRS. ALVING: Do you think Alving was any purer when we went to the altar than Johanna was when Engstrand got himself married?

PASTOR MANDERS: But there's all the difference in the world between—

MRS. ALVING: Not so much. In fact—there was, however, a big difference in the price. A miserable three hundred dollars against a whole fortune.

PASTOR MANDERS: How can you compare two completely different things? You were responding to your family's wishes, and your own heart.

MRS. ALVING: *(Not looking at him.)* I thought you knew where what you call my heart was wandering at the time.

PASTOR MANDERS: *(Distantly.)* If I'd known anything like that I certainly wouldn't have been a daily guest in your husband's house.

MRS. ALVING: Still, the fact remains that I really didn't pay any attention to what I wanted.

PASTOR MANDERS: Well, you listened to your nearest relatives anyway—just as you're supposed to—your mother and your two aunts.

MRS. ALVING: Yes, that's very true. The three of them totaled it all up for me. Ah, it's just incredible how neatly they figured out that it would be insane to turn down that offer. If Mother could look down and see the strings that came attached to all that splendor—

PASTOR MANDERS: No one can be held responsible for the way it turned out. None the less, there's one solid fact: your marriage was founded in strict accord with the principles of law and order.

MRS. ALVING: *(By the window.)* Yes—law and order. I often think they cause all the misery in the world.

PASTOR MANDERS: Mrs. Alving, you're heading toward sin—

MRS. ALVING: Well, be that as it may. I just can't stand all these restrictions and obligations any more—I can't stand them! I've got to work my way to freedom.

PASTOR MANDERS: What does that mean?

MRS. ALVING: *(Drumming on the windowpane.)* I should never have covered up the truth about Alving's life. But I didn't dare do otherwise, not at the time. And not just for my own sake, either. I was so cowardly!

PASTOR MANDERS: Cowardly?

MRS. ALVING: If people found out about it they'd just have said something like: "Poor man, no wonder he strays a bit at times—with a wife who runs off and leaves him."

PASTOR MANDERS: And they'd have had some justification.

MRS. ALVING: *(Looking hard at him.)* If I were everything I should be, I would have taken Osvald aside and told him. "Listen, my son, your Father was a fallen man."

PASTOR MANDERS: Merciful God!

MRS. ALVING: And then I would have told him everything I've told you, word for word.

PASTOR MANDERS: Mrs. Alving, you're almost horrifying me.

MRS. ALVING: Yes, I know! I know! I horrify myself when I think about it. *(Walks from the window.)* What a coward I am!

PASTOR MANDERS: What you call cowardice, I call doing your duty, living up to your responsibility! Have you forgotten that a child should love and honor his father and mother?

MRS. ALVING: Let's not talk abstractions. Let's ask: should Osvald love and honor Chamberlain Alving?

PASTOR MANDERS: Doesn't some voice in your mother's heart cry out to you not to shatter your son's ideals?

MRS. ALVING: What about the truth?

PASTOR MANDERS: What about ideals?

MRS. ALVING: Ideals, ideals! If only I weren't such a coward!

PASTOR MANDERS: Don't throw away ideals, Mrs. Alving—that can set a terrible vengeance in motion. Especially in Osvald's case. Osvald's not long on ideals, unfortunately. But as far as I can tell, his father does represent some sort of ideal for him.

MRS. ALVING: You're right about that.

PASTOR MANDERS: You stirred those ideals up yourself, and kept them alive, in your letters to him.

MRS. ALVING: Yes, I was under the spell of duty and convention—so I lied to my boy, year after year. Ah, what a coward—what a coward.

PASTOR MANDERS: You've created a joyful illusion for your son, Mrs. Alving—don't underrate the value of that.

MRS. ALVING: Hmm. I wonder if it's such a good thing after all? But I just won't put up with him fooling around with Regina. He's not going to ruin that poor girl's life.

PASTOR MANDERS: Good God, no. That would be terrible!

MRS. ALVING: If I thought he was serious about—if I thought it could make him happy—

PASTOR MANDERS: Yes, what then?

MRS. ALVING: It still wouldn't work. Regina's not that kind of person.

PASTOR MANDERS: What do you mean?

MRS. ALVING: If I weren't such a coward, I'd say to him. "Go ahead and marry her, or come up with some other arrangement, only do it openly and honestly."

PASTOR MANDERS: May God forgive you—marriage? Of all the terrifying—it's unheard of!

MRS. ALVING: Unheard of? Oh yes! Raise your right hand now—don't you think that you could find plenty of couples just as closely related out here in the country?

PASTOR MANDERS: I absolutely don't understand you.

MRS. ALVING: Oh yes you do.

PASTOR MANDERS: Well—you must be thinking of those instances of—well, yes, unfortunately, family life isn't always as pure as it should be. But in the world you're talking about, you can't really know for certain. In this case, on the other hand—where a Mother would willingly permit her own son to—

MRS. ALVING: I'm not willing. I don't want to let this happen for anything in the world—that's exactly what I was saying.

PASTOR MANDERS: No, because you said you were a coward. But what if you weren't a coward—then, in the Creator's name, what a monstrous union—!

MRS. ALVING: Well, when it comes to that, they say we're all descended from that kind of union. And whose idea was that, Pastor Manders?

PASTOR MANDERS: We won't discuss that subject now, Mrs. Alving. You're hardly in the right frame of mind for it. How could you dare to say that it was cowardice on your part—?

MRS. ALVING: Let me tell you what I mean by that. I'm terrified—and it's made me something of a coward—because my mind is haunted by the dead among us, and I'm afraid I can never be completely free from them.

PASTOR MANDERS: What did you call them?

MRS. ALVING: The dead among us—ghosts. When I heard Regina and Osvald in there, I saw ghosts. I almost believe we are ghosts, all of us. It's not just what we inherit from our fathers and mothers that walks again in us—it's all sorts of dead old ideas and dead beliefs and things like that. They don't exactly live in us, but there they sit all the same and we can't get rid of them. All I have to do is pick up a newspaper, and I see ghosts lurking between the lines. I think there are ghosts everywhere you turn in this country—as many as there are grains of sand—and then there we all are, so abysmally afraid of the light.

PASTOR MANDERS: Aha! This is your profit after all that reading. Excellent, isn't it? Ach, these detestable, rabble-rousing, free-thinking writings.

MRS. ALVING: You're wrong, my dear Pastor. You're the one who egged me on to do my own thinking. You can take all the credit, all the praise for that.

PASTOR MANDERS: I!

MRS. ALVING: Yes—when you forced me to submit to what you called duty and responsibility; when you praised as right and proper what my own mind found hideous and revolting. Then I started to look over your teaching thread by thread. I only wanted to pull apart a knot or two—but when they came loose, the whole thing unraveled. What I thought was a handmade garment turned out to be a mass-produced imitation.

PASTOR MANDERS: *(Softly, moved.)* Is this all I won in my life's hardest battle?

MRS. ALVING: Call it your most pitiful defeat.

PASTOR MANDERS: No, Helene—it was my greatest victory—over myself.

MRS. ALVING: It was a crime against us both.

PASTOR MANDERS: When I commanded you to go home—when I said "Woman, your place is with your lawful husband"—when you came to me crying, pleading, "take me—here I am"—was that a crime?

MRS. ALVING: Yes, I think so.

PASTOR MANDERS: We don't understand each other at all.

MRS. ALVING: At least not any more.

PASTOR MANDERS: Never—not once—not even in my most private thoughts, have I ever thought of you as anything other than another man's wife.

MRS. ALVING: You believe that?

PASTOR MANDERS: Helene—!

MRS. ALVING: Some things are easy to forget, I guess.

PASTOR MANDERS: No, no—I'm the same now as I always was.

MRS. ALVING: *(Changing her tone.)* Well, well, well. Let's not talk about the old days any more. Here you are up to your ears in committee work and boards of trustees, and I'm running around doing battle with ghosts—both inside and out.

PASTOR MANDERS: I can help you with the outer ones at least. After listening to everything you've said today—with growing horror, I'm telling you—I can't in good conscience allow a young, defenseless girl to remain in your house.

MRS. ALVING: Don't you think it would be best to get her settled—I mean married?

PASTOR MANDERS: Absolutely. I think that would be best all around. Regina is at that age right now when—well, I don't really know much about these things—

MRS. ALVING: Regina has matured pretty fast.

PASTOR MANDERS: Yes, she has, hasn't she? I was impressed at how remarkably well developed she was when I was preparing her for her confirmation. Anyway, for the time being she should go home, live with her father—ah—of course—Engstrand's not—and he—he's been lying to me this way!
(A knock at the hall door.)

MRS. ALVING: Who can that be? Come in.

ENGSTRAND: *(In the doorway, dressed in Sunday clothes.)* Begging your pardon—

PASTOR MANDERS: Aha! Hmm—

MRS. ALVING: Engstrand—it's you.

ENGSTRAND: There weren't any maids around, so I took the great liberty of knocking, as they say.

MRS. ALVING: All right, come in. You have something to say to me?

ENGSTRAND: *(Entering.)* No, thanks anyway. I really wanted a word with the pastor.

PASTOR MANDERS: *(Pacing up and down.)* Hmm. Really? A word with me? That's what you want?

ENGSTRAND: Yes, I'd be terribly glad—

PASTOR MANDERS: *(Stops in front of him.)* All right, but quickly.

ENGSTRAND: You see, it's like this, Pastor—now that we've gotten paid down there—can't thank you enough, ma'am—now that everything's finished, I was thinking it would be so proper and perfect for all of us who've been working together so beautifully—well, I was thinking we ought to finish up this evening with a little prayer.

PASTOR MANDERS: A prayer? Down at the Memorial?

ENGSTRAND: Yes. But if the pastor thinks it's not proper—

PASTOR MANDERS: Oh, it most certainly is, but—hmm—

ENGSTRAND: I used to hold a little evening prayer service down there myself.

MRS. ALVING: Did you?

Henrik Ibsen: GHOSTS—*Act Two*

ENGSTRAND: Yes, now and then. A little uplift, you might say. But I'm just a simple, ordinary man with no real spiritual gifts, God help me—so I was thinking that since Pastor Manders happened to be out here—

PASTOR MANDERS: I have to ask you a question first. Are you in the right frame of mind for a gathering like this? Do you feel your conscience is free and clear?

ENGSTRAND: God help us, let's not waste our time talking about my conscience, Pastor—

PASTOR MANDERS: That's exactly what we're going to talk about. So, what's your answer?

ENGSTRAND: Oh, that conscience of mine—it can sure be tough sometimes.

PASTOR MANDERS: At least you recognize the fact. Tell me now, and don't try to talk around the question: What is the truth about Regina?

MRS. ALVING: *(Quickly.)* Pastor Manders!

PASTOR MANDERS: *(Reassuringly.)* Just let me—

ENGSTRAND: Regina? Lord, you're scaring me. *(Looks at Mrs. Alving.)* Nothing bad's happened to her, has it?

PASTOR MANDERS: We certainly hope not. I'm talking about you and Regina—what's the truth there? You claim to be her father, don't you? Well?

ENGSTRAND: *(Uncertainly.)* Well—hmm—the Pastor already knows about the business between me and the dearly departed Johanna—

PASTOR MANDERS: No more twisting the truth! Your late wife confided everything to Mrs. Alving before she left the house here.

ENGSTRAND: But it was supposed to be—she did that?

PASTOR MANDERS: So you're exposed, Engstrand.

ENGSTRAND: So she—after taking an oath and swearing to heaven—

PASTOR MANDERS: She swore!

ENGSTRAND: She took an oath, I mean. So sincerely, too.

PASTOR MANDERS: And you've been hiding the truth from me all these years. From me, who trusted you completely.

ENGSTRAND: Yes, sorry, but that's what I did.

PASTOR MANDERS: Have I deserved this from you, Engstrand? Haven't I always extended a helping hand to you, in word and deed, if it was in my power to do so? Answer. Haven't I done that?

ENGSTRAND: Things would have looked bad for me plenty of times if it hadn't been for Pastor Manders.

PASTOR MANDERS: And this is how you repay me. Get me to enter false records into the parish register—keep me in the dark, for years, about this information which you owed both to me and the truth. Your conduct is completely unpardonable, Engstrand. From now on I have nothing more to do with you.

ENGSTRAND: *(With a sigh.)* I suppose that's that.

PASTOR MANDERS: Yes. How can you possibly justify yourself now?

ENGSTRAND: But was she supposed to go around here making her shame even worse by talking about it? If the pastor could just imagine himself—for one moment—in poor Johanna's shoes—

PASTOR MANDERS: I?

ENGSTRAND: Oh Lord, I don't mean exactly the same shoes. But if the pastor had something to be ashamed of in the eyes of the world, as they say. We men shouldn't judge a poor woman too severely, Pastor.

PASTOR MANDERS: I'm not doing that. My reproach is for you and you alone.

ENGSTRAND: Do I have permission to ask the Pastor just one little question?

PASTOR MANDERS: Well, ask it.

ENGSTRAND: Isn't it right and proper for a man to raise up the fallen?

PASTOR MANDERS: Yes, of course.

ENGSTRAND: And a man's obliged to keep his word of honor, isn't he?

PASTOR MANDERS: Of course he is, but—

ENGSTRAND: When Johanna fell into her misfortune because of that Englishman—or maybe he was an American or a Russian, whatever they're called—well, that was when she came into town. Poor thing, she'd already turned me down a time or two before—she only had eyes for the handsome gentlemen, and I had this bum leg, you see—well, the pastor remembers how I took it upon myself to go into that dance hall where there was a drunken riot going on—and how when I tried to admonish those seafaring men, as they say, to turn over a new leaf—

MRS. ALVING: *(Over by the window.)* Hmm—

PASTOR MANDERS: I know, Engstrand—they threw you down the stairs. You've told me about that before. You bear your cross honorably.

ENGSTRAND: I don't pride myself on it, Pastor. But here's what I wanted to say: she came to me and confessed everything, crying and groaning and gnashing her teeth. I have to tell you, Pastor, it broke my heart to hear her.

PASTOR MANDERS: Did it really, Engstrand? So. What then?

ENGSTRAND: Well, I said to her. That American, he's off roaming the seven seas. And you, Johanna, I said, have sinned and are a fallen creature. But Jakob Engstrand, I said, he stands on his own two strong legs, and—well, in a manner of speaking, Pastor—

PASTOR MANDERS: I understand. Please go on.

ENGSTRAND: And that's how I raised her up righteously and married her so that no one would ever find out about her wild ways with foreigners.

PASTOR MANDERS: This was all very admirable on your part. But I still can't condone accepting money for—

ENGSTRAND: Money? Me? Not a bit.

PASTOR MANDERS: *(With a glance at Mrs. Alving.)* But—?

ENGSTRAND: Ah, ah, ah—wait a minute—yes, I remember now. Johanna had a little money with her. But I wouldn't have anything to do with it. Fie, Mammon, I said, the wages of sin! We'll throw this dirty gold—or bills, I can't remember what it was—right into that American's face, I said. But by then he was gone off across the wild oceans, Pastor.

PASTOR MANDERS: Was he, my dear Engstrand?

ENGSTRAND: That's right. And so Johanna and I agreed that the money should go for bringing up the child, and it did; I can give you an accurate account of every last penny.

PASTOR MANDERS: This changes things considerably.

ENGSTRAND: That's the way things are, Pastor. I think I can say I've been a good Father to Regina—as good as I could be, since unfortunately I'm a poor weak mortal—

PASTOR MANDERS: There, there, Engstrand—

ENGSTRAND: But I still think I can say I raised the child and built a loving home with my dear Johanna, as it is written. But it would never have occurred to me to go to Pastor Manders, priding myself on this and taking credit for having done a good deed for once in this world, no, no. When something like that happens to Jakob Engstrand, he keeps quiet about it. It's just too bad it doesn't happen very often. When I go to see Pastor Manders, it's all I can do to fit in everything weak and sinful—like I said, this conscience can be awfully tough on me sometimes.

PASTOR MANDERS: Give me your hand, Jakob Engstrand.

ENGSTRAND: Oh for heaven's sake, Pastor.

PASTOR MANDERS: Don't hang back. *(Grasps his hand.)* There now.

ENGSTRAND: And if I could dare the happiness of asking the Pastor's forgiveness—

PASTOR MANDERS: You! No, it's the other way around. I should beg your forgiveness.

ENGSTRAND: Oh, in God's name, no, no.

PASTOR MANDERS: Yes, I insist. With all my heart. Forgive me for misjudging you so completely. If I could only think of some sign of my remorse—something to show you my good will—

ENGSTRAND: Is that what the pastor wants?

PASTOR MANDERS: Yes, absolutely.

ENGSTRAND: Because there's a great opportunity for that right now. With the honest savings from my work out here I'm thinking of setting up some kind of seaman's home in town.

MRS. ALVING: You are!

ENGSTRAND: Yes—it'll be a kind of asylum, you might say. Temptations are legion for the seaman who wanders ashore. But in this house of mine, I was thinking, he could be under a watchful, fatherly eye.

PASTOR MANDERS: What about that, Mrs. Alving?

ENGSTRAND: I don't have a lot to start out with—may the Lord increase and multiply it—but if I could get a friendly helping hand—

PASTOR MANDERS: Yes, yes! Let's consider this idea thoroughly. Your project interests me greatly. Now go ahead and get everything ready—light the candles for the celebration. Then we can have an edifying hour together, Engstrand—now I really believe you're in the proper frame of mind.

ENGSTRAND: I think so too. Good-bye, Mrs. Alving, and thanks. Take extra good care of Regina for me. *(Brushes a tear from his eye.)* Dear Johanna's child—isn't it amazing—she's grown right into my own heart. Yes, she really has. *(He bows and leaves through the hall.)*

PASTOR MANDERS: Well—what do you have to say about the man now, Mrs. Alving? That was a completely different perspective on things, wasn't it?

MRS. ALVING: It certainly was.

PASTOR MANDERS: You see how incredibly careful you have to be when judging your fellow man. But it's such a great joy to discover that you've been in error. So then—what do you say?

MRS. ALVING: I say you are and will always be such a child, Pastor.

PASTOR MANDERS: I?

MRS. ALVING: *(Places both hands on his shoulders.)* And I also say I'd like to wrap you up in a big hug.

PASTOR MANDERS: *(Quickly retreating.)* No, no, God bless you. What an impulse!

MRS. ALVING: *(With a smile.)* Now, you mustn't be afraid of me.

PASTOR MANDERS: *(By the table.)* Sometimes you have the most extravagant means of expressing yourself. I'll just get these documents together and put them in my brief case. *(As he does so.)* There. Now good-bye for the time being. And when Osvald gets back, be on the alert. I'll look in on you later.
(He takes his hat and goes out through the hall doorway. Mrs. Alving sighs, looks out the window a moment, tidies up a little in the room and starts to go into the dining room, but stops with a stifled cry in the doorway.)

MRS. ALVING: Osvald—still at the table!

OSVALD: *(From the dining room.)* Just finishing my cigar.

MRS. ALVING: I thought you were taking a little walk up the road.

OSVALD: In this weather?
(A glass clinks. Mrs. Alving lets the door stay open and sits with her knitting on the sofa by the window.)

OSVALD: *(Still inside.)* Wasn't that Pastor Manders?

MRS. ALVING: Yes. He went down to the Memorial.

OSVALD: Hmm.
(The glass and decanter clink again.)

MRS. ALVING: *(With a worried look.)* Osvald dear, be careful with that liqueur. It's very strong.

OSVALD: It works wonders against the dampness.

MRS. ALVING: Don't you want to come in here with me?

OSVALD: But I can't smoke in there.

MRS. ALVING: You know you can smoke a cigar.

OSVALD: All right. I'll come in. Just a splash more. There. *(He enters the room with a cigar and closes the door after him.)* Where's the Pastor gone to?

MRS. ALVING: I told you he went down to the Memorial.

OSVALD: Oh yes. That's right.

MRS. ALVING: You shouldn't sit at the table so long, Osvald.

OSVALD: *(With the cigar behind his back.)* But it's so nice, Mother. *(Patting and fondling her.)* Just imagine what this is for me—coming home, sitting at my mother's own table, in my mother's room, eating my mother's wonderful food.

MRS. ALVING: My dear boy.

OSVALD: *(Somewhat impatiently, pacing and smoking.)* And what else can I do here? I can't get started on anything—

MRS. ALVING: You can't?

OSVALD: In this murk? Not a glimpse of sunlight all day. *(Paces around the room.)* And then this—not being able to work.

MRS. ALVING: Maybe you shouldn't have come home.

OSVALD: No, Mother. I had to.

MRS. ALVING: Because I'd ten times rather give up my happiness at having you here than—

OSVALD: *(Stopping by the table.)* Tell me, Mother—does my being home really make you that happy?

MRS. ALVING: Does it make me happy?!

OSVALD: *(Crumpling a newspaper.)* I'd have thought it was pretty much the same for you here, with me or without me.

MRS. ALVING: You have the heart to say that to your own mother, Osvald?

OSVALD: You got along without me very well before.

MRS. ALVING: Yes, I got along—that's true.
(Silence. The twilight slowly increases, Osvald paces back and forth. He has set his cigar down.)

OSVALD: *(Stops by Mrs. Alving.)* Mother, may I sit next to you?

MRS. ALVING: *(Making a place for him.)* Yes, my boy. Please do.

OSVALD: Now, Mother. I have something to tell you.

MRS. ALVING: *(Tense.)* Well?

OSVALD: *(Staring into space.)* I can't carry it around any longer.

MRS. ALVING: Carry what? What is it?

OSVALD: *(As before.)* I couldn't bring myself to write you about it, and since I came home—

MRS. ALVING: *(Gripping his arm.)* Osvald, what is this?

Henrik Ibsen: GHOSTS—*Act Two*

OSVALD: Yesterday and again today I tried to get rid of these thoughts—to break free. But it's no use.

MRS. ALVING: *(Rising.)* Now you've got to tell me, Osvald.

OSVALD: *(Pulls her down to the sofa again.)* Sit down, and I'll try. I've been complaining so much about being tired out by my trip—

MRS. ALVING: Yes? So what?

OSVALD: But that's not what's wrong with me—no ordinary tiredness—

MRS. ALVING: *(Tries to rise.)* You're not sick, Osvald!

OSVALD: *(Pulls her down again.)* Sit still, Mother. Just take it easy. I'm not exactly sick; not what you usually think of as sick, anyway. *(Puts his hand to his head.)* Mother, my mind is sick—broken down—I will never be able to work again. *(With his hands over his face he throws himself down in her lap and bursts into sobbing tears.)*

MRS. ALVING: Osvald! Look at me! No, this isn't true.

OSVALD: *(Looks up with despairing eyes.)* Never work again! Never—never! That's living death! Mother—can you imagine anything so horrible?

MRS. ALVING: My poor boy! How did this terrible thing happen to you?

OSVALD: *(Sitting up again.)* That's exactly what I can't figure out. I haven't lived a wild life. Not in any way. You mustn't think that of me, Mother—I've never done that!

MRS. ALVING: I didn't think so, Osvald.

OSVALD: And this happens to me anyway! This horrible thing.

MRS. ALVING: Everything will turn out right, my blessed boy. It's nothing more than overwork. Please believe me.

OSVALD: *(Heavily.)* That's what I thought at first—but it's not true.

MRS. ALVING: Tell me everything, beginning to end.

OSVALD: It started right after the last time I was home—just after I got back to Paris. I got this piercing pain in my head—mostly toward the back of the head, it seemed. Like an iron band was squeezing tight from the neck up—

MRS. ALVING: And then?

OSVALD: First I thought it was just my usual headaches again—the ones I've had off and on since I was fourteen or so.

MRS. ALVING: Yes, yes—

OSVALD: But that wasn't it. I realized that soon enough. I couldn't work any more. I'd start working on a new painting, a large canvas; but it was as if my powers had left me; my strength was paralyzed; I couldn't concentrate on any particular project; I felt giddy, things would swim in and out of focus. That was a horrible feeling. Finally I saw a doctor, and learned the truth.

MRS. ALVING: What do you mean?

OSVALD: He was one of the foremost doctors in Paris. He made me describe my symptoms; then he started asking me a whole series of questions that I didn't think had anything to do with my case—I couldn't understand what he was getting at.

MRS. ALVING: So—?

OSVALD: Finally he said, "You've been worm-eaten since birth."

MRS. ALVING: *(Tensely.)* What did he mean by that?

OSVALD: I didn't understand either—so I asked him to explain it more clearly. Then the old cynic said ... *(Clenches his fist.)* Oh ...

MRS. ALVING: Said what?

OSVALD: He said: "The sins of the fathers are visited on the children."

MRS. ALVING: *(Slowly rises up.)* The sins of the fathers—!

OSVALD: I almost hit him in the face—

MRS. ALVING: *(Walks across the room.)* The sins of the fathers—

OSVALD: *(Smiles sadly.)* Yes, what do you think of that? Of course I told him that was impossible. But he was adamant; only when I showed him your letters, and translated all the passages where you talked about Father—

MRS. ALVING: And then—?

OSVALD: Well, then he had to admit he was on the wrong track and I finally learned the truth. The incredible truth! This beautiful, blissful young life I was leading with my comrades—it was beyond my capacity. I should never have indulged in it. So I actually destroyed myself.

MRS. ALVING: Osvald! No! Don't think that way!

OSVALD: He said that no other explanation made any sense. That's the horrible thing. Wrecked—beyond cure—for the rest of my life—because of my own irresponsibility. Everything I wanted to do in the world—I don't even dare think about it any more—I can't let myself think about it. If I could only live my life over again—undo what I've done.
(He throws himself face down on the sofa. Mrs. Alving struggles with her inner feelings and paces back and forth. After a moment, Osvald looks up, propped up on his elbows.)

Henrik Ibsen: GHOSTS—*Act Two*

OSVALD: If only it was inherited—unavoidable—but this! To throw away health, happiness, everything in the world—the future—life itself!—on trivia!

MRS. ALVING: No, no, my blessed boy. This is impossible. *(Bending over him.)* Things aren't as desperate as you think.

OSVALD: Oh, what do you know? *(Jumps up.)* And on top of it all, Mother, to be causing you all this pain! Lately I've almost been wishing that you didn't care so much about me.

MRS. ALVING: Osvald—my only boy! The only thing I have in the world—the only thing I care about.

OSVALD: *(Holds both her hands and kisses them.)* Yes, yes—now I see. Now that I'm home, I see that you do. And that's one of the hardest things to bear. So—now you know. Now we won't talk about it any more today. I can't stand to think about it for very long. *(Walks around the room.)* Get me something to drink, Mother!

MRS. ALVING: Drink? What do you want to drink now?

OSVALD: Oh, whatever you have. Maybe there's some cold punch?

MRS. ALVING: Yes, but Osvald, my dear—!

OSVALD: Don't deny me this, Mother. Just be kind. I've got to have something to drown all these thoughts that keep nagging at me! *(Goes into the conservatory.)* And it's so dark here!
(Mrs. Alving pulls the bell-rope.)

OSVALD: This rain never stops. It can go on week after week; months at a time. Never a glimpse of sun. All the times I've been home, I can't ever remember seeing the sun shine.

MRS. ALVING: Osvald—you're thinking of leaving me.

OSVALD: Hmm—*(Sighs deeply.)* I'm not thinking of anything. I can't think of anything. *(In a low voice.)* I've given up on that.

REGINA: Did you ring, ma'am?

MRS. ALVING: Yes, bring the lamp in here.

REGINA: Right away, ma'am. It's already lit. *(Goes out.)*

MRS. ALVING: *(Goes over to Osvald.)* Osvald, don't hide anything from me!

OSVALD: I'm not, Mother. *(Goes to the table.)* I think I've told you a lot.
(Regina brings the lamp and sets it on the table.)

MRS. ALVING: Oh, and Regina—you might bring us a half-bottle of champagne.

REGINA: All right, madam. *(Goes out again.)*
OSVALD: *(His arm around Mrs. Alving's neck.)* That's the way it should be. I knew my mother wouldn't let her boy go thirsty.
MRS. ALVING: Poor, dear Osvald—how can I deny you anything now?
OSVALD: *(Eagerly.)* Is that true, Mother? You mean it?
MRS. ALVING: What?
OSVALD: That you can't deny me anything?
MRS. ALVING: But Osvald—
OSVALD: Sssh!
(Regina brings a tray with a half-bottle of champagne and two glasses, which she sets on the table.)
REGINA: Should I open—?
OSVALD: No thank you, I'll do it myself.
(Regina goes out again.)
MRS. ALVING: *(Sitting at the table.)* What did you mean—about not denying you anything?
OSVALD: *(Busy opening the bottle.)* First a glass—or two.
(The cork pops. He fills one glass and is about to fill the other.)
MRS. ALVING: Thanks, not for me.
OSVALD: No? More for me then! *(He empties the glass, refills it, empties it again, then sits at the table.)*
MRS. ALVING: *(Expectantly.)* Well?
OSVALD: *(Without looking at her.)* Listen—tell me—I thought you and Pastor Manders were awfully—hmm—quiet at dinner.
MRS. ALVING: You noticed?
OSVALD: Yes. Hmm—*(After a short silence.)* Tell me—what do you think of Regina?
MRS. ALVING: What do I think?
OSVALD: Yes. Isn't she magnificent?
MRS. ALVING: You don't know her as well as I do, Osvald—
OSVALD: So?
MRS. ALVING: Regina lived at home too long. I should have taken her in earlier.
OSVALD: Yes, but she's magnificent to look at, Mother. *(He fills his glass.)*
MRS. ALVING: Regina has problems, Osvald—some serious ones—
OSVALD: Yes? So what? *(Drinks again.)*

Henrik Ibsen: GHOSTS—*Act Two*

MRS. ALVING: But I'm fond of her anyway, and I'm responsible for her. Under no circumstances would I let anything happen to her.

OSVALD: *(Jumps up.)* Mother, Regina is my only hope.

MRS. ALVING: *(Rising.)* What do you mean?

OSVALD: I can't bear this agony all alone any more.

MRS. ALVING: Don't you have your mother to help you with it?

OSVALD: Yes, that's what I thought, that's why I came home. But it's not working. I can see it; it can't work. I can't have a life out here!

MRS. ALVING: Osvald!

OSVALD: I have to live a different way, Mother. That's why I've got to leave you. I don't want you to have to see all this.

MRS. ALVING: My unhappy child! Ah, Osvald, when you're as sick as you—

OSVALD: If it were just the illness, I'd stay with you. You're the best friend I have in the world.

MRS. ALVING: That's true, Osvald, isn't it?

OSVALD: *(Uneasily paces around.)* But it's the agony, the torment, the remorse—and most of all—the sense of dread. This horrible dread.

MRS. ALVING: *(Following him.)* Dread? What do you mean?

OSVALD: Don't ask me—I don't know. I can't describe it.
(Mrs. Alving walks over and pulls the bell-rope.)

OSVALD: What's going on?

MRS. ALVING: I want my boy to be happy. He's not going to go around brooding. *(To Regina who has appeared at the door-way.)* More champagne—a whole bottle.

OSVALD: Mother!

MRS. ALVING: Don't you think we know how to live out here in the country?

OSVALD: Isn't she great looking? The way she's built—and so incredibly strong and healthy—

MRS. ALVING: *(Sitting by the table.)* Sit down, Osvald. Let's talk calmly together.

OSVALD: *(Sits.)* You probably don't know this—I have something to set straight with Regina. A wrong I did her.

MRS. ALVING: You!

OSVALD: You might just call it an indiscretion. Perfectly innocent, in fact. When I was home the last time—

MRS. ALVING: Yes?

OSVALD: —well, she kept asking me about Paris and I started describing how things are down there. One thing led to another and I remember I happened to say: "Would you like to go there yourself?"

MRS. ALVING: Well?

OSVALD: She turned blood-red and finally she said "Yes—I'd really like to do that." "All right," I said, "that could probably be arranged."—or words to that effect.

MRS. ALVING: And then?

OSVALD: I'd forgotten the whole thing, of course, but the day before yesterday I asked her in passing if she was glad I would be home so long—

MRS. ALVING: Yes?

OSVALD: —and she looked at me strangely and asked "But what about my trip to Paris?"

MRS. ALVING: Her trip?

OSVALD: And then I got it out of her: she'd taken the whole thing seriously, she'd been up here thinking about me the whole time, started trying to learn French—

MRS. ALVING: So that's why—

OSVALD: Mother, when I saw that magnificent, beautiful, vivacious girl standing in front of me—until that moment I hadn't really noticed her—but now she was right there, arms open wide, ready to take me to her—

MRS. ALVING: Osvald!

OSVALD: —and then it came to me, all of a sudden—she was salvation. I saw the joy of life in her.

MRS. ALVING: The joy of life? There's salvation in that?

REGINA: *(Entering from the dining room with a bottle of champagne.)* I'm sorry it took so long, but I had to go down to the cellar—*(Sets the bottle on the table.)*

OSVALD: And bring another glass.

REGINA: *(Looks at him in surprise.)* Madam's glass is right there, Mr. Alving.

OSVALD: Yes—one for you, Regina.
(Regina starts. Throws a swift, timid glance at Mrs. Alving.)

OSVALD: Well?

Henrik Ibsen: GHOSTS—*Act Two*

REGINA: *(Softly, hesitantly.)* Does Madam—?
MRS. ALVING: Bring the glass, Regina.
  (Regina goes into the dining room.)
OSVALD: *(Looking at her.)* Have you noticed the way she walks—so firm and fearless?
MRS. ALVING: This can't happen, Osvald!
OSVALD: It's decided. You must see that. There's no point discussing it.
  (Regina enters with an empty glass which she keeps in her hands.)
OSVALD: Please have a seat, Regina.
  (Regina looks inquiringly at Mrs. Alving.)
MRS. ALVING: Sit down, Regina.
  (Regina sits on a chair near the dining room door, holding the empty glass in her hands.)
MRS. ALVING: Osvald—what were you saying about the joy of life?
OSVALD: Yes, Mother—the joy of life. You don't seem to know much about it. I never feel it here at home.
MRS. ALVING: Not even when you're home with me?
OSVALD: Not when I'm home at all. But you can't understand.
MRS. ALVING: Yes, yes—I think I'm close to understanding—now.
OSVALD: That and the joy of work as well. They're basically the same thing at heart. But none of you knows anything about that.
MRS. ALVING: You're probably right. Osvald, tell me more about it.
OSVALD: What I mean is that people here are taught that work is a curse—a punishment for sin—and that life's one long misery, to be gotten over with as soon as possible.
MRS. ALVING: Yes, a vale of misery. And we work hard at making it that way, with all our honorable and virtuous labors.
OSVALD: But that kind of thinking isn't accepted out there in the world. Nobody believes in that tradition any more. Out there people think it's pure bliss just to be alive. Mother, have you noticed that all my paintings spring from this joy of life? Every one—invariably—about the joy of life. Light and sunshine, and a holiday spirit—people's faces happy and glowing—and that's why I'm afraid to stay here with you at home.
MRS. ALVING: Afraid? What are you afraid of here?
OSVALD: I'm afraid of everything that's best in me degenerating into ugliness.
MRS. ALVING: *(Looks straight at him.)* You think that would happen?

OSVALD: I'm certain of it. Live the exact same way here as out there, and it still wouldn't be the same life.

MRS. ALVING: *(Who has been listening intently, rises with big, thoughtful eyes and says.)* Now I see how it all fits!

OSVALD: What do you see?

MRS. ALVING: I see it for the first time. And now I can speak.

OSVALD: *(Rising.)* Mother, I don't understand you.

REGINA: *(Who has also risen.)* Should I go?

MRS. ALVING: No, stay here. Now I can speak. Now, my boy, you're going to know everything. And then you can choose. Osvald! Regina!

OSVALD: Quiet—the pastor.

PASTOR MANDERS: *(Entering through the hall door.)* Ah, ah, ah—we've had a really heart-warming session down there.

OSVALD: So have we.

PASTOR MANDERS: Engstrand must be helped with his seaman's home. Regina will go with him, and give him a helping hand—

REGINA: No, thank you, Pastor.

PASTOR MANDERS: *(Noticing her for the first time.)* What—? Here. And with a glass in your hand?

REGINA: *(Quickly puts down the glass.)* Beg pardon!

OSVALD: Regina is going with me, Pastor.

PASTOR MANDERS: Going! With you!

OSVALD: Yes, as my wife—if she wants that.

PASTOR MANDERS: Good Lord—

REGINA: It's not my doing, Pastor.

OSVALD: Or she'll stay here, if I stay.

REGINA: *(Involuntarily.)* Here!

PASTOR MANDERS: Mrs. Alving, I'm astounded!

MRS. ALVING: None of these things will happen—because now I can speak out freely.

PASTOR MANDERS: You can't do that—! No, no, no!

MRS. ALVING: Yes, I can and will. And even so, not a single ideal will fall.

OSVALD: Mother, what are you hiding from me?

REGINA: *(Listening.)* Madam—listen! People are shouting out there. *(She goes into the garden room.)*

OSVALD: *(Going to the window, left.)* What's going on? Where's that light coming from?

REGINA: *(Crying out.)* Something's burning in the asylum!

PASTOR MANDERS: A fire? Impossible! I was just down there.

OSVALD: Where's my hat? Never mind—! Father's Memor—! *(He runs out through the garden door.)*

MRS. ALVING: My shawl, Regina! It's all in flames!

PASTOR MANDERS: Dreadful! Mrs. Alving, this is a fiery judgment on this wayward house!

MRS. ALVING: Yes, of course. Come on, Regina!
(She and Regina hurry out through the hall.)

PASTOR MANDERS: *(Clasping his hands.)* And no insurance! *(Goes out the same way.)*

End of Act Two

Act Three

(The room as before. All the doors stand open. The lamp still burns on the table. Dark outside, except for a faint glow of fire in the background left. Mrs. Alving, with a large shawl over her head, is standing in the garden room, looking out. Regina, also with a shawl, stands a little behind her.)

MRS. ALVING: Everything burned. Right to the ground.

REGINA: The basement's still burning.

MRS. ALVING: Where's Osvald? There's nothing left to save.

REGINA: Should I take his hat down to him?

MRS. ALVING: He doesn't even have his hat?

REGINA: *(Pointing to the hall.)* No, it's hanging up in there.

MRS. ALVING: Leave it. He's got to come up soon. I'll go look for him. *(She goes out through the garden door.)*

PASTOR MANDERS: *(Enters from the hall.)* Mrs. Alving's not here?

REGINA: She just went down to the garden.

PASTOR MANDERS: This is the most terrible night I've ever lived through.

REGINA: It's an awful piece of luck, isn't it Pastor?

PASTOR MANDERS: Don't talk about it! I can hardly even let myself think about it.

REGINA: How could it happen?

PASTOR MANDERS: Don't ask me, Miss Engstrand! How should I know? Are you also—? Isn't it enough that your Father—?

REGINA: What about him?

PASTOR MANDERS: He's about driven me out of my mind, that's what!

ENGSTRAND: *(Entering through the hall.)* Pastor—!

PASTOR MANDERS: *(Turning in terror.)* You're after me here too?

ENGSTRAND: Yes, God strike me dead, but it's what I have to do. Lord! this is a real mess, Pastor.

PASTOR MANDERS: *(Pacing back and forth.)* Terrible. Terrible.

ENGSTRAND: And all because of that prayer service down there. *(Softly to Regina.)* Now we've got him, girl! *(Aloud.)* And to think that it's my fault that Pastor Manders is to blame for something like this!

PASTOR MANDERS: But, Engstrand, I swear—

ENGSTRAND: Nobody but the pastor was in charge of those candles.

PASTOR MANDERS: *(Stopping.)* Yes. So you claim. But I absolutely cannot remember ever holding a candle in my hands.

ENGSTRAND: And I had such a clear view of how the Pastor took the candle, snuffed the flame with his fingers, and threw the wick down into some shavings.

PASTOR MANDERS: You saw that?

ENGSTRAND: Yes, I saw that for sure.

PASTOR MANDERS: That's what I find impossible to believe. I never snuff candles with my fingers.

ENGSTRAND: Yes, it looked horribly careless. But Pastor—is it really going to be that big a loss?

PASTOR MANDERS: *(Pacing uneasily back and forth.)* Oh, don't ask me!

ENGSTRAND: *(Walking with him.)* Not insured. And then to walk over there and set fire to the whole heap. Lord, oh Lord, what a mess!

PASTOR MANDERS: *(Wiping his brow.)* Yes, Engstrand, you can certainly say that again.

ENGSTRAND: And for something like this to happen to a charitable institution—a place that, so to speak, was to serve the whole community. I don't suppose the papers will handle you too gently.

PASTOR MANDERS: No, that's exactly what I'm thinking. That's almost the worst thing about this whole business. All those attacks and insinuations—it's too awful to think about!

MRS. ALVING: *(Entering from the garden.)* He won't be talked into leaving the ruins.

PASTOR MANDERS: Ah, Mrs. Alving. There you are.

MRS. ALVING: So you didn't have to make your speech, Pastor Manders.

PASTOR MANDERS: Oh, I would have been only too glad—

MRS. ALVING: *(Subdued.)* What's done is done, and for the best. This "Home" would not have turned out a blessing to anyone.

PASTOR MANDERS: You don't think so?

MRS. ALVING: You do think so?

PASTOR MANDERS: Still, it was a terrible disaster.

MRS. ALVING: We'll treat it as a business matter, that's all. Engstrand, are you waiting for the pastor?

ENGSTRAND: *(By the hall door.)* Yes, as a matter of fact, I am.

MRS. ALVING: Well, just sit there for the time being.

ENGSTRAND: Thanks, I'd just as soon stand.

MRS. ALVING: *(To Manders.)* You'll be taking the next steamer?

PASTOR MANDERS: Yes—it leaves in an hour.

MRS. ALVING: Would you be good enough to take all the paperwork back with you? I don't want to hear one more word about any of it. I've got other things to think about—

PASTOR MANDERS: Mrs. Alving—

MRS. ALVING: Later I'll send you full authorization to arrange everything as you see fit.

PASTOR MANDERS: I'll gladly see to that, of course. The original terms of the bequest, unfortunately, will have to be modified.

MRS. ALVING: That's understood.

PASTOR MANDERS: Yes. I think that for the moment, I could arrange it so that the Solvik estate can be turned over to the parish. The land certainly can't be written off as worthless, it can always be put to some good use. And as for the interest on the capital in the bank, perhaps I could find some venture to support with it—something that would benefit the town.

MRS. ALVING: Whatever you want. I'm not interested in any of it.

ENGSTRAND: Think about my seamen's home, Pastor!

PASTOR MANDERS: Yes, you may have something there—well, it must all be carefully considered.

ENGSTRAND: Why the devil do you have to consider—aw, Lord.

PASTOR MANDERS: *(With a sigh.)* And unfortunately, I don't know how long I'll be able to remain in charge. Public opinion might compel me to resign. It all depends on the findings of the official inquiry into the fire.

MRS. ALVING: What?

PASTOR MANDERS: And those findings can't be predicted in any way.

ENGSTRAND: *(Edging closer.)* Oh yes they can. Because Jakob Engstrand's here.

PASTOR MANDERS: Yes, yes, but—

ENGSTRAND: *(In a low voice.)* And Jakob Engstrand's not the man to abandon a worthy benefactor in his hour of need, as they say.

PASTOR MANDERS: But—my good—how?

ENGSTRAND: Jakob Engstrand's a ministering angel, Pastor, yes he is!

PASTOR MANDERS: No, no, I couldn't possibly accept that.

ENGSTRAND: Ah, but that's how it'll be, all the same. I know somebody who's taken the blame for somebody else once before, yes I do.

Henrik Ibsen: GHOSTS—*Act Three*

PASTOR MANDERS: Jakob! *(Shakes his hand.)* You are a rare individual. Well, you'll get your support for your seamen's home; you can count on it.
(Engstrand tries to thank him, but is so choked up with emotion that he can't.)

PASTOR MANDERS: *(Slings his traveling bag over his shoulder.)* So, we're off. We'll travel together.

ENGSTRAND: *(By the dining room door, softly to Regina.)* Follow me, girl! You'll be as cozy as the yolk in an egg.

REGINA: *(Tosses her head.)* Merci!
(She goes out into the hall and fetches the pastor's traveling things.)

PASTOR MANDERS: Good-bye, Mrs. Alving. May the spirit of law and order find an open door into this house.

MRS. ALVING: Good-bye, Manders!
(She goes into the garden room as she sees Osvald enter through the garden door.)

ENGSTRAND: *(While he and Regina help the pastor with his coat.)* Good-bye, my girl. If anything happens to you, you know where to find Jakob Engstrand. *(Quietly.)* Little Harbor Street—! *(To Mrs. Alving and Osvald.)* And my establishment for wayfaring sailors—I'll call it "Captain Alving's Home," that's right. And if I get to run things the way I want, I promise you it'll be a worthy memorial to the sainted Captain.

PASTOR MANDERS: *(In the doorway.)* Hmm—hmm! Come on now, my dear Engstrand. Good-bye, good-bye!
(Pastor Manders and Engstrand go out through the garden door.)

OSVALD: *(Goes over to the table.)* What was this establishment he was talking about?

MRS. ALVING: Some kind of home that he and the pastor want to start.

OSVALD: It'll burn down, just like this one.

MRS. ALVING: What makes you say that?

OSVALD: Everything will burn. Nothing of Father's memory will remain. And here I am, burning up too.
(Regina looks at him in astonishment.)

MRS. ALVING: Osvald! My poor boy, you shouldn't have stayed down there so long.

OSVALD: *(Sits at the table.)* I almost think you're right about that.

MRS. ALVING: Let me dry your face, Osvald. You're still wet.

OSVALD: *(Looking indifferently in front of himself.)* Thank you, Mother.

MRS. ALVING: Are you tired? Do you want to sleep?

OSVALD: *(Fearfully.)* No, no—no sleep! I never sleep. I only pretend to. *(Dully.)* Soon enough, soon enough.

MRS. ALVING: Yes, my dear, dear boy, you're really ill after all.

REGINA: *(Tense.)* Is Mr. Alving ill?

OSVALD: *(Impatiently.)* Now shut the doors! This deathly fear—

MRS. ALVING: Shut them, Regina.
(Regina shuts the doors and remains standing by the hall door. Mrs. Alving takes off her shawl. Regina does the same.)

MRS. ALVING: *(Pulls a chair up to Osvald and sits beside him.)* There, now I'm here beside you—

OSVALD: Yes, that's good, and Regina should be here too. Regina will always be near me. You'll give me a helping hand, Regina. You will, won't you?

REGINA: I don't understand—

MRS. ALVING: Helping hand?

OSVALD: When it becomes necessary.

MRS. ALVING: Osvald, isn't your mother right here to give you a helping hand?

OSVALD: You? *(Smiles.)* No, Mother, I don't think you'd ever give me the hand I need. *(Laughs dully.)* You! *(Looks earnestly at her.)* And yet you're certainly the closest one. *(Vehemently.)* Regina, why can't you be easier with me? Why won't you call me Osvald?

REGINA: *(Softly.)* I don't think Mrs. Alving would like it.

MRS. ALVING: You'll have every right to in a little while. So sit here with us—yes, you too.
(Regina sits modestly and hesitantly at the other side of the table.)

MRS. ALVING: Now, my poor, suffering boy. Now I'll get rid of this burden on your mind—

OSVALD: You, Mother?

MRS. ALVING: All your self-reproach and remorse and blame—

OSVALD: You think you can?

MRS. ALVING: Yes, Osvald, now I can. You were talking before about the joy of life. Right then it was as if new light began to shine on my whole existence.

OSVALD: *(Shaking his head.)* I don't understand any of this.
MRS. ALVING: You should have known your father when he was just a young lieutenant. You could certainly see the joy of life in him!
OSVALD: That much I know.
MRS. ALVING: Just to look at him was like a sunny day. All that untamed energy, all that vitality!
OSVALD: And so?
MRS. ALVING: And so this child, born out of the joy of life—and he was like a child then—he had to go around here in this perfectly average town—no real joy to offer, only the usual pleasures. He had to try to live without goals, just bogged down in endless paperwork. There was nothing here to challenge his soul, nothing engaged his heart—it was all just routine business. He didn't have a single comrade who had any idea about the joy of life, only loafers and drunks—
OSVALD: Mother!
MRS. ALVING: And so what had to happen, happened.
OSVALD: What had to happen?
MRS. ALVING: You said yourself earlier what would happen to you if you stayed here.
OSVALD: Are you trying to say that Father—
MRS. ALVING: Your poor father could never find any outlet for the overwhelming joy of life in him. And I'm afraid I didn't bring any sunshine into his home either.
OSVALD: No?
MRS. ALVING: No, they'd made me learn all about duty and such, and I went around here believing in those things for the longest time. Everything came down to duty—my duties, his duties—and, well, I'm afraid I made this house unbearable for your poor father.
OSVALD: Why haven't you ever written me about this?
MRS. ALVING: Until today I've never seen it as something to be discussed with his son.
OSVALD: How did you see it?
MRS. ALVING: *(Slowly.)* I saw only one thing: that your father was a broken man before you were born.
OSVALD: *(In a smothered voice.)* Ah—!*(He gets up and goes to the window.)*

MRS. ALVING: And every day, I had one thought on my mind. That Regina, in all honesty, belonged here in this house—as much as my own son.

OSVALD: *(Turns swiftly.)* Regina!

REGINA: *(Springing up and asking, in a choked voice.)* Me—!

MRS. ALVING: Yes. Now both of you know.

OSVALD: Regina!

REGINA: *(To herself.)* So my mother was—

MRS. ALVING: Your mother was good in many ways, Regina.

REGINA: Yes, but all the same she was like that. I've often thought it—well, madam, may I have permission to leave right now?

MRS. ALVING: Do you really want to, Regina?

REGINA: Yes, I certainly do!

MRS. ALVING: Of course, you have to do what you want, but—

OSVALD: *(Goes to Regina.)* You're leaving? But you belong here.

REGINA: *Merci*, Mr. Alving. Oh—I guess I can call you Osvald now. But this certainly isn't the way I planned to.

MRS. ALVING: Regina, I know I haven't been completely open with you—

REGINA: No, you can say that again! If I'd known that Osvald was sick—and anyway now there can't be anything serious between us—no, I really can't stay out here in the country working myself to death for invalids.

OSVALD: Not even someone so close to you?

REGINA: Not if I can help it. A poor girl's got her youth, that's all. If she doesn't make something out of it, she'll find herself out in the cold before she knows what hit her. And I've got the joy of life in me, ma'am!

MRS. ALVING: Yes, I'm afraid you do. But don't throw yourself away.

REGINA: Oh, if it happens it happens. Osvald takes after his father, I guess I take after my mother. May I ask madam if Pastor Manders knows anything about this?

MRS. ALVING: Pastor Manders knows everything.

REGINA: Well, I'd better make sure I get on that steamer as fast as I can. The pastor's so easy to get along with—and I really think I've got as much right to some of that money as he does—that filthy carpenter.

Henrik Ibsen: GHOSTS—*Act Three*

MRS. ALVING: You're welcome to it, Regina

REGINA: *(Looking sharply at her.)* You could have brought me up like a gentleman's daughter—that would have been a better fit. *(Tosses her head.)* But what the hell—it's all the same! *(With a bitter glance at the unopened bottle.)* I'll be drinking champagne in the best society, wait and see.

MRS. ALVING: If you ever need a home, Regina, come to me.

REGINA: No thank you ma'am. Pastor Manders will take care of me. And if that doesn't work out, I know a house where I'll always be welcome.

MRS. ALVING: Where's that?

REGINA: Captain Alving's Home.

MRS. ALVING: Regina, I can see it now—you're heading for disaster.

REGINA: Ah—ffft! *Adieu! (She nods and goes out through the hall.)*

OSVALD: *(Standing by the window, looking out.)* Is she gone?

MRS. ALVING: Yes.

OSVALD: *(Muttering to himself.)* It's all insane.

MRS. ALVING: *(Goes over behind him and lays her hands on his shoulders.)* Osvald—my dear boy—all this has given you an awful shock, hasn't it?

OSVALD: *(Turning his face towards her.)* About Father, you mean?

MRS. ALVING: Yes, your unfortunate father. I'm afraid it's been too much for you.

OSVALD: How can you think that? It was a surprise, of course—but finally it can't make much difference to me.

MRS. ALVING: *(Withdrawing her hands.)* No difference—that your father was so incredibly unhappy?

OSVALD: Naturally I'm sympathetic, as I would be for anyone else, but—

MRS. ALVING: And that's all? For your own father.

OSVALD: Oh yes, Father, Father! I never knew anything about my father. All I remember is the time he made me throw up.

MRS. ALVING: That's terrible, to think like that! Shouldn't a child love his father no matter what?

OSVALD: When the child had nothing to thank his father for? Never knew him? You're so enlightened in so many ways—can you really cling to that old superstition?

MRS. ALVING: You say it's only a superstition?
OSVALD: Yes—you see that, Mother, I'm sure. It's just one of those ideas that gets started in the world and then—
MRS. ALVING: *(Shaken.)* Ghosts!
OSVALD: *(Walks across the floor.)* Yes, you certainly could call them ghosts.
MRS. ALVING: *(Crying out.)* Osvald—then you don't love me either!
OSVALD: But at least I know you.
MRS. ALVING: Yes—but that's all?
OSVALD: And I know how much you care for me and I'm very grateful for that. You can be enormously useful to me now that I'm sick.
MRS. ALVING: Yes, I can, Osvald, can't I! I could almost bless this illness that drove you home to me. Because now I can see it: I don't have you yet, I'll have to win you.
OSVALD: *(Impatiently.)* Yes, yes, yes. This is all just talk. Remember I'm a sick man, Mother. I can't worry about others; I have enough to do just thinking about myself.
MRS. ALVING: *(Softly.)* I'll be patient and calm.
OSVALD: And cheerful, Mother!
MRS. ALVING: Yes, my dear, dear boy, you're right. *(Goes over to him.)* Now have I taken away all your remorse? No more reproaching yourself?
OSVALD: Yes, you have. But who will take away the dread?
MRS. ALVING: Dread?
OSVALD: *(Walks across the room.)* Regina would have done it at a word from me.
MRS. ALVING: I don't understand. What's this about dread—and Regina?
OSVALD: Is it late, Mother?
MRS. ALVING: Early morning. *(Looking out through the garden room.)* Up in the mountains the day is beginning to break. And it's going to be a clear day, Osvald! In a little while you'll get to see the sun.
OSVALD: That'll be a joy. Oh, there can be so much to live for—
MRS. ALVING: Yes, I know!
OSVALD: And even if I can't work—
MRS. ALVING: Oh, you'll be able to work again soon. Now that you don't have to brood about these depressing ideas any more.

OSVALD: No, that's true. It's good that you could knock down all those delusions of mine. And when I get rid of this one last thing—*(Sits on the sofa.)* Now, Mother, we've got to have a talk.

MRS. ALVING: All right. *(She pushes an armchair over to the sofa and sits beside him.)*

OSVALD: And then the sun will rise. And then you'll know. And then I'll no longer have this dread.

MRS. ALVING: What will I know? Tell me.

OSVALD: *(Not listening to her.)* Mother, didn't you say that you'd do anything for me, anything in the world, if I asked you?

MRS. ALVING: That's what I said.

OSVALD: Do you stand by that?

MRS. ALVING: You can depend on it, my only boy. You're what I live for now, nothing else.

OSVALD: All right. Now you'll hear it. Mother, you have a strong mind, I know you can take this in—so now you must sit calmly while you hear what it is.

MRS. ALVING: What could be so horrible?

OSVALD: And don't scream. You hear me? Promise me that? We'll sit and talk about it quietly. Promise me that, Mother?

MRS. ALVING: Yes, yes. I promise—just tell me!

OSVALD: Well, all this talk about my being tired—about not being able to think about work—that isn't the illness, only the symptoms.

MRS. ALVING: What is the illness?

OSVALD: The illness I received as my inheritance—*(Points to his forehead.)* It sits right here.

MRS. ALVING: *(Almost speechless.)* Osvald! No, no!

OSVALD: Don't scream. I can't stand it. Yes, Mother, it sits right here, lurking, ready to break out any day, any time.

MRS. ALVING: Horrible!

OSVALD: Just be calm. That's how it is with me.

MRS. ALVING: *(Jumping up.)* It's not true, Osvald! It's impossible! It can't be!

OSVALD: I had one attack down there, it didn't last long. But when I found out what had happened to me, this dread began pursuing me, relentlessly, and so I started back home to you as fast as I could.

MRS. ALVING: And that's the dread—!

OSVALD: Yes, it's revolting beyond words. Don't you see that? Some plain old terminal disease I could—I'm not afraid of dying, even though I'd like to live as long as I can.

MRS. ALVING: Yes, Osvald—you've got to!

OSVALD: But this is beyond disgusting. To be turned into a helpless child again—to have to be fed, to have to be—it's unspeakable!

MRS. ALVING: My child has his mother to take care of him.

OSVALD: *(Leaps up.)* Never, that's exactly what I don't want. I can't stand the idea of lying there for years like that, turning old and gray. And meanwhile you might die before me. *(Sits in Mrs. Alving's chair.)* The doctor said it wouldn't necessarily be fatal right away. He called it a kind of softening of the brain, or something like that. *(Smiles sadly.)* I think that sounds so charming—it always makes me think of red velvet curtains—something soft and delicate to stroke.

MRS. ALVING: *(Screaming.)* Osvald!

OSVALD: *(Leaps up again and walks across the room.)* And now you've taken Regina away from me! If only I had her. She'd have given me a helping hand, yes she would.

MRS. ALVING: *(Goes over to him.)* What do you mean, my boy? What help is there in the world that I wouldn't give you?

OSVALD: When I'd recovered from my attack down there, the doctor told me that when it came again—and it will come again—that then it'd be beyond hope.

MRS. ALVING: He was heartless enough to—

OSVALD: I demanded it. I told him I had plans to make—*(Smiles slyly.)* And so I had. *(Takes a little box from his inside breast pocket.)* See this, Mother?

MRS. ALVING: What is it?

OSVALD: Morphine powder.

MRS. ALVING: *(Looks at him in horror.)* Osvald—my boy!

OSVALD: I've managed to save twelve capsules.

MRS. ALVING: *(Grabbing for it.)* Give me the box, Osvald!

OSVALD: Not yet, Mother! *(He puts it back in his pocket.)*

MRS. ALVING: I can't live through this!

Henrik Ibsen: GHOSTS—*Act Three*

OSVALD: You have to live through it. If Regina were here I'd have told her how things are, and begged her for this last bit of help. And she would have helped me, I'm sure of it.

MRS. ALVING: Never!

OSVALD: When the horrible thing happened, and she saw me lying there like an imbecile, like a child, helpless, lost, beyond hope of rescue—

MRS. ALVING: Regina would never have done that!

OSVALD: Regina would have done it! She was so splendid, so light-hearted, she would have gotten tired pretty fast of looking after an invalid like me.

MRS. ALVING: Well then. Give thanks that Regina's not here!

OSVALD: So—now you have to give me that helping hand, Mother.

MRS. ALVING: *(With a loud scream.)* I!

OSVALD: Who else? Who's closer?

MRS. ALVING: I! Your Mother!

OSVALD: Exactly why.

MRS. ALVING: I, who gave you life!

OSVALD: I didn't ask you for life. And what kind of life have you given me? I don't want it. Take it back!

MRS. ALVING: Help, help! *(She runs into the hall.)*

OSVALD: *(Pursuing her.)* Don't leave me! Where are you going?

MRS. ALVING: *(In the hall.)* To get the doctor, Osvald! Let me go!

OSVALD: *(In the hall.)* You're not leaving. And no one's coming in. *(A key is turned in a lock.)*

MRS. ALVING: *(Coming in again.)* Osvald! Osvald!—my child!

OSVALD: *(Following her.)* Where's your Mother's heart? Can you stand to see me suffer this unspeakable dread?

MRS. ALVING: *(After a moment's silence, says firmly.)* Here's my hand on it.

OSVALD: Will you—?

MRS. ALVING: If necessary. But it won't be necessary. No, never—it's not possible!

OSVALD: Well, let's hope so. And let's live together as long as we can. Thank you, Mother.
(He sits in the armchair that Mrs. Alving had moved over to the sofa. The day is breaking. The lamp is still burning on the table.)

MRS. ALVING: *(Approaching him cautiously.)* Do you feel more at peace now?

OSVALD: Yes.

MRS. ALVING: *(Bends over him.)* You've been carrying a terrible delusion inside, Osvald—but it was all a delusion. Of course you couldn't bear all these agonies. But now you'll get your rest, here at home with your mother, my blessed boy. Anything you want, anything you point out to me, you'll have it! Just like when you were a little child. See, there. The sickness is gone—see how easily it went away! I knew it would. And look, Osvald, what a beautiful day we're going to have. Brilliant sunshine. Now you can really see your home.
(She goes over to the table and puts out the lamp. Sunrise. The glaciers and peaks in the background lie in brilliant morning light.)

OSVALD: *(Sits in the armchair with his back to this view, without stirring. Suddenly he says.)* Mother, give me the sun.

MRS. ALVING: *(By the table, looks at him, startled.)* What did you say?

OSVALD: *(Repeats dully and tonelessly.)* The sun. The sun.

MRS. ALVING: *(Goes over to him.)* Osvald, what's the matter with you? *(Osvald seems to shrink in the chair. All the muscles loosen. His face is expressionless. His eyes stare vacantly.)*

MRS. ALVING: *(Shaking in terror.)* What is this? *(Screams loudly.)* Osvald! What's the matter with you! *(Throws herself down on her knees beside him and shakes him.)* Osvald! Osvald! Look at me! Don't you know me!

OSVALD: *(Tonelessly, as before.)* The sun. The sun.

MRS. ALVING: *(Springs up in anguish. Tears at her hair with both hands and screams.)* This is unbearable! *(Whispers as though terrified.)* Unbearable! Never! *(Suddenly.)* Where did he put them? *(Fumbling hastily in his pocket.)* Here! *(Retreats a few steps and screams.)* No, no, no!—Yes! No, no! *(She stands a few steps from him, her hands clutching her hair, staring at him in speechless horror.)*

OSVALD: *(Sits motionless as before, and says.)* The sun. The sun.

End of Play

Mavourneen Dwyer as Ms. Alving and Dikran Tulaine as Osvald in the Alliance Theatre Company of Atlanta's production of *Ghosts*.

In a caricature of Pear's soap advertisement, Clement Scott attempts to disinfect Ibsen, as the ghosts of Archer, Grien and Gosse hover in the background.

William Archer

Ghosts and Gibberings

This piece is from the *Pall Mall Gazette*, 8 April 1891.

> *Ghosts* was performed only once at the Independent Theatre Society in London on 13 March 1891. That single performance, however, ignited a firestorm of public controversy. William Archer referred to these criticisms as " ... amazing feats of vituperation." To emphasize this point, Archer brought together the most abusive statements from the press into a single article titled "Ghosts and Gibberings." This compilation illustrates, reveals, and ridicules the hysterical nature of the opposition to Ibsen.
>
> —D.M.

"Ibsen's positively abominable play entitled *Ghosts*.... This disgusting representation.... Reprobation due to such as aim at infecting the modern theatre with poison after desperately inoculating themselves and others.... An open drain: a loathsome sore unbandaged; a dirty act done publicly; a lazar-house with all its doors and windows open.... Candid foulness.... Kotzebue turned bestial and cynical.... Offensive cynicism.... Ibsen's melancholy and malodorous world. Absolutely loathsome and fetid.... Gross, almost putrid indecorum.... Literary carrion.... Crapulous stuff.... Novel and perilous nuisance."—*Daily Telegraph* (leading article). "This mess of vulgarity, egotism, coarseness, and absurdity."—*Daily Telegraph* (criticism). "Unutterably offensive.... Prosecution under Lord Campbell's Act.... Abominable piece.... Scandalous."—*Standard*. "Naked loathsomeness.... Most damned and repulsive production."—*Daily News*. "Revoltingly suggestive and blasphemous.... Characters either contradictory in themselves, uninteresting or abhorrent."—*Daily Chronicle*. "A repulsive and degrading work."—*Queen*. "Morbid, unhealthy, unwholesome and disgusting story.... A piece to bring the stage into disrepute and dishonour with every right-thinking man and woman."—*Lloyd's*. "Merely dull dirt long drawn out."—*Hawk*. "Morbid horrors of the hideous tale.... Ponderous dullness of the didactic talk.... If any repetition of this outrage be attempted, the authorities will doubtless wake from their lethargy."—*Sporting and Dramatic News*. "Just a wicked nightmare"—*The Gentlewoman*. "Lugubrious diagnosis of sordid impropriety.... Characters are prigs, pedants and profligates.... Morbid caricatures.... Maunderings of nookshotten Norwegians.... It is no more of a play than an average Gaiety burlesque."—W. St. Leger in *Black and White*. "Most loathsome of all Ibsen's plays ... Garbage and offal."—*Truth*. "Ibsen's putrid play called *Ghosts* ... So loathsome an enterprise."—*Academy*. "As foul and filthy a concoction as has ever been allowed to disgrace the boards of an English theatre.... Dull and disgusting.... Nastiness and malodorousness laid on thickly as with a trowel."—*Era*. "Noisome corruption."—*Stage*.

Henrik Ibsen.—"An egotist and a bungler."—*Daily Telegraph*. "A crazy fanatic and determined Socialist.... A crazycranking being.... Not only consistently dirty but deplorably dull."—*Truth*. "As a dramatist, I consider the poet Calmour his superior."—*Hawk*. "The Norwegian pessimist in *petto(!)*."—W. St. Leger in *Black and White*. "Ugly, nasty, discordant, and downright dull.... A gloomy sort of ghoul, bent on groping for horrors by night, and blinking like a stupid old owl when the warm sunlight of the best of life dances into his wrinkled eyes."—*Gentlewoman*. "A teacher of the aestheticism of the Lock Hospital."—*Saturday Review*.

Ibsenites (i.e., persons who omit to foam at the mouth when the name of Ibsen is mentioned).—"Lovers of prurience and dabblers in impropriety who are eager to gratify their illicit tastes under the pretence of art."—*Evening Standard*. "Ninetyseven per cent. [Nothing like accuracy!] of the people who go to see *Ghosts* are nasty-minded people who find the discussion of nasty subjects to their taste, in exact proportion to their nastiness."—*Sporting and Dramatic News*. "The socialistic and the sexless.... The unwomanly women, the unsexed females, the whole army of unprepossessing cranks in petticoats.... Educated and muck-ferretting dogs.... Effeminate men and male women.... They all of them—men and women alike—know that they are doing not only a nasty but an illegal thing.... The Lord Chamberlain left them alone to wallow in *Ghosts*.... Outside a silly clique, there is not the slightest interest in the Scandinavian humbug or all his works.... A wave of human folly." —*Truth*.

These are a few extracts from a little book I am compiling—on the model of the Wagner *Schimpf-Lexicon*—to be entitled "Ibsenoclasts: or, an Anthology of Abuse. It will be an entertaining little work, I promise you; but the time for publication has not yet come. The materials, it is true, are already abundant; but they keep on pouring in every day, and are likely to do so for some time to come. I am anxious to make the compilation a complete and classic handbook of obloquy—a Baedeker to Billingsgate, as it were; and such is the wealth of our incomparable mothertongue that, despite the industry of a hundred "frumious" critics during the past month or so, I cannot suppose that the well of wormwood is as yet exhausted, or that such virtuosos in vituperation will for the future be forced ingloriously to repeat themselves. Besides, the full irony and humour of the situation cannot be quite apparent to the general reader, or to the critics themselves, until a certain time shall have elapsed. As yet, the contributors to the above florilegium can barely have recovered from the moral epilepsy into which *Ghosts*—so far, and so far only, justifying their denunciations—appears to have thrown them. By the time I publish my complete Manual of Malediction, they will have come to themselves again, and will be able to read with a smile—though perhaps a somewhat sickly one—the babble of their delirium.

For the present I would fain "assist nature" and hasten their recovery by confronting, in one particular, the *Ghosts* of their heated imagination with the actual play as it was represented and as he who runs may read it. That the average man should profess himself bored by it, is only natural and proper. If it were pleasant and acceptable to the average man, it would entirely fail of its aim. The "ghosts" of the moral world are not to be "laid" by a single exorcism. The first effect of any disturbance of their repose is naturally to make them "squeak and gibber in the Roman streets." It is not even to be expected that the average man, in his exasperation, should take the slightest trouble to think out what the poet means, or to represent truthfully what he says. Yet I own I am surprised at the unanimity with which the critics have averred that the tragedy is mainly, if not exclusively, concerned with what the *Anti-Jacobin* calls the "loathsome details of disease born of depravity." Scarcely a paper but says the same thing, in almost the same words. The most precise of all, perhaps, is the *St. James Gazette:* "No detail is omitted. We see the patient before us. His symptoms are described with revolting minuteness; the quivering of an eyelid or the drooping of a lip is duly noted: the course of the disease, in its origin, development, and culmination, traced with a precision worthy of a professor of anatomy. The very theatre seems to be turned into a hospital." Nothing can be more explicit than this statement; yet it is absolutely without foundation. Oswald tells his mother that he is suffering from softening of the brain—not a pleasant announcement, certainly, but with nothing particularly "loathsome" about it. The only "symptoms" mentioned are a severe headache and bodily and mental lassitude, which cannot surely be called "revolting" phenomena. There is not a single allusion to "quivering eyelids" or "drooping lips"; the "origin, development, and culmination" of Oswald's disease are not "traced with precision," for they are not traced at all. Instead of no detail being omitted, no detail is given. I do not for a moment suggest that the writer deliberately stated what he knew to be false. He wrote under the overpowering impression of what is undoubtedly a very terrible scene or series of scenes. The intense reality of the thing was vividly present to his mind, and he lacked time, and perhaps energy, to consider very closely how that effect of reality had been produced. In assuming that it must have been produced by "revoltingly minute" descriptions, of which, as a matter of fact, there is no trace, he bore unconscious testimony to the subtle art of the poet. Of course it may be argued that the horror of the scene, by whatever means produced, is beyond human endurance, and consequently outside art. That is a rational position, which may be rationally discussed when the critics have quite recovered from their convulsions. But the fact remains that in Ibsen's dialogue there are none of the "loathsome" medical details which bulk so hugely before the "red and rolling eye" of the critical imagination.

There is a scene in *Truth*—one of those fragrant and wholesome plays beside which Ibsen, of course, seems unendurably "fetid" and "malodorous"—in which a party of men who have been lying egregiously to their womenfolk through two whole acts at last determine that they must tell the truth. After they have expatiated for some time on the moral elevation begotten by this resolve, one of them demurely suggests that they had better settle what the truth is to be. I would make the same suggestion to the Ibsenoclasts. Members of the same staff, at any rate, might surely arrive at a working agreement as to what is to be the truth about Ibsen. I print side by side two extracts from the *Daily Telegraph* of March 14, the first from a dramatic criticism on page 3, the second from a leading article on page 5:

> There was very little to offend the ear directly. On the Ibsen stage their nastiness is inferential, not actual. They call a spade a spade in a roundabout and circumlocutory fashion.
>
> It can no more be called Greek for its plainness of speech and candid foulness than could a dunghill at Delphi or a madhouse at Mitylene.

What is the bewildered man in the street to make of such conflicting oracles? Is Ibsen "candidly foul" or only "inferentially nasty"? Where doctors (of indecorum) differ, who shall decide? Mr. Macdougall perhaps? But now we are met by a still more baffling discrepancy of judgment. When we find Mr. Clement Scott and the critic of the *Daily Telegraph* flatly contradicting each other, chaos seems to have come again. Towards the close of last month Mr. Clement Scott was invited to take part in a debate on *Ghosts* at the Playgoer's Club. He was unable to attend, but sent a letter to represent him in the discussion. In this letter, as reported in the *Detroit Free Press* of February 28, there occurs the following sentence:— "None can doubt the cleverness, the genius, the analytical power of the 'Master'." After so emphatic a deliverance from so high an authority we began to take heart of grace, and to imagine that Ibsen might not be such a blockhead after all. But, alas! we reckoned without the critic of the *Daily*

William Archer: Ghosts and Gibberings

Telegraph. Ghosts, he assured us on March 14, not much more than a fortnight after the date of Mr. Scott's letter, "might have been a tragedy had it been treated by a man of genius. Handled by an egotist (!) and a bungler, it is only a deplorably dull play. There are ideas in *Ghosts* that would have inspired a tragic poet. They are vulgarized and debased by a suburban Ibsen. You want a Shakespeare, or a Byron (!), or a Browning to attack the subject-matter of *Ghosts* as it ought to be attacked. It might be a noble theme. Here it is a nasty and a vulgar one." Now, which are we to believe—Mr. Scott, or the literary oracle of the largest circulation, who reckons Byron among the great tragic poets? Is Ibsen a genius or merely an egotist and a bungler? I fear the weight of the evidence is in favour of the latter judgment; for I observe that a third eminent authority, the critic of *Truth,* sides with his colleague of the *Telegraph* against Mr. Scott. He writes of "the Ibsen dust-bin," and exclaims: "Literature forsooth! Where is a page of literature to be found in the whole category of Ibsen's plays? It is an insult to the word." This settles the matter! The man who can write of "the whole category" of Ibsen's plays must be an unimpeachable authority on literature. Mr. Scott and the rest of us must even yield to this categorical assurance, and own Ibsen no genius but a suburban egotist.

This article, I shall be told, is purely negative, and contains no rational discussion of the merits and demerits of *Ghosts.* True; but who can carry on a rational discussion with men whose first argument is a howl for the police?

Archer's *staunch* defense of Ibsen was itself the source of ridicule for the journalist. —D.M.

Francis Fergusson

Ghosts and The Cherry Orchard: The Theater of Modern Realism

Fergusson, Francis; *The Idea of a Theater: A Study of Ten Plays, The Art of Drama in Changing Perspective.* Copyright ©1949 by Princeton University Press. Reprinted by permission of Princeton University Press.

The Plot of *Ghosts:* Thesis, Thriller, and Tragedy

Ghosts is not Ibsen's best play, but it serves my purpose, which is to study the foundations of modern realism, just because of its imperfections. Its power, and the poetry of some of its effects, are evident; yet a contemporary audience may be bored with its old-fashioned iconoclasm and offended by the clatter of its too-obviously well-made plot. On the surface it is a *drame à thèse*, of the kind Brieux was to develop to its logical conclusion twenty years later: it proves the hollowness of the conventional bourgeois marriage. At the same time it is a thriller with all the tricks of the Boulevard entertainment: Ibsen was a student of Scribe in his middle period. But underneath this superficial form of thesis-thriller—the play which Ibsen started to write, the angry diatribe as he first conceived it—there is another form, the shape of the underlying action, which Ibsen gradually made out in the course of his two-years' labor upon the play, in obedience to his scruple of truthfulness, his profound attention to the reality of his fictive characters' lives. The form of the play is understood according to two conceptions of plot, which Ibsen himself did not at this point clearly distinguish: the rationalized concatenation of events with a univocal moral, and the plot as the "soul" or first actualization of the directly perceived action.

Halvdahn Koht, in his excellent study *Henrik Ibsen*, has explained the circumstances under which *Ghosts* was written. It was first planned as an attack upon marriage, in answer to the critics of *A Doll's House*. The story of the play is perfectly coherent as the demonstration and illustration of this thesis. When the play opens, Captain Alving has just died, his son Oswald is back from Paris where he had been studying painting, and his wife is straightening out the estate. The Captain had been accepted locally as a pillar of society but was in secret a drunkard and a debauchee. He had seduced his wife's maid, and had a child by her; and this child, Regina, is now in her turn Mrs. Alving's maid. Mrs. Alving had concealed all this for something like twenty years. She was following the advice of the conventional Pastor Manders and endeavoring to save Oswald from the horrors of the household: it was for this reason she had sent him away to school. But now, with her husband's death, she proposes to get rid of the Alving heritage in all its forms, in order to free herself and Oswald for the innocent, unconventional "joy of life." She wants to endow an orphanage with the Captain's money, both to quiet any rumors there may be of his sinful life and to get rid of the remains of his power over her. She encounters this power, however, in many forms, through the Pastor's timidity and through the attempt by Engstrand (a local carpenter who was bribed to pretend to be Regina's father) to blackmail her. Oswald wants to marry Regina and has to be told the whole story. At last he reveals that he has inherited syphilis from his father—the dead hand of the past in its most sensationally ugly form—and when his brain softens at the end, Mrs. Alving's whole plan collapses in unrelieved horror. It is "proved" that she should have left home twenty years before, like Nora in *A Doll's House*; and that conventional marriage is therefore an evil tyranny.

In accordance with the principles of the thesis play, *Ghosts* is plotted as a series of debates on conventional morality, between Mrs. Alving and the Pastor, the Pastor and Oswald, and Oswald and his mother. It may also be read as a perfect well-made thriller. The story is presented with immediate clarity, with mounting and controlled suspense; each act ends with an exciting curtain which reaffirms the issues and promises important new developments. In this play, as in so many others, one may observe that the conception of dramatic form underlying the thesis play and the machine-made Boulevard entertainment is the same: the logically concatenated series of events (intriguing thesis or logical intrigue) which the characters and their relationships merely illustrate. And it was this view of *Ghosts* which made it an immediate scandal and success.

But Ibsen himself protested that he was not a reformer but a poet. He was often led to write by anger and he compared the process of composition to his pet scorpion's emptying of poison; Ibsen kept a piece of soft fruit in his cage for the scorpion to sting when the spirit moved him. But Ibsen's own spirit was not satisfied by the mere discharge of venom; and one may see, in *Ghosts*, behind the surfaces of the savage story, a partially realized tragic form of really poetic scope, the result of Ibsen's more serious and disinterested brooding upon the human condition in general, where it underlies the myopic rebellions and empty clichés of the time.

In order to see the tragedy behind the thesis, it is necessary to return

Francis Fergusson: The Theater of Modern Realism

to the distinction between plot and action, and to the distinction between the plot as the rationalized series of events, and the plot as "the soul of the tragedy." The action of the play is "to control the Alving heritage for my own life." Most of the characters want some material or social advantage from it—Engstrand money, for instance, and the Pastor the security of conventional respectability. But Mrs. Alving is seeking a true and free human life itself—for her son, and through him, for herself. Mrs. Alving sometimes puts this quest in terms of the iconoclasms of the time, but her spiritual life, as Ibsen gradually discovered it, is at a deeper level; she tests everything—Oswald, the Pastor, Regina, her own moves—in the light of her extremely strict if unsophisticated moral sensibility: by direct perception and not by ideas at all. She is tragically seeking; she suffers a series of pathoses and new insights in the course of the play; and this rhythm of will, feeling, and insight underneath the machinery of the plot is the form of the life of the play, the soul of the tragedy.

The similarity between *Ghosts* and Greek tragedy, with its single fated action moving to an unmistakable catastrophe, has been felt by many critics of Ibsen. Mrs. Alving, like Oedipus, is engaged in a quest for her true human condition; and Ibsen, like Sophocles, shows on-stage only the end of this quest, when the past is being brought up again in the light of the present action and its fated outcome. From this point of view Ibsen is a plot-maker in the first sense: by means of his selection and arrangement of incidents he defines an action underlying many particular events and realized in various modes of intelligible purpose, of suffering, and of new insight. What Mrs. Alving sees changes in the course of the play, just as what Oedipus sees changes as one veil after another is removed from the past and the present. The underlying form of *Ghosts* is that of the tragic rhythm as one finds it in *Oedipus Rex*.

But this judgment needs to be qualified in several respects: because of the theater for which Ibsen wrote, the tragic form which Sophocles could develop to the full, and with every theatrical resource, is hidden beneath the clichés of plot and the surfaces "evident to the most commonplace mind." At the end of the play the tragic rhythm of Mrs. Alving's quest is not so much completed as brutally truncated, in obedience to the requirements of the thesis and the thriller. Oswald's collapse, before our eyes, with his mother's screaming, makes the intrigue end with a bang, and hammers home the thesis. But from the point of view of Mrs. Alving's tragic quest as we have seen it develop through the rest of the play, this conclusion concludes nothing: it is merely sensational.

The exciting intrigue and the brilliantly, the violently clear surfaces of *Ghosts* are likely to obscure completely its real life and underlying form. The tragic rhythm, which Ibsen rediscovered by his long and loving attention to the reality of his fictive lives, is evident only to the histrionic sensibility. As Henry James put it, Ibsen's characters "have the extraordinary, the brilliant property of becoming when represented at once more abstract and more living": i.e., both their lives and the life of the play, the spiritual content and the form of the whole, are revealed in this medium. A Nazimova, a Duse, could show it to us on the stage. Lacking such a performance, the reader must endeavor to respond imaginatively and directly himself if he is to see the hidden poetry of *Ghosts*.

Mrs. Alving and Oswald: The Tragic Rhythm in a Small Figure

As Ibsen was fighting to present his poetic vision within the narrow theater admitted by modern realism, so his protagonist Mrs. Alving is fighting to realize her sense of human life in the blank photograph of her own stuffy parlor. She discovers there no means, no terms, and no nourishment; that is the truncated tragedy which underlies the savage thesis of the play. But she does find her son Oswald, and she makes of him the symbol of all she is seeking: freedom, innocence, joy, and truth. At the level of the life of the play, where Ibsen warms his characters into extraordinary human reality, they all have moral and emotional meanings for each other; and the pattern of their related actions, their partially blind struggle for the Alving heritage, is consistent and very complex. In this structure, Mrs. Alving's changing relation to Oswald is only one strand, though an important one. I wish to consider it as a sample of Ibsen's rediscovery, through modern realism, of the tragic rhythm

Oswald is of course not only a symbol for his mother, but a person in his own right, with his own quest for freedom and release, and his own anomalous stake in the Alving heritage. He is also a symbol for Pastor Manders of what he wants from Captain Alving's estate: the stability and continuity of the bourgeois conventions. In the economy of the play as a whole, Oswald is the hidden reality of the whole situation, like Oedipus' actual status as son-husband: the hidden fatality which, revealed in a series of tragic and ironic steps, brings the final peripety of the action. To see how this works, the reader is asked to consider Oswald's role in Act I and the beginning of Act II.

The main part of Act I (after a prologue between Regina and Engstrand) is a debate, or rather agon, between Mrs. Alving and the Pastor. The Pastor has come to settle the details of Mrs. Alving's bequest of her husband's money to the orphanage. They at once disagree about the purpose and handling of the bequest; and this disagreement soon broadens into the whole issue of Mrs. Alving's emancipation versus the Pastor's conventionality. The question of Oswald is at the center. The Pastor wants to think of him, and to make of him, a pillar of society such as the Captain was supposed to have been, while Mrs. Alving wants him to be her masterpiece of liberation. At this point Oswald himself wanders in, the actual but still mysterious truth underlying the dispute between his mother and the Pastor. His appearance produces what the Greeks would have called a complex recognition scene, with an implied peripety for both Mrs. Alving and the Pastor, which will not be realized by them until the end of the act. But this tragic development is written to be acted; it is to be found, not so much in the actual words of the characters, as in their moral-emotional responses and changing relationships to one another.

The Pastor has not seen Oswald since he grew up; and seeing him now he is startled as though by a real ghost; he recognizes him as the very reincarnation of his father: the same physique, the same mannerisms, even the same kind of pipe. Mrs. Alving with equal confidence recognizes him as her own son, and she notes that his mouth-mannerism is like the Pastor's. (She had been in love with the Pastor during the early years of her marriage, when she wanted to leave the Captain.) As for Oswald himself, the mention of the pipe gives him a Proustian intermittence of the heart: he suddenly recalls a childhood scene when his father had given him his own pipe to smoke. He feels again the nausea and the cold sweat, and hears the Captain's hearty laughter. Thus in effect he recognizes himself as his father's, in the sense of his father's *victim*, a premonition of the ugly scene at the end of the play. But at this point no one is prepared to accept the full import of these insights. The whole scene is, on the surface, light and conventional, an accurate report of a passage of provincial politeness. Oswald wanders off for a walk before dinner, and the Pastor and his mother are left to bring their struggle more into the open.

Oswald's brief scene marks the end of the first round of the fight, and serves as prologue for the second round, much as the intervention of the chorus in the agon between Oedipus and Tiresias punctuates their struggle, and hints at an unexpected outcome on a new level of awareness. As soon as Oswald has gone, the Pastor launches an attack in form upon Mrs. Alving's entire emancipated way of life, with the question of Oswald, his role in the community, his upbringing and his future, always at the center of the attack. Mrs. Alving replies with her whole rebellious philosophy, illustrated by a detailed account of her tormented life with the Captain, none of which the Pastor had known (or been willing to recognize) before. Mrs. Alving proves on the basis of this evidence that her new freedom is right; that her long secret rebellion was justified; and that she is now about to complete Oswald's emancipation, and thereby her own, from the swarming ghosts of the past. If the issue were merely on this rationalistic level, and between her and the Pastor, she would triumph at this point. But the real truth of her situation (as Oswald's appearance led us to suppose) does not fit either her rationalization or the Pastor's.

Oswald passes through the parlor again on his way to the dining room to get a drink before dinner, and his mother watches him in pride and pleasure. But from behind the door we hear the affected squealing of Regina. It is now Mrs. Alving's turn for an intermittence of the heart: it is as though she heard again her husband with Regina's mother. The insight which she had rejected before now reaches her in full strength, bringing the promised pathos and peripety; she sees Oswald, not as her masterpiece of liberation, but as the sinister, tyrannical, and continuing life of the past itself. The basis of her rationalization is gone; she suffers the breakdown of the moral being which she had built upon her now exploded view of Oswald.

At this point Ibsen brings down the curtain in obedience to the principles of the well-made play. The effect is to raise the suspense by stimulating our curiosity about the facts of the rest of the story. What will Mrs. Alving do now? What will the Pastor do—for Oswald and Regina are half-brother and sister; can we prevent the scandal from coming out? So the suspense is raised, but the attention of the audience is diverted from Mrs. Alving's tragic quest to the most literal, newspaper version of the facts.

The second act (which occurs immediately after dinner) is ostensibly concerned only with these gossipy facts. The Pastor and Mrs. Alving debate ways of handling the threatened scandal. But this is only the literal surface: Ibsen has his eye upon Mrs. Alving's shaken psyche, and the actual dramatic form of this scene, under the discussion which Mrs. Alving keeps up, is her pathos which the Act I curtain broke off. Mrs. Alving is suffering the blow in courage and faith; and she is rewarded with her deepest insight: "I am half inclined to think we are all ghosts, Mr. Manders. It is not only what we have inherited from our fathers and mothers that exists again in us, but all sorts of dead ideas and all kinds of old dead beliefs and things of that kind. They are not actually alive in us; but they are dormant all the same, and we can never be rid of them. Whenever I take up a newspaper and read it, I fancy I see ghosts creeping between the lines. There must be ghosts all over the world. They must be as countless as the grains of sand, it seems to me. And we are so miserably afraid of the light, all of us." This passage, in the fumbling phrases of Ibsen's provincial lady, and in William Archer's translation, is not by itself the poetry of the great dramatic poets. It does not have the verbal music of Racine, nor the freedom and sophistication of Hamlet, nor the scope of the Sophoclean chorus, with its use of the full complement of poetic and musical and theatrical resources. But in the total situation in the Alving parlor which Ibsen has so carefully established, and in terms of Mrs. Alving's uninstructed but profoundly developing awareness, it has its own hidden poetry: a poetry not of words

Francis Fergusson: The Theater of Modern Realism

but of the theater, a poetry of the histrionic sensibility. From the point of view of the underlying form of the play—the form as "the soul" of the tragedy—this scene completes the sequence which began with the debate in Act I: it is the pathos-and-epiphany following that agon.

It is evident, I think, that insofar as Ibsen was able to obey his realistic scruple, his need for the disinterested perception of human life beneath the clichés of custom and rationalization, he rediscovered the perennial basis of tragedy. The poetry of *Ghosts* is under the words, in the detail of action, where Ibsen accurately sensed the tragic rhythm of human life in a thousand small figures. And these little "movements of the psyche" are composed in a complex rhythm like music, a formal development sustained (beneath the sensational story and the angry thesis) until the very end. But the action is not completed: Mrs. Alving is left screaming with the raw impact of the calamity. The music is broken off, the dissonance unresolved—or, in more properly dramatic terms, the acceptance of the catastrophe, leading to the final vision or epiphany which should correspond to the insight Mrs. Alving gains in Act II, is lacking. The action of the play is neither completed nor placed in the wider context of meanings which the disinterested or contemplative purposes of poetry demand.

The unsatisfactory end of *Ghosts* may be understood in several ways. Thinking of the relation between Mrs. Alving and Oswald, one might say that she had romantically loaded more symbolic values upon her son than a human being can carry; hence his collapse proves too much—more than Mrs. Alving or the audience can digest. One may say that, at the end, Ibsen himself could not quite dissociate himself from his rebellious protagonist and see her action in the round, and so broke off in anger, losing his tragic vision in the satisfaction of reducing the bourgeois parlor to a nightmare, and proving the hollowness of a society which sees human life in such myopic and dishonest terms. As a thesis play, *Ghosts* is an ancestor of many related genres: Brieux's arguments for social reform, propaganda plays like those of the Marxists, or parables á la Andreev, or even Shaw's more generalized plays of the play-of-thought about social questions. But this use of the theater of modern realism for promoting or discussing political and social ideas never appealed to Ibsen. It did not solve his real problem, which was to use the publicly accepted theater of his time for poetic purposes. The most general way to understand the unsatisfactory end of *Ghosts* is to say that Ibsen could not find a way to represent the action of his protagonist, with all its moral and intellectual depth, within the terms of modern realism. In the attempt he truncated this action, and revealed as in a brilliant light the limitations of the bourgeois parlor as the scene of human life.

IBSEN'S GHOSTS: A DRAMATURGICAL SOURCEBOOK

The End of *Ghosts:* The Tasteless Parlor and the Stage of Europe

Oswald is the chief symbol of what Mrs. Alving is seeking, and his collapse ends her quest in a horrifying catastrophe. But in the complex life of the play, all of the persons and things acquire emotional and moral significance for Mrs. Alving; and at the end, to throw as much light as possible upon the catastrophe, Ibsen brings all of the elements of his composition together in their highest symbolic valency. The orphanage has burned to the ground; the Pastor has promised Engstrand money for his "Sailor's Home" which he plans as a brothel; Regina departs, to follow her mother in the search for pleasure and money. In these eventualities the conventional morality of the Alving heritage is revealed as lewdness and dishonesty, quickly consumed in the fires of lust and greed, as Oswald himself (the central symbol) was consumed even before his birth. But what does this wreckage mean? Where are we to place it in human experience? Ibsen can only place it in the literal parlor, with lamplight giving place to daylight, and sunrise on the empty, stimulating, virginal snow-peaks out the window. The emotional force of this complicated effect is very great; it has the searching intimacy of nightmare. But it is also as disquieting as a nightmare from which we are suddenly awakened; it is incomplete, and the contradiction between the inner power of dream and the literal appearances of the daylight world is unresolved. The spirit that moved Ibsen to write the play, and which moved his protagonist through her tragic progress, is lost to sight, disembodied, imperceptible in any form unless the dreary exaltation of the inhuman mountain scene conveys it in feeling.

Henry James felt very acutely the contradiction between the deep and strict spirit of Ibsen and his superb craftsmanship on one side, and the little scene he tried to use—the parlor in its surrounding void—on the other. "If the spirit is a lamp within us, glowing through what the world and the flesh make of us as through a ground-glass shade, then such pictures as Little Eyolf and John Gabriel are each a chassez-croisez of lamps burning, as in tasteless parlors, with the flame practically exposed," he wrote in *London Notes.* [Jan.–Aug., 1897] "There is a positive odor of spiritual paraffin. The author nevertheless arrives at the dramatist's great goal—he arrives for all his meagerness at intensity. The meagerness, which is after all but an unconscious, an admirable economy, never interferes with that: it plays straight into the hands of his rare mastery of form. The contrast between this form—so difficult to have reached, so 'evolved,' so civilized—and the bareness and bleakness of his little northern democracy is the source of half the hard frugal charm he puts forth."

James had rejected very early in his career his own little northern democracy, that of General Grant's America, with its ugly parlor, its dead conventions, its enthusiastic materialism, and its "non-conducting atmosphere." At the same time he shared Ibsen's ethical preoccupation, and his strict sense of form. His comments on Ibsen are at once the most sympathetic and the most objective that have been written. But James's own solution was to try to find a better parlor for the theater of human life; to present the quest of his American pilgrim of culture on the wider "stage of Europe" as this might still be felt and suggested in the manners of the leisured classes in England and France. James would have nothing to do with the prophetic and revolutionary spirit which was driving the great continental authors, Ibsen among them. In his artistry and his moral exactitude Ibsen is akin to James; but this is not his whole story, and if one is to understand the spirit he tried to realize in Mrs. Alving, one must think of Kierkegaard, who had a great influence on Ibsen in the beginning of his career.

Kierkegaard (in *For Self-Examination*) has this to say of the disembodied and insatiable spirit of the times: " ... thou wilt scarcely find anyone who does not believe in—let us say, for example, the spirit of the age, the *Zeitgeist*. Even he who has taken leave of higher things and is rendered blissful by mediocrity, yea, even he who toils slavishly for paltry ends or in the contemptible servitude of ill-gotten gains, even he believes, firmly and fully too, in the spirit of the age. Well, that is natural enough, it is by no means anything very lofty he believes in, for the spirit of the age is after all no higher than the age, it keeps close to the ground, so that it is the sort of spirit which is most like will-o'-the-wisp; but yet he believes in spirit. Or he believes in the world-spirit *(Weltgeist)* that strong spirit (for allurements, yes), that ingenious spirit (for deceits, yes); that spirit which Christianity calls an evil spirit—so that, in consideration of this, it is by no means anything very lofty he believes in when he believes in the world-spirit; but yet he believes in spirit. Or he believes in 'the spirit of humanity,' not spirit in the individual, but in the race, that spirit which, when it is god-forsaken for having forsaken God, is again, according to Christianity's teaching, an evil spirit—so that in view of this it is by no means anything very lofty he believes in when he believes in this spirit; but yet he believes in spirit.

"On the other hand, as soon as the talk is about a holy spirit—how many, dost thou think, believe in it? Or when the talk is about an evil spirit which is to be renounced—how many, dost thou think, believe in such a thing?"[1]

This description seems to me to throw some light upon Mrs. Alving's

---

[1] Kierkegaard, *For Self-Examination and Judge for Yourselves* (Princeton University Press, 1944), p. 94.

quest, upon Ibsen's modern-realistic scene, and upon the theater which his audience would accept. The other face of nineteenth century positivism is romantic aspiration. And Ibsen's realistic scene presents both of these aspects of the human condition: the photographically accurate parlor, in the foreground, satisfies the requirements of positivism, while the empty but stimulating scene out the window—Europe as a moral void, an uninhabited wilderness—offers as it were a blank check to the insatiate spirit. Ibsen always felt this exhilarating wilderness behind his cramped interiors. In *A Doll's House* we glimpse it as winter weather and black water. In *The Lady from the Sea* it is the cold ocean, with its whales and its gulls. In *The Wild Duck* it is the northern marshes, with wildfowl but no people. In the last scene of *Ghosts* it is, of course, the bright snow-peaks, which may mean Mrs. Alving's quest in its most disembodied and ambivalent form; very much the same sensuous moral void in which Wagner, having totally rejected the little human foreground where Ibsen fights his battles, unrolls the solitary action of passion. It is the "stage of Europe" before human exploration, as it might have appeared to the first hunters.

There is a kinship between the fearless and demanding spirit of Kierkegaard, and the spirit which Ibsen tried to realize in Mrs. Alving. But Mrs. Alving, like her contemporaries whom Kierkegaard describes, will not or cannot accept any interpretation of the spirit that drives her. It may look like the *Weltgeist* when she demands the joy of living, it may look like the Holy Ghost itself when one considers her appetite for truth. And it may look like the spirit of evil, a "goblin damned," when we see the desolation it produces. If one thinks of the symbols which Ibsen brings together in the last scene: the blank parlor, the wide unexplored world outside, the flames that consumed the Alving heritage and the sunrise flaming on the peaks, one may be reminded of the condition of Dante's great rebel Ulysses. He too is wrapped in the flame of his own consciousness, yet still dwells in the pride of the mind and the exhilaration of the world free of people, *il mondo senza gente*. But this analogy also may not be pressed too far. Ulysses is in hell; and when we explore the Mountain on which he was wrecked, we can place his condition with finality, and in relation to many other human modes of action and awareness. But Mrs. Alving's mountains do not place her anywhere: the realism of modern realism ends with the literal. Beyond that is not the ordered world of the tradition, but *Unendlichkeit,* and the anomalous "freedom" of undefined and uninformed aspiration.

Perhaps Mrs. Alving and Ibsen himself are closer to the role of Dante than to the role of Ulysses, seeing a hellish mode of being, but free to move on. Certainly Ibsen's development continued beyond *Ghosts,* and toward the end of his career he came much closer to achieving a consistent theatrical poetry within the confines of the theater of modern realism. He himself remarked that his poetry was to be found only in the series of his plays, no one of which was complete by itself.

But my purpose is, of course, not to do justice to Ibsen but to consider the potentialities of modern realism; and for this purpose Chekhov's masterpiece is essential. Chekhov did not solve the problem which Ibsen faced in *Ghosts*. He was not trying to show a desperate quest like Mrs. Alving's, with every weapon of the mind and the will. By his time the ambitious machinery of thesis and thriller had begun to pall; the prophetic-revolutionary spirit, grown skeptical and subtle, had sunk back into the flesh and the feelings, into the common beggarly body, for a period of pause, in hope and foreboding. Chekhov does not have Ibsen's force and intellect but he can accept the realistic stage much more completely, and use it with greater mastery for the contemplative purpose of art.

Rolf Fjelde *Foreword*

"Foreword" by Rolf Fjelde, from *Four Major Plays, Vol. II* by Henrik Ibsen, translated by Rolf Fjelde. Translation copyright (c) 1970 by Rolf Fjelde. Used by permission of Dutton Signet, a division of Penguin Books USA Inc.

In the dramatic world of *Ghosts* the equivocal purveyor both of abstract demands categorically imposed and of codes and norms surrendering to conformity is Pastor Manders. The situation calling for appropriate response occurred two decades previous: the marriage with young Lieutenant Alving. The intelligent and sympathetic examination of all the factors involved thus takes place after long delay and constitutes the retrospective action of the drama, the recovery of the lost reality of the past. And the burden of the play's lament, cumulatively achieved through the brooding scenic images, the subtly nuanced language, the slow sacrifice of its ritual victim, Osvald, is: "What worth have truth and freedom, realized twenty years too late?"

Francis Fergusson, in his justly famed interpretation of *Ghosts*, has defined its binding action, through a Stanislavskian infinitive phrase, as "to control the Alving heritage for my own life." But this formulation, as he observes, confines the action chiefly to the plane of maneuver for material or social advantage, a motive shared by only three of the five characters. Helene Alving, however, is seeking a nobler objective, namely, a true and free human life, an ideal for which her artist son, Osvald, stands as the incarnation. Thus her action, on a higher plane, could be rephrased as "to regain my son" and all he ideally is, as a symbol of the fulfillment of her quest. This motivation has as well a negative corollary: "to repudiate Captain Alving" and all *he* really was, under that cloak of respectability she wove to conceal him, blessed and abetted by Pastor Manders. Toward this end the orphanage has been built, to absorb every last trace of the Alving inheritance. The ceremony of dedication is now at hand; the maltreated wife, the solicitous mother hopes then to be as free as the son. Except that Osvald, in the grippingly theatrical conclusion of Act I, proves to be inhabited by a ghost. Mrs. Alving is thrust into a paralyzing impasse, able neither to regain nor repudiate, having discovered to her horror the hated father subsisting in the loved son.

Nothing has prepared her for this revelation. Before and during her marriage, she had been conventionally devout, oriented toward duty, easily subject to direction by her relatives and pastor. In the ten years since her husband's death, she has arduously made herself over into a model of enlightenment, a liberal, a rationalist, a freethinker—without, however, confronting the ultimate truth that arises out of the indefinable depth of the personality, determining the profound ambiguities in all human relationships, including her own complicity in the wasted possibilities of Captain Alving. "I can't stand it!" she cries out at one point, in belated recognition of default. "I've got to work my way out to freedom." The great, the moving spiritual action of the drama then commences, when "to regain my son" gradually becomes "to regain my husband, young Lieutenant Alving," and all he *really* was. Inga-Stina Ewbank has shown how delicately Mrs. Alving's deepening perception of the truth is conveyed, even to the thematic repetition of the tiny modal verb "had to." In Act I it expresses a litany of self-centered complaint: *because* Alving was thus-and-so, "I *had to* become his drinking companion ... I *had to* sit alone with him ... I *had to* pull the whole load ... " The rankling resentment in the phrase, the certitude of its premise are both reflexes of the diminished consciousness instilled by Manders' rigidly codified view of morality. By Act III the subject has shifted from "I" to "he." The underlying content of the litany has altered to a recognition that "this child [Alving] ... *had to* make his life here ... he *had to* get along with no real goal in life," and so on. The little phrase is now resonant with Mrs. Alving's new, intensely felt awareness of human limitation and suffering, of the pathos of irreplaceable gifts stifled by enveloping mediocrity and by misunderstanding, not the least of which has been her own.

On the reduced stage of Ibsen's realism, Mrs. Alving's spiritual struggle, her anguished expansion of consciousness into the truth of an antithetical human being's existence gives the play a heroically sustained impetus toward self-liberation that moves counter to Osvald's gathering despair and disintegration. But as with *Enemy*, that movement implies larger parallels as well. The ghosts of the title are also "all kinds of old dead doctrines and opinions and beliefs." From the initial opposition of the wife's righteous moralism vs. the husband's joy of life, the play comes to resemble, as Brian Johnston has brilliantly indicated, an immense séance that raises the essential spirits of the main "intellectual currents" *(åndelig strømninger)* that have formed Western civilization. From the Judeo-Christian tradition, the action is haunted by specters of the temptation and fall of man, the trinity, the *pietà* (shockingly reenacted at the end), and the millennium of Ibsen's Second Empire dominated by Pauline religious orthodoxy; and, from the eclipsed Hellenic tradition, by reminiscences of a lost paganism, the search for which proved such a vital element in the historical Enlightenment, as both reductively paralleled and awesomely reproved for lack of sufficient depth in the tragic quest for self-recovery by the woman significantly named Helene. With so large a field of world-historical forces

Rolf Fjelde: Foreword

at work, it might be well as a final note to reaffirm, echoing Peter Brook, that for all its seriousness, the play is still play; that it already prefigures, particularly in the Manders-Engstrand exchanges, the sly and buoyant humor that will burst forth shortly in *Enemy*; and that any stage production is remiss if it neglects a comic lightness of touch that, in its intermittent way, is as amusing as anything in James Joyce's delightfully racy verse "Epilogue to Ibsen's *Ghosts.*"

Brian Johnston

Archetypal Repetition in Ghosts

Brian Johnston, *The Ibsen Cycle: The Design of Plays from* Pillars of Society *to* When We Dead Awaken, (University Park: The Pennsylvania State University Press, 1992), 189–236 Copyright 1992 by the Pennsylvania State University. Reproduced by permission of the publisher.

> It is strange how history repeats itself in different forms like variations on a musical theme.
> —*Ibsen in a letter to John Grieg*

We are first of all, of course, struck by the title *Gengangere* (Ghosts), those who return to walk again, which immediately suggests the fearful, primitive, and occult. The feared return of the dead to plague the living is one of the most primitive and basic of all human fears, considered by many anthropologists to be the origin of religious practice and myth. Such a fear begot elaborate burial and memorial practices, even including the actual binding of the dead body before burial to prevent its returning from the grave.[1] It may seem a long way from this prehistorical nightmare to the sophisticated structure of Ibsen's family drama, but it is just this nightmare that is reexperienced by the modern consciousness in the famous climax in Act I when Helene Alving cries out:

> Ghosts. Those two in the greenhouse have come back!

In fact, close analysis will show that the play's major action consists of a desperate but futile attempt (and by means of a memorial to the dead) to keep the dead buried in their graves. Though consciousness has advanced beyond physically tying the dead body to prevent its return, Helene Alving has attempted the same action by sophisticated modern means: by legal deeds, by an alien moralism that only faintly disguises the animus felt by the living wife toward the dead husband. Beyond the immediate dead, too, hover the hosts of the spirit's past, always ready to overwhelm and repossess the little foreground world of human reason.

The Greek quality of *Ghosts* has been recognized by a number of commentators. Almost as soon as the play appeared, a countryman of Ibsen's, the classical scholar P. O. Schjøtt, saw its similarity to classical Greek drama. G. Wilson Knight observes that the heritage of guilt in *Ghosts* "is like the curse on the house of Atreus in the *Oresteia.*"² Other critics have pointed out the Greek structure of the play: how its method of recollecting the past within the *agon* of the present resembles the method of *Oedipus Tyrannos,* how its almost obsessive mathematical procedure (reducing the characters onstage one by one) has a stark Sophoclean rationality. The subtitle of the play, too, *A Family Drama* (*Et familiedrama*), recollects the subject matter of Greek tragedy. When, therefore, we recognize that the dialectic of the play follows Hegel's account of the ethical society, whose conflicts are illustrated by Greek tragedy, we are not violating but substantiating the most perceptive of accepted commentary upon the play. It should, therefore, be possible to suggest, without incurring too much protest, that Ibsen, concerned with resurrecting the spirit of Greek drama, has drawn upon the greatest achievements of the three major tragedians of Athens: the *Oresteia,* the *Oedipus Tyrannos,* and *The Bacchae.*

Though, in structure, and in theme, *Ghosts* is Greek, its total spiritual subject matter is that of Ibsen's own day, so that there is no contradiction in the fact that within this Greek structure we can find spiritual archetypes obviously deriving from other mythological traditions, such as the Germanic and the Judeo-Christian. These other forces, however, are assembled for a distinctly Greek dialectic so that even the Christian priest, Manders, is a social rather than a spiritual leader, his function expressing itself in terms of social convention and social *duties.* Manders is the reflection of orthodox social mores (his conventional piety would be as happy with one religious tradition as with another) so that Ibsen is not setting him up as an easy anti-Christian target but is using him to portray the somewhat pathetic inadequacies of a level of consciousness that attempts to function entirely in terms of conventional pieties. Thus there is, in Ibsen's portrait of Manders, no bias to be outgrown (somewhat late in life!) in the later plays; I think Ibsen can be taken as speaking the truth when he observed, "in the whole book there is not a single opinion, not a single remark to be found that is there on the dramatist's account...." The method, the technique underlying the form of the book, was in itself quite enough to prevent the author making himself apparent in the dialogue.³

The world of *Ghosts* is a historically determined one, in which the condition of the present can be understood only by a process of imaginative historical recollection and analysis. Identities on the stage, for all their vivid particularity and immediacy, also are universal and archetypal: the priest, Manders; his "satanic" complement, Engstrand; the intellec-

---

[1] *Larousse Encyclopedia of Mythology* (London, 1959), 5–7.
[2] G. Wilson Knight, *Henrik Ibsen,* 51.
[3] Letter to Sophus Scharndorph, 6 January 1882.

tually inquiring Helene; the artist, Osvald. These characters exist firmly as modern figures in a modern situation, but only the most superficial judgment would claim that the modern consciousness is truncated from the history that has shaped it or that the poet who was to give us an adequate portrait of the present would not have to explore the evolution of human consciousness. Religion, art, and intellectual inquiry, which are as important to the play's meanings as the life histories and destinies of fictional individuals, did not drop full-blown from heaven onto the modern scene, but became what they are through the process of history: a point acknowledged by Ibsen in a note to the play:

> The key-note is to be: The prolific growth of our intellectual life, in literature, art, etc.—and in contrast to this; the whole of mankind gone astray.[4]

Very obviously, here, Ibsen is considering a culture crisis within a moment in history, and if it is protested that this does not apply to the *individual* within that culture crisis, that here, at least, we can dispense with that historical awareness that Ibsen insisted was indispensable to a modern author, another note to *Ghosts* shows that the individual human being is also a product of culture and history:

> The complete human being is no longer a product of nature, he is an artificial product like corn, and fruit-trees, and the Creole race and thoroughbred horses and dogs, the vine, etc.,
>
> The fault lies in that all mankind has failed. If a man claims to live and develop in a human way it is megalomania. All mankind, and especially the Christian part of it, suffers from megalomania.[5]

Let us consider the earlier suggestion that Ibsen's play resurrects themes and situations from the major Greek tragedians, for here the parallels are striking.

1. In the *Oresteia*, the military father, Agamemnon, is slain by his wife, Clytemnestra (twin sister of Helen), who has sent her son out to strangers. To set right her troubled and frightened conscience, the wife attempts to placate the wronged and buried father (many years later when her son has grown into a young man) by a fraudulent memorial ritual at his grave. The son returns from abroad at this moment and leagues with his sister to avenge his father. (These details are repeated in Sophocles' treatment of this myth.)

In *Ghosts*, the dead military father, Alving, has been wronged by his

---

[4] Archer, trans., XII, 185.
[5] Ibid., 186.

wife Helene, who has sent her son out to strangers. Helene tries to allay the ghost of her husband once and for all with a fraudulent ritual: as she is making arrangements for this, her son, Osvald, returns from abroad and soon will league with his sister, Regine, against the whole world of pious untruth created by Helene against the values represented by her husband. In *The Libation Bearers*, as in *Ghosts*, after the father has been avenged, there is a powerful invocation of the sun.

2. In *Oedipus Tyrannos* the present action of investigation of a present distress (the plague at Thebes) uncovers more and more of the polluted past. In the Oedipus myth the son was sent from the house to avert the catastrophe that the action fulfills. Mrs. Alving's tragic journey into enlightenment parallels that of Oedipus. There are minor similarities, perhaps, in Oedipus's duel with Tiresias and Helene's with *her* priest, Manders, and in the incest motif of both plays, though these parallels are very slight. The major parallel is the theme of the tragic family history, the polluted house, and the action of passionate and tragic retrospection.

3. Between *Ghosts* and *The Bacchae* the parallels are mostly thematic, but still powerfully striking. In Euripides' play the god of wine and joy-of-life, Dionysos, avenges himself upon the family that attempts to deny his divinity. The play ends with the mother, Agave, confronted by the mutilated body of her son, killed by herself—a terrible testimony to the power of the god she has offended. In *Ghosts*, Helene Alving, representing the pietistic and life-denying traditions of puritan Christianity, had set herself against the force of "joy-of-life" (*livsglede*, an untranslatable word that means something much more profound, such as the life impulse itself) and had erected, over her victory over this power, a triumphant lie that will be terribly destroyed (as in Euripides' play, there is the fiery destruction of a building). *Ghosts* ends with the mother confronting the wreckage of the son whom her crime helped to destroy.

These parallels can no more be coincidental than the parallels between other plays in the Cycle and their completely appropriate sources in Hegel and world literature and history. In Hegel's account of the ethical society, we move through an ever-widening circle of conflicts, the circumference of meaning continuously being pushed through individual, familial, societal, ethical, cultural, and religious dimensions of reality until the whole structure of reality is encompassed. The central conflict (symbolized by the conflict between Antigone and Creon, or Oedipus and his fate) detonates the devastation of the whole substance of this particular worldview (the ethical consciousness); and this is true, too, of the action of *Ghosts*, which involves:

> (1) The struggle of the individual consciousness against the structure of conventional society. (Helene and Osvald.)

(2) The conflicts within the family of husband-wife, parent-child, brother-sister relationships.

(3) A social and cultural world whose divisions are illustrated in the discrepancies between Captain Alving's orphanage and Chamberlain Alving's brothel; Osvald's "Parisian" values versus Manders' pietism; the collision between enlightened knowledge and conventional orthodoxy.

(4) The metaphysical discrepancy between Manders' careful, spiritual orthodoxy and the lonely spiritual quest of Helene Alving, brought to test the validity of her entire conventional instruction.

The detonation at the nucleus of the drama sets off a reaction not completed until the whole substance of this worldview is destroyed: a destruction, in the Hegelian paradox, essential to the continuing life of Spirit.

The somewhat dreadful nature of Ibsen's humor can be gauged from *Ghosts*' subtitle, *A Family Drama*. It brings to mind the familiar nineteenth-century phrase "family novel" or "family play," an assurance, to a squeamish public, that the "wholesome" contents are fit to be enjoyed by the entire family. The subject of *Ghosts* is the family, and its central metaphor, syphilis, destroys the generative source of all families, a superbly *tasteless* irony calculated to offend in the same way as the even more tasteless joke embedded in the situation of *Oedipus Tyrannos*. From Latin, Ibsen might well have been aware of the pun on *spiritus*, familiar to the Elizabethans, for example, equating it with semen ("the expense of spirit in a waste of shame ... "), which would make the metaphor of syphilis stand duty for the polluted spirit in a double sense: an appropriate synthesis of physical and metaphorical meaning. For if, as the powerful note to *Ghosts* implies, "all mankind is on the wrong track," this is not to be attributed to local moral and medical causes but to a major crisis in the history of the human spirit. This, admittedly, is a big subject, but I am convinced that Ibsen was interested only in big subjects—of the magnitude, in fact, that kept him occupied so long on the world-historical drama *Emperor and Galilean*. If the whole of mankind is on the wrong track then the error of misdirection began far back in history, near the spiritual origins of modern man. Thus it will repay considering the subject of physical and psychical origins in terms of polluted streams, and of the interconnection of these two realms. Infected or diseased spiritual streams will set up the cultural conditions of repressed Eros in rebellion, and syphilis will extend from being a mere medical symptom into a genuine tragic Nemesis. It is genuinely tragic, not only for its appropriateness (poetic justice in the very prose of prose), but also for its universal scale of reference, which is nothing less than the history of Europe. Thus the horrible suffering of Osvald and his mother, which has struck so many commentators as rooted in a pessimism, or in a merely local criticism of a particular morality—and in either case thus denied tragic dignity—completes a *universally* tragic pattern.

The main action of *Ghosts*—what, in fact, constitutes Helene Alving's fate—is the comprehension and exoneration of the life values, or laws, of Captain Alving; at first they are seen merely as a material inheritance tarnished by corruption and deception, a ghost to be laid forever to rest, but they are finally comprehended as a violated right whose suppression has resulted in a terrible Nemesis. The dialectical crisis of the play, interrupted by the outbreak of the orphanage fire, is the moment when Helene, stirred by her son's remark about *livsglede* (joy-of-life), suddenly "sees it all"—the whole pattern in which she recognizes herself, for the first time, as a destructive agent. The central figure in this pattern is that of the young, life-craving lieutenant before he was broken by the net of duties that his wife enlisted from that pietistic community of which Manders is the representative and spokesman. This image is the last and most powerful ghost to haunt the play, achieving that unity of recognition scene and reversal that Aristotle praised as the most perfect of tragic effects, for when Helene Alving is brought to recognize the nature of her husband and the nature of her crime against him, not only does her life work "burn up," but the entire direction of her quest—to be free of the influence of the hated husband—is reversed into its opposite: to rescue and rehabilitate all that he stood for.

Captain Alving, though dead, is Helene's invisible antagonist, striking back, like Agamemnon, through his children. He thus is of far more consequence as a dialectical presence than Manders or Engstrand who never risk the level of essential dialectical confrontation. Like a Socratic dialogue, the play's argument proceeds from error and misconception to final comprehension, and Helene's journey into light through recognition of error and guilt is a miniature model of the modern spirit's difficult recognition of the misdirection of its own spiritual history: the recognition that prompts the note to *Ghosts* that "all mankind is on the wrong track."

Ghosts is able to contain, within an action recognizably of Ibsen's own times, both the historical perspectives that have gone into the making of the modern consciousness, and one of the major (or archetypal) forms of that consciousness—the Hellenic. Thus the condition of consciousness esthetically enacted by the play and, it is to be hoped, activated in the audience, is a complete form, being archetypal, historical, and contemporary.

Brian Johnston: Archetypal Repetition in GHOSTS

This continuous interaction of more than one plane of reality throughout the total action must be kept in mind in our analysis of action and character, if our response is to be adequate to Ibsen's challenge.

Our analysis of character, for instance, must involve more than preoccupation with individual motives and character assessment, to a concern with the ethical, intellectual, and esthetic implications of the interaction of the total character grouping—the total consciousness—depicted by the play. That is to say, we should look at *Ghosts* as if it were, in the Miltonic phrase, a "great argument," the characters of which carry as many thematic as psychological qualities, and draw our attention outward, to the expanding supertext of meaning and implication, as well as inward, to the motives, velleities, and nuances of the individual psyche. It might help, in fact, to look at the character grouping of the play, for a moment, as if it were a visual design:

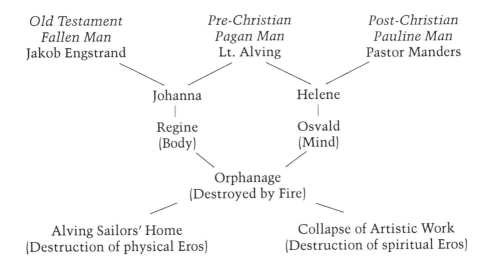

The three male figures, Engstrand, Alving, and Manders, all are involved in the past of Helene Alving, and are the subjects of choices and decisions she has made and now, in the action of the play, must reexamine and revalue. On the purely psychological and moral level they represent her old revulsion from Alving's life-style, her attachment to Manders' pietism, and her bad conscience over the consequences of her husband's way of life—all of these valuations emerging from her own particular upbringing and worldview. This is a very important area of the play's existence and of its full meaning, but it also serves to embody, or actualize, a wider realm of consequences and causes, and to see the characters also in terms of this wider range of meanings is not to violate the nature of the play but to be faithful to its *full* rhythm and resonance. I would even say that, as a *limitedly* realistic play, in which the poet makes a fairly narrow range of consciousness (e.g., psychological and social) carry the full richness of his meaning, *Ghosts* is as unsatisfactory as *Antigone* or *Oedipus the King* would be; it is only with our awareness of the greater dimensions of its intention that the subtle and complex artistry begins to work, and that the language and the dramatic method, which otherwise might seem "stagey" and nonrealistic, are shown to be dramatically far more complex than strict realism; this method expresses a continuous interplay of universal and particular reference in which *both*, universal *and* particular, or text and supertext, must be simultaneously present.

The significantly named *Jakob* Engstrand should impress us, not merely as a particular fallen and graceless individual, but as vividly representative of fallen man in whom the pagan categories of eros and *livsglede* have degenerated into "sin" and the brothel. Young Lieutenant Alving, with his baffled "joy-of-life," is suggestive of an alternative, guilt-free, energetic, and *creative* eros whose values have been unhappily *divided* in his children. The virginal, life-denying Pastor Manders, while being a plausible individual "character," transmits into the play's dialectic the spiritual tradition of Pauline Christianity, which has helped to shape the structure of modern culture and of the modern consciousness: the culture and consciousness of the audience before which the play, *Ghosts*, is presented as a mirror held up to Nature. In Ibsen's theater, the "characters" are significant enough to find a place in the Cycle when, in fact, they are strong enough to carry archetypal identities.

From this perspective, the Alving family history becomes the "diagram" of a wider spiritual history; not, of course, a dogmatic assertion on the course of Western history, but a model that can help us better meditate upon and understand its salient aspects.

Each offspring of Alving has an actual and a pseudofather and a different mother. Regine's putative father is Engstrand but actually Alving. Osvald is the legitimate son of Alving, but his mother's emotional allegiance to "pastor" Manders (to the point where she claims Osvald actually resembles Manders) gives him, too, a second father. (In fact, the pillar of society that Helene brought up Osvald to consider his father to be is Alving remade in the image of Manders.) Alving's two partners, the unwilling but legitimate Helene, and the willing but illegitimate Johanna, are each "infected" by their own previous alliances, Johanna with Engstrand, Helene with Manders. The appropriate shortcomings of the two offspring, Regine healthy in body but disastrously lacking in mind, Osvald intellectually creative but crippled physically,[6] are thematically linked to the shortcomings of Alving's two partners, Johanna and Helene. The two children divide between each other aspects (physical and mental) that can function creatively only in union and mutual interaction, and though these two functions or aspects are capable of being reduced to individual inadequacies, they quite obviously bring to mind the whole area of life subsumed under the categories of Flesh and Spirit. Regine's destination, Chamberlain Alving's sailors' home, should carry all the resonance of the most moralistic Victorian use of such emblems, as much as the collapse of Osvald's function as an artist should imply all that the nineteenth-century use of the figure of the Poet or the Artist in decline implies; our modern embarrassment with such archetypal identities (though Ibsen subtilizes them more than his contemporaries) is not necessarily to our credit.

A central metaphor of the play is that of the "asylum." We notice that all the living characters are involved in it. It is Helene's memorial which (contrary to a true memorial) attempts to *eliminate* the memory of her husband. Manders will assist in this process of elimination or obliteration, by his conventionally pious memorial service. Engstrand is employed to work in the children's home and this, too, seems to be Regine's destined task (in Helene's mind). Osvald has returned home to be present at the memorial ceremony. An orphanage is a place for homeless children just as a sailors' home (which also will bear Alving's name) is a place for homeless adults, and in both instances the sexual connotations of illegitimacy and sexual license are obvious. (It is likely that the sailors will create the need for the children's home, so that the Alving name on both institutions recognizes the connection.) Ibsen is not likely to be morally outraged by this: it is the peculiar *dreariness* of these institutions in the modern world that more likely offended him, a dreariness deriving from a lack of faith in either the Hellenic or the Christian worldviews. The lack of parentage, in the larger design of the play, could represent the truncation of the modern world from these two spiritual sources, so that the buildings of this orphanage, schoolhouse (Hellenic), and chapel (Christian) are, indeed, memorials to a dead past. In *Emperor and Galilean* Ibsen explicitly affirms this. The Church (Act I) and the University (Act II) are both shown to be spiritually bankrupt, and it is only a further degree of reification to translate Church and University (standing for Faith and Learning) into local

---

[6]There is an ambiguity here, for Osvald is physically afflicted in the *brain*, the result of which is the disintegration of his mind and his art. Nevertheless, Osvald obviously represents the intellectual sublimation of his father's *livsglede*, as Regine represents its physical manifestation.

chapel and schoolhouse. The diagram of the play set out on page 145 is not the whole play but it *can* alert us to the universal and abstract argument that the details of scene, character, action, and dialogue render in terms of tangible reality and tangible art.

The scene of *Ghosts* is a coastal town in western Norway, seemingly set apart from the large world (as in *The Pillars of Society*) and from large spiritual conflicts. We learn, from details that emerge in the dialogue, that this local community is suspicious and watchful, moralistic and unforgiving to those who are morally vulnerable. This community has to be placated, its opinions, however narrow, having to be taken into careful consideration, and Manders, the committee pastor with neither time nor talent for larger spiritual realities, goes in fear of it.

At the entrance to this world, in "Little Harbour Street," Engstrand intends to set up his "sailors' home" in order to lure in the "wandering seafarers of the world's oceans." This portentous phrase, used by Engstrand, seems to be echoed in Manders' account, to Helene, of the "intellectual currents" (*aandelige strømninger*) "in the larger world—where you've let your son wander so long."[7] These two images—the sailors wandering on the seas, to be lured into the "home," and the son wandering among the intellectual currents of the wide world, to return to the life-lie of his society—suggest, again, both flesh and spirit "on the wrong track."

Set apart from this community, and reached by boat, is Rosenvold, now a center of some enlightenment with its books, periodicals, and the belatedly freethinking (i.e., Hellenic) Helene. "Rosenvold" suggests an aristocratic vantage point, somewhat like "Rosmersholm," and if Ibsen chooses his names with the same care as other details in his play, there may be connotations, here, of the pagan categories of love (*Rosen* = rose) and force (*vold*) more decisively concentrated in the philandering Lieutenant Alving. Part of the Rosenvold estate is Solvik, which Helene will relinquish, reckoning it to represent the "value" of Alving as a marriage partner. It is to be noted that this particularly sordid interpretation of the relationship is Helene's, not Alving's, and alerts us to view skeptically her whole account of that marriage. Upon Solvik is erected the schoolhouse and chapel of the orphanage: both vehicles of an orthodoxy that Helene has, in fact, outgrown, thus compounding her hypocrisy in erecting the memorial. *Sol*vik brings to mind that constant sun metaphor in Ibsen's work (*Sol*, of course, is sun) and Helene's relinquishment of Solvik is at least in keeping with her whole sacrifice of *livsglede*, the Dionysiac energy

---

[7]It is possible that the phrase *aandelige strømninger* is a recollection of Georg Brandes's famous work, *Main Streams [Hovedstrømninger] of Nineteenth-Century Literature.*

indispensable to the health of the human spirit; Osvald's collapse, with the words, "Give me the sun, mother," brings home the full disastrousness of this sacrifice.

The geography—or topography—of the world of *Ghosts*, therefore, is a metaphoric landscape where even the most prosaic-seeming details (schoolhouse, chapel, sailors' home, orphanage, and family home) carry universal as well as particular connotations, and when Ibsen invades this landscape with historical and cultural consciousness, larger perspectives open up. We must, I believe, be alerted to visual echoes and quotations in Ibsen's work as well as verbal ones, and some such visual suggestion is evoked, surely, when the limping Jakob Engstrand attempts to enter a garden room and is intercepted by a young girl, Regine, who brandishes a weaponlike garden syringe and tries to prevent his entering. The satanic figure, entering a garden and being intercepted by an at least visually angelic figure, is continued in the dialogue with its debate on "the Lord's rain" and "the Devil's rain." In Norwegian, there is probably intended a pun on the word *regne* which means both "rain" and "reckon," for this day of rain is also a day of awful reckoning.[8] Regine calls attention to Manders' foot as Peer calls attention to the priest-devil's hoof in *Peer Gynt* and warns Engstrand not to clump about and awaken the "young master" (*den unge herren*) sleeping above. The words "Lord" and "young master" (*Vaarherre* and *den unge herren*) follow closely in the dialogue and Ibsen might, here, intend an at least thematic correspondence, a point we shall take up a little later. The Engstrand-Regine dialogue forcefully confirms Engstrand's "satanic" character: he speaks continually of temptations, orgies, weak and fallen humanity, and his oaths are usually associated with the devil (*fanden*) or with blasphemous allusions to the Bible, such as *jøss* (for Jesus), *kors* (cross), *døde og pine* (death and torment). He complains that he always is being blamed for everything and Regine's response to this (somewhat legitimate) satanic complaint is, "Ugh, and then that leg!" In the dialectical pattern of the play, Engstrand's satanism with its "brothel" world and un-Greek ugliness derives from the hostility to the world of the flesh of Pauline Christianity.

An important element in Ibsen's symmetrical design is the character of Johanna, who is in ghostly union with Alving, a union reincarnated in Regine, who, with Osvald, reenacts a scene once played by the dead couple. Regine is a vehicle of this Johanna identity as Osvald is of Alving's. Regine, for example, refuses to join Engstrand's sailors' home with the same words that Johanna once used, in the same house, to refuse Engstrand:

---

[8]The ambiguity of *regne*, for rain, making up accounts, and judgment, is exploited in the play.

> REGINE: ... *Me*, who's been brought up by a lady like Mrs. Alving, a chamberlain's wife? Who's been treated almost like a part of the family?

Engstrand, soon after this, recalls the words of Johanna's refusal:

> ENGSTRAND: ... The way she played the fine lady! *(Imitating her)* "Let me go, Engstrand! Leave me alone! I've served three years in the household of Chamberlain Alving, of Rosenvold!"

Both women, we notice, are "threatened" by Engstrand's overtures and, in defense, take refuge in the elevated social rank of the "Kammerherre" (Chamberlain) identity of Alving. In the course of the play we shall see that the "metaphoric" power of the secondary, Engstrand plot, is out of all proportion to Engstrand's social standing, or to any *primary* dramatic function of the character. For about this figure is associated the entrapment of Manders, the fiery destruction of the Alving orphanage, the possible capture of Regine for his brothel and the destruction of the value of eros in the play. Whereas the Alving household of husband, wife, and son finally undergoes a tragic "ethical" history elevated above, and thus immune to, that of the Engstrand-Manders-Regine plot, this secondary plot does contain a lurid, melodramatic force that is centered, I believe, on the "satanic" identity of Engstrand. That is, though the melodramatic secondary plot detaches itself from the primary tragic plot of Alving, Helene, and Osvald, it nevertheless sets up a sardonic, subethical, (i.e., non-Hellenic) parallel to it. The two plots, the tragic and the melodramatic, tell two quite separate stories peopled by characters on two separate planes of ethical reality. It is this juxtaposition of the two plots, tragic and melodramatic, that allows the ethical distinction of the tragic characters to emerge so clearly and to reveal so tellingly, Pastor Manders' damning spiritual fall from (tragic) distinction.

The details we hear of Engstrand's career are not only a squalid and lowlife counterpoint to the Alving family's story: they also build up, in the form of a supertextual narrative, an intriguingly rich mythopoeic identity in terms of his "satanic" function. In the course of the Engstrand-Regine dialogue we hear something of Engstrand's past. He was "thrown downstairs" and lamed, which, in conjunction with his satanic identity, recollects also the myth of Hephaistos, "thrown by angry Jove." Hephaistos, whose own notoriously unfaithful wife was seduced by the military Ares, was, like Satan, associated with fire, and Engstrand is "sometimes very careless with matches." The parallels between Satan-Hephaistos and Loki, the Scandinavian mischief-making god, were pointed out by Jacob Grimm in his *Deutsche Mythologie* (1844), a major work of that "German scholarship" that Ibsen praised so highly. Satan, Hephaistos, and Loki were all associated with fire;[9] all three were lame;[10] Satan and Hephaistos were thrown from heaven;[11] Satan and Loki both were punished and made to suffer torment.[12] Engstrand, of course, is a very solid nineteenth-century Norwegian carpenter of the west coast, with precise physical and psychical traits; but this dimension of reality, fascinating though it is, is only a small part of Ibsen's total artistic intention. Engstrand's actions and speeches,[13] unknown to himself, involve other dimensions of reality; and this is nothing new, for comparative mythology did not begin in the nineteenth century. Milton, for one, saw archetypal identities repeating themselves behind the particular identities of different mythologies. Engstrand's first name, Jakob, looks back to the Judaic tradition of myth. Jakob Engstrand resembles the biblical Jacob in deceit, cunning, and an unscrupulous self-interest that allows him to profit under his employer as Jacob profited under Laban. The last book of the Old Testament, Malachi, opens, as it closes, with images reminding us of details in *Ghosts*: for God promises "Jacob" success and, more grimly, foretells that Edom "shall build, but I will throw down," an idea that Ibsen may have remembered in the destruction of the Alving memorial compared with Jakob Engstrand's more successful building plans. In his *Deutsche Mythologie* Grimm notes the Christian practice of erecting Christian buildings upon pagan holy sites, and Helene's action of erecting on Solvik a building that represents the opposite of everything that Alving stood for, may carry its own supernatural Nemesis. Though this idea does not account with the strictest notions of everyday realism, it has the merit of assuming an imaginative continuity between the author of *Emperor and Galilean* and the author of the Cycle: that, in fact, they are the same man.

The satanic connotations (which, of course, are not solemnly horrendous, but to a great extent due to Ibsen's intellectual playfulness—or *galskap*, as he called it) of Engstrand's identity are only further reinforced by his close association with Pastor Manders, an association that, already established in the past, is further cemented in the progress of the play. We have mentioned that Engstrand and Manders are on the same, somewhat low, level in the play's dialectic, incapable of the tragic insights of Helene and Osvald. At the beginning of the play, Engstrand hurriedly exits through one door before Manders enters by another, but in the course of

---

[9] *Teutonic Mythology*, I, 241.
[10] Ibid., II, 447.
[11] Ibid., III, 994.
[12] Ibid.
[13] And perhaps even his surname, Engstrand? It is of course dangerous for a non-Norwegian to see meanings in Norwegian names: but a portmanteau pun on *Eng-el* (angel) and *strand* (wrecked, as in the English "stranded") at least fits the first name, Jakob.

the play, the two figures come closer together until their handclasp and resolve to travel by "the same boat" together, and they exit from the ethically devastated household as unenlightened as ever. This, at first glance, odd alliance of "devil" and priest is new neither in Ibsen nor in European literature. It is, in fact, one of Ibsen's stock metaphors, employed first in *The Pretenders* where, at the sacrifice of realistic credibility, Ibsen brings back the ghost of Bishop Nicholas[14] dressed as a monk, to speak the words of Satan to Christ when he promises Earl Skule: "I will take you up into a high mountain and show you all the glory of the world," and he informs the earl that there are over fifty popes and hundreds of clerics in the lower regions. In *Peer Gynt* the devil actually is dressed as a priest and has a deformed foot, or hoof, which has some resemblance to Engstrand's lameness. In *Ghosts* the satanic and priestly halves of the same identity are separated. This seemingly audacious joke actually is quite ancient: Goethe's Mephistopheles is dressed as a medieval cleric, and Marlowe's Dr. Faustus is even more explicit:

> Go, and return an old Franciscan Friar;
> That Holy shape becomes a devil best.

In *Ghosts* this melodramatic, satanic-priestly identity is symptomatic of the moral atmosphere (so un-Hellenic) against which the Hellenic spirit rises, representing the obstacle, in fact, which a resurrected Hellenism would have to overcome and which, in fact, Helene and Osvald have, finally, overcome. It is for this reason that Engstrand and Manders are mainly subordinate melodramatic figures, shut out of the tragic dialectic in which Alving, Helene, and Osvald are engaged.

The similarity of identity between Engstrand and Manders appears in a number of ways. If, for instance, we analyze the Manders-Regine dialogue that follows immediately upon the Engstrand-Regine dialogue, we discover that it is, point for point, a more innocent version of the same themes. It opens, again, with the subject "rain"—Regine this time artfully reversing her earlier judgment and calling it "blessed" (*velsignet*). Manders, just like Engstrand, attempts to persuade Regine to join the highly dubious "sailors' home," using much the same arguments of family duty. Engstrand piously opines that Regine needs a father's care; Manders, over Regine's strong objections, expostulates, "But a daughter's duty, my good girl ... " Like Engstrand, Manders observes that Regine has "grown"—

---

[14]I do not know whether the devil was known as "Old Nick" in Europe as in England; but Bishop Nicholas foretells that whenever there is ill-doing in Norway, it is a sure sign that he is around. Old Nick could not say more!

though he is less explicit as to the nature of this development. The pastor's oaths are the pious complement of the carpenter's, swearing by God (*Gud*).

Manders, like the Church, needs a sick and sinful world to minister to and to sustain his own identity—a symbiotic role that Engstrand willingly performs for him, but which a healthy paganism would contemn. Equally, Engstrand needs Manders, for his "sailors' home" will be built with the bricks of religion. We see, and hear of, frequent episodes of Engstrand's asking forgiveness of the minister in order better to manipulate him: confessing his sins, repenting, and usefully taking the blame for all wrongdoing. At the beginning of the play he tells Regine he is "blamed for everything," and in Act III he offers to take the blame for the orphanage fire, thus getting the pastor out of an awkward situation. "I am," he tells Manders, "your guardian angel." (The fact that Engstrand most likely *is* responsible for the fire does not alter Manders' ethically dubious behavior in allowing another to take on his possible guilt.)

A tremendous moment in the play, dramatically powerful yet bristling with complexities, is when Manders turns upon Helene the full weight of his reproachful, righteous moralism. Like Tiresias confronting Oedipus, he charges her with willfulness and headstrong rebelliousness, and then glances at her role in marriage and parenthood. Yet, unlike Tiresias, Manders, in invoking tradition, duty, and a higher power, manifests his total inability to comprehend these glibly indicated realities. The great traditional, Christian moral authority that he enlists in his denunciation is discredited by its damning remoteness from the complexities of life, so that his denunciation, for all its force, is a demonstration of his intellectual helplessness.[15]

When Helene rouses herself to demolish Manders' whole worldview, the complexities deepen. For Helene's defense of herself, with its exposure of Alving, while effectively destroying Manders' authority by demonstrating the disparity between his moral position and his knowledge of the facts, is itself based upon a misconception of values almost as drastic as that of Manders himself: so that these two are stabbing at each other in the dark. In Helene's account, Alving is the great punishment inflicted upon her by Manders, the great wrong from which she still suffers, whose revelation justifies her whole life and shows her to deserve Manders' approbation, from *his* moral standpoint; but in the course of the play she must learn that she, as plausibly, was the great wrong inflicted upon Alv-

---

[15] Apart from the Tiresias-Oedipus confrontation, Manders' outburst irresistibly calls to mind the magnificent confrontation of Philip and the Grand Inquisitor in Schiller's *Don Carlos*, where a great traditional, but blind, authority is set against a struggling intellectual enlightenment.

ing and that her whole life is an elaborate self-deceit and deceit of others to hide that crime. Thus she is *more* guilty than Manders charges!

If we consider the "argument" of *Ghosts* as it emerges, so far, we will find it to be startlingly Nietzschean. There is the same judgment on the Christian tradition, the same exoneration of joy and health, and Nietzsche's aphorism, "Christianity gave Eros poison to drink: he did not die of it but he degenerated into vice," might stand as the motto of *Ghosts*, with Engstrand's "sailors' home" and Alving's syphilis as the motto's terrible emblems. The concept of eros, in this play, too, is Hellenic, involving the physical, the intellectual, the communal, the esthetic, the religious, and the philosophical levels of consciousness as in Plato's ladder of Eros in *The Symposium*: a concept of eros resurrected in modern times by Freud, as he acknowledged.[16]

The history of the Alving marriage emerges on two levels in the play. In Act I we hear about it through the shocked voice of Helene and the responses of pious horror from Manders who earlier had accused Helen of "throwing off the cross" of her marriage and had congratulated himself on forcing her once again to take up her marriage as a cross. Helene (like Aline Solness in *The Master Builder*) was brought up to place *duties* (*plikter*) above *livsglede* (joy of life). This was the side of Helene's character that was attracted to the Manders who can ask, "What right have people to happiness?" and it was this aspect of her character, rather than any inherent viciousness in Alving, that corrupted the marriage, as Helene will discover by the end of the play. The fact that she arrives at this discovery by the fine exercise of her duty-bound nature *at its best,* by putting aside concern for herself in order to understand and console her son, is another irony in the dialectic of the play, which, of course, is doing something more serious than making a one-sided criticism of Christian moralism. Poor Manders' moral principles are now revealing themselves to be fatal to the lives of those nearest to him: none more so than the strange perversion of human sexuality that sees marriage as a "cross" to be borne! Beneath the moral complacency of Manders' accounts of his motives and actions, and Helene's justification of herself, something of the *real* tragedy of the Alving marriage is beginning to emerge. At this moment in the play, however, though Helene is *intellectually* liberated from the past represented by Manders' pious orthodoxy, the depths of her nature still are not freed from this training, so that she is yet unable to prefer the finer vitality of Alving to the life-fearing pietism of Manders.

---

[16] Sigmund Freud, *Three Essays on the Theory of Sexuality.* Preface to the Fourth Edition, xix.

Brian Johnston: Archetypal Repetition in GHOSTS

It is only when she is brought to witness the possible destruction of this vitality or creativity in her son that the enormity of the crime against Alving is vividly present to her.

On a first viewing of the play, one is likely to be trapped into either accepting Helene's account of her marriage or rejecting it as an example of Ibsen's own limited puritanism. The verbal counterpoint is extremely subtle; Helene's revelations of the "horrors" of her married life ironically reveal, unknown to herself or to Manders, the *real* horror of her actions. She recounts to her pastor Alving's "excesses," which forced her to sit up night after night with him, getting him drunk and listening to his silly stories. These cheerless and unsympathetic travesties of bacchanals led to Alving's decline, to Helene, in her own words, having "a weapon against him" (*For nu hadde jeg våpen imot ham*) and to her taking over his property, improving it, and disguising "the true nature" of her husband from the world.

Helene's whole account, given to justify herself, actually describes her crime against Alving: a crime that, like the protagonist of a Greek drama, she was, by her very nature, fated to commit, for she represented a law totally opposed to his. At first Alving's energies were confined to the pietistic little town that so thoroughly reflected Helene's hostile attitude toward all he stood for, then they were forced into drunken impotence leading to his loss of control over his estate.

At one point in her revelation Helene tells Manders, in the same tone of horror, how her maid once was bringing water for the flowers when the irrepressible pagan, Alving, pursued her. Beneath the outraged moralism of Helene's voice, and Manders' shocked responses, is buried a lively episode that, in its human terms, is not so unlike such pursuits as Pan and Syrinx, Apollo and Daphne. Helene concedes that Alving was "charming" (*hjertevinnende*) and one begins to detect, beneath Helene's narration, something of that incorrigible pagan joy that Ibsen's Julian so admired in Alcibiades.[17]

It is important, for our understanding of the play, to see that Helene's version of the past is a distortion; we have, here, a form of dramatic counterpoint where the account of reality given by Helene is played off against what we begin to detect as the actual truth of the situation. At this point in the play, the gulf between Helene and her husband indicates the irreconcilable opposition of the two life principles they represent: of life

---

[17] Once again, one must accept Ibsen's insistence on the central importance of *Emperor and Galilean* to an understanding of his whole work, even if we are forced to go against accepted Ibsen commentary. The writer of *Emperor and Galilean* is not likely to share Helene's attitude toward Alving's sexual peccadillos.

as duty or life as spontaneity, joy. This gulf can be bridged only by Helene's abandoning her principle and recognizing the value of its opposite.

The dialectical antagonisms within the *language* of the play thus enact one of the play's themes—the tragic one-sidedness and mutual exclusiveness of the opposing forces in the emperor-Galilean conflict. As the play progresses, Helene is forced to discover a language more adequate to the reality of the situation until, finally, her Christian conscientiousness incorporates Alving's life-craving consciousness, so that the language of the latter moves from the suppressed background to the foreground, as Helene actually begins to speak with Alving's voice.[18]

The offspring of this joyless marriage, Osvald, brings into the play the Parisian (and Alving) values of joyful, spontaneous, guilt-free living. Paris in the nineteenth century not only was synonymous in the northern world with "immorality":[19] it was also, since the days of the *philosophes* and despite the restoration of Church and monarchy and the consequent reaction recorded by Georg Brandes, the center of the most determined intellectual onslaught upon Christianity until Nietzsche. The little exchange between Osvald and Manders on the life-style of the Parisian artists, therefore, reflects an actual hostility between orthodox moralism and the most adventurous imaginative thought in the spirit of the age, so that Ibsen's audience would have been able to supply the wider dimension of references that are mostly lost to us.

Osvald's doctor, in Paris, cynically repeated the Old Testament saying, "the sins of the fathers are visited upon the children," but Osvald, knowing nothing of his father's life but Helene's idealistic lie, takes the blame upon himself and pronounces upon his carefree life in Paris the judgment that Helene and Manders already have pronounced upon his father.

> ... and I finally learned the truth. The incredible truth! This beautiful, blissful young life I was leading with my comrades—it was beyond my capacity. I should never have indulged in it. So I actually destroyed myself.

One sees that it is *life itself* that is being slandered here: its whole possibility of fullness, joy, achievement, represented supremely, perhaps,

---

[18] Inga-Stina Ewbank has a perceptive account of this episode in the anthology *Contemporary Approaches to Ibsen*, 106.

[19] Bjørnson wrote from Paris on its immorality, from which Norway was free. His remarks far outdo Pastor Manders' denunciations. Norway, and its literature, continually was invoked as a pure and wholesome antidote to the moral sickness of Europe, both by the unhappy Europeans themselves and by the Norwegians. (Cf. Robert Buchanan's article on "the fleshly school of poetry" of Rossetti and Swinburne.)

by the Athenian experiment, and decried ever since by the vision of life that can ask, "What right have human beings to happiness?" Manders is unsparingly depicted by Ibsen as being anti-life; not only is he virginal, but he fears the manifestation of life in art or the life-styles out of which art arises. Helene, intellectually, has detached herself from Manders' opinions and can side with Osvald in the discussion on the life-style of his artist-friends, but this intellectual emancipation is superficial: in the depths of her spirit she is still with Manders and it will require the full shock of Osvald's disintegration to bring home to her the offense against life that her own values represent. When she attempts to remove Osvald's feelings of guilt, she starts upon a course that will remove the guilt from Alving, too, and she will stand self-condemned—the ironic reversal of the opening of the play which was to celebrate her great self-vindication. Her past idealization of her husband, like the memorial, was a lie, ostensibly to hide *his* guilt from the world, but which actually hid her own, for the attitude of mind that saw Alving's life as guilty was itself based upon a lie. In the end Helene exonerates Alving, not by means of lies and a fraudulent memorial, but by means of the truth: a complexity and subtlety of situation and development typical of Ibsen.

Act I, in which Mrs. Alving presents her husband's past in the most lurid light, ends with the ghost of that husband reemerging through his children, who, though unconsciously, become his avengers, as in the Orestes story. Helene has told Manders that on the next day, at the dedication of the memorial to Alving, "the whole comedy" of the past will have been played out. Immediately there follows the famous noise in the conservatory and Helene's terrified whisper: "Ghosts! Those two in the conservatory. Come back to haunt us," as this Clytemnestra and her Aegisthus go in to the unwittingly avenging Orestes and Electra.

The offstage flirtation, covered up by the embarrassed Osvald, which seems, at first, a quaint nineteenth-century inhibition, one of the limitations under which Ibsen worked, becomes, in his hands, an appropriate metaphor in itself for suppressed sexuality. Osvald not only reenacts his father's philandering; he reenacts its furtiveness and the shock it occasioned in his mother. One's response to this episode, like one's response to Helene's revelations of her husband's offenses, will depend to a great extent on how far one has grasped the meaning of the play whose theme is the calamitous suppression of eros by forces that still are thwarting its liberation. If one takes the view of sexuality of Manders and Helene, this episode, and Alving's past, is shocking; however, if one looks back at the play from the vantage point of a Hilde Wangel of Maia and Ulfheim, the situation is shocking in quite another way!

Osvald, as the child of both parents, is the battleground on which their opposing laws fight to the death, and if one side of his nature is

Alving's pagan values that will be cleared of guilt, the other, which has honored the false image of his father and condemned himself and his life in Paris, derives from Helene's Christian values. Osvald is invested with something of a messianic destiny by his mother who tells Manders that her son will "speak out" the new ideas and beliefs that she, in her solitude, has been formulating. More than once she addresses Osvald as "blessed boy" (*velsignede gutt*), which reinforces Regine's term for Osvald, young master/lord (*den unge herren*), and these overtones of a Christ-like identity surely are powerfully caught up in the closing moments of the play in which Helene wipes Osvald's face, kneels before him, and, as the sun streams behind his collapsed figure, recollects the traditional *pietà* of mother and crucified son. The recollection of Christ's fate is present in the fact that Osvald atones for the guilt of the past, of which he is innocent, and must suffer a "spiritual breakdown" (*aandelige nedbrudd*). Hugh Kenner has pointed out that the syphilis in *Ghosts* really is a metaphor for Original Sin[20]—which, again, refers the pattern of the little local drama to a universal drama. The disease also calls to mind the pagan images of plague and pollution—the unclean presence that dooms an entire family. We notice that, in this first group, the image of pollution develops from *A Doll House* to *An Enemy of the People*, providing a dark undercurrent to the pagan imagery and themes of these plays.

Osvald is torn in half by the collision of the two ethical forces in the dialectic that are designated Duty and Joy-of-life. He has been brought up by his mother to respect the former principle and to honor its supposed existence in his father, but his own nature, both in his life and in his art, impels him toward the latter. One metaphor for his ineffectual attempt to return to sources of greater instinctual and creative energy and freedom is the champagne, for drink is a frequent and important metaphor, in Ibsen's writing, for the release of the imagination from a repressive reality. G. Wilson Knight observes:

> ... as we watch Osvald asking for drink and yet more drink, we may regard him as a modern successor to Emperor Julian, soliciting the Dionysian fire to re-awake a dead culture and centuries of Christianity-gone-sour from the nature-born and sun-impregnated elixirs.[21]

---

[20] In the essay "Joyce and Ibsen's Naturalism."
[21] *Henrik Ibsen*, 52. The wine, brought up from the cellar, and resurrecting this sunlight and happiness, is similar to Keats' famous vintage "Cool'd a long age in the deep delved earth" (and thus literally buried like a corpse) and resurrecting, in Keats's imagination, the vanished "dance, and Provencal song, and sunburned mirth" ("Ode to a Nightingale").

Brian Johnston: Archetypal Repetition in GHOSTS

The desire for drink is an indication in the character of energies and potentialities that cannot find a creative or permissible outlet in a repressive structure of reality. Weaker or less imaginative natures, such as Manders', can accept the repressive order and function smoothly within it. A strong nature, such as Helene's, can adapt the repressive order to her own purposes, without an acute awareness of loss. But, in Ibsen's plays, there is an interesting class of characters, imaginative, creative, or of wider vision, who, unable to accept the repressive order or adapt it to firm but narrow purposes, and incapable of altering it, are driven to a somewhat desperate rediscovery of the repressed content of their psyches through drink—the equivalent of the contemporary use of drugs. In Osvald, the character's desire to escape through drink will link him to the central tragic insight of the play: the offense against joy-of-life.

At a moment when young Lieutenant Alving is about to be resurrected, Osvald asks for glass after glass of champagne so that Regine must twice go to the cellar for the bottles. Osvald, drinking the champagne, tells his mother how his art had always "turned on this joy of life.... Light and sunshine and a holiday spirit ... and radiantly happy faces." But, in his mother's home and the society surrounding it, all these impulses would, he claims, degenerate into "something ugly." Thus, by means of the drink, Osvald has traced the course of his father's fall, and it is at this point that Helene "sees it all." She is about to speak out to her son—and speaking out would express her belated but vivid awareness of the value, joy-of-life, her husband represented; but Ibsen delays this moment: Helene will not be able to articulate to Osvald and the theater audience her insight into this suddenly understood conflict, until she, as well as that audience, also is brought to comprehend its full calamity. The moment of insight, therefore, is interrupted by a piece of obvious but effective and appropriate symbolism: the children's home, that fraudulent memorial that violates the truth of both Alving's and Helene's life values, now burns up, and with it the possibility of perpetuating this pious fraud in the future, for the building was uninsured.[22] Everything of the past that is inessential to the dialectic is cleared away as the play moves toward the full disclosure of the truth.

---

[22]The particular emphasis given to the fact that the orphanage is uninsured (Manders' exclamation, "And no insurance!" is the curtain of Act II) is also emphatically prepared for in a quite lengthy discussion on the merits of insurance. "Insurance" suggest a faith in the avoidability of *tragedy:* the discussion draws attention to the hypocrisy of Manders, who insures his *private* goods but not this exemplary *public* asset; insurance, too, might characterize the lack of genuine concern with the permanent value of the actions by which Helene builds up the false image of Alving: the memorial is concerned only to whitewash the Past, not lay foundations for the Future.

IBSEN'S GHOSTS: A DRAMATURGICAL SOURCEBOOK

In the action of Act III, Manders, Engstrand, and Regine are one by one removed from the scene as we move to this play's ultimate confrontation. Helene stares at the wreckage of her son and of a life's work founded upon the disastrous denial of the instinctual, spontaneous, creative values caught up in the meaning of *livsglede!* It is an indication of the control Ibsen has over the material of this play that he can develop it upon so many levels, one of these levels being fairly broad comedy. Act III opens with the distressed Manders fleeing into Rosenvold pursued by the limping Engstrand and, in an ironic reversal of their situation in Act II, Engstrand now fastens guilt on Manders and magnanimously absolves him of it, thereby binding the minister close to him and his scheme for setting up a "sailors' home," Chamberlain Alving's Home,[23] and metaphorically emphasizing the collusion of the "fallen" and the pietistic views of the world. To further the founding of Chamberlain Alving's Home, Manders and Engstrand leave to travel by the same boat together, taking with them this now irrelevant and superseded phase of the play's dialectic. With the departure of Manders and Engstrand, the room is sealed off from the outside world (Osvald asks that the doors be shut), and the remaining figures group for a final reckoning. The whole rhythm of the play now shifts from the "busy" realism of the previous action, with its comic villainies, its shocking disclosures, the burning orphanage, to the grave truth-telling, and unadorned anguish of Helene's confrontation with her son. This is a height of consciousness, like that of Greek tragedy attained by nearly unbearable insight and not to be sustained for long; the rest of the Cycle will not present us with such a starkly terrible confrontation again, for it will be concerned to resurrect other modes of spirit and other responses from us. But, for the moment, the Greek aspect of our consciousness is to be awakened for its resurrection day, as we, the audience, are encouraged to rise up to something like the ethical courage of that mode of spirit.

Helene attempts to take the burden from Osvald's mind by at last truthfully exonerating Alving and so exonerating Osvald's own belief in the life value, joy-of-life, to which he has given seemingly disastrous allegiance. She has been shocked and awakened to a new level of perception, and now acknowledges the right, and even primacy, of the law, *livsglede,* that she previously had violated. In a sensitive analysis of Ibsen's language, Inga-Stina Ewbank has pointed out how, at this moment, Helene "is seeing Alving's life from *his* point of view, and so [her] speech gives

---

[23] Alving's titles, we notice, increase in earthly importance as he declines intrinsically. His highest peak is as Lieutenant; as Captain he graces the fraudulent memorial; but his grandest title, *Kammerherre* (Chamberlain), to which Johanna and Regine are attached, is reserved for the sailor's home, a point missed in most translations.

us, through the new dimension of understanding, an interaction of two minds."[24] This interaction, one might say, articulates the lost potential marriage of Helene and Alving, glimpsed now through the wreckage of so many lives. Alving is seen as a "child," full of joyous energy but crushed by the silent conspiracy of a joyless society bent only on business and bureaucracy, to whom Helene herself had brought only cheerless ideas of "duty and things of that kind." "Everything came down to duty—*my* duties, *his* duties—and, well, I'm afraid I made this house unbearable for your poor father."

The full disclosure, like many recognition scenes in Greek drama, involves also the discovery of blood ties: Regine is revealed to be Alving's daughter; but, ironically, instead of this revelation cementing the family together, as in the brother-sister recognition scenes of Orestes and Electra, or Orestes and Iphigenia, it serves, like the discovery of consanguinity in *Oedipus the King*, to destroy the family. Regine now leaves Rosenvold to league with her false father in setting up the home named after her true father, so that the stage is left to Helene and the son of the husband she has learned to love too late. Now the doors are not only closed, but locked, sealing off the confrontation of mother and son from the outside world, and giving the audience the sense of unbearable claustrophobia, the dialectical rhythm having reached its ultimate destination in an inescapable prison of logic as Helene is forced violently to face in her son the disintegration that she, long ago, helped to initiate. This terrible scene, with Osvald driving his mother back into the house as she attempts to escape, calling for help, vividly reenacts the confrontation of Orestes and his mother, as does the whole concept of the mother's fate, waiting for years, finally catching up with her in the figure of her son. The modern melodramatic movement of the play, like its dialectic, reaches back and rediscovers (and reactivates) the archetypal tragic situation.

The last stage, or spasm, of this dialectical rhythm, is hideously ironic: Osvald now asks his mother to do *consciously* what she *unconsciously* has done to his father—to destroy him. In the final stage of her emancipation from the past Helene is brought, by the reincarnation of her husband in Osvald, to a fate worse than that which Clytemnestra suffered: to repeat her earlier crime when her whole spirit cries out against it. She had helped to destroy her husband and the memory of him, through hatred; now, when she has come to love her husband in her son, she must, out of this same love, repeat the action she has come to loathe. Much of the great intensity and power of this moment in the play—the most powerful moment in the whole of the Cycle—derives from the terrible

---

[24] *Contemporary Approaches to Ibsen* (1966), 102.

Sophoclean ironies that it gathers together into one action. All the earlier substance of the play is recollected like the many themes of a contrapuntal recapitulation, but they reappear, now, in a sharp new light, with all the force of *Nemesis*.[25]

Against the image of the exonerated father, recovered in the language of Helene Alving's memory, there is counterpointed the visual image of the sacrificed son, horribly present to our view. It is here that the *pietà* aspect of this last image—of mother and son—would carry such tremendous cultural-historical connotations, implying the collapse of a whole spiritual order behind the agony-in-the-drawing-room of the Alving family tragedy. It is this capacity of Ibsen's art, to move intensively inward and extensively outward at the same time, that gives his drama its unique power in the modern theater.

In the dialectical development of the play, the final perception we are brought to is not just the tragedy of Helene, nor just that of Osvald, but of the dead father, too. His suffering, confinement, and decline emerge as the unexpiated wrong that has brought about this day of reckoning. This second, subterranean movement of the play, in which the rights of the dead man, once thrust into the background, as in the dialogues of the opening of the play, now powerfully emerge into the foreground and into the light, is a positive movement in the dialectic that rescues the play from either the cynical pessimism or the lugubrious moralism often attributed to it. This movement is something much stronger, healthier, saner, and far less fashionable than pessimism: the dramaturgy is expressing a complex, thoroughly thought-out *concept,* and this intellectual intention behind the emotionally effective dramaturgy, like counterpoint in music, gives Ibsen's art the toughness and complexity and above all the *sanity* that are essential to the highest art. The action of *Ghosts,* then, is not merely the necessary negative one of the destruction of false appearance, but one, also, of recovery of tabooed reality. A false mode of consciousness is painfully discarded and the possibility of a truer mode of consciousness indicated. The rehabilitation of young Alving is rather similar to a process of pictorial restoration, where centuries of accumulated error or distortion are cleaned away to reveal the brilliant original. There are, we notice, many references in the play to false accounts, false teachings, lies, hypocrisies, the concealment and distortion of the truth, both consciously and, more

---

[25] Osvald's spiritual/mental destruction (*aandelige nedbrudd*) of course reminds us of the Furies that afflicted Orestes; but in the wider dialectic of the play that looks back to *Emperor and Galilean,* Osvald, as the younger generation, would represent the modern spirit itself, which, deriving from a broken, defeated paganism and a life-denying Paulism, is destined only for collapse. Any renewal or "third empire" must return to the more vital sources of both traditions—a theme typical of nineteenth-century writers and thinkers.

deeply, unconsciously. The memorial is the flagrant emblem and example of this, but the false documents of Regine's birth, Mrs. Alving's lying letters to her son, Manders' slander of Parisian bohemia, Engstrand's deceptions of the minister, the euphemisms for his "sailors' home," etc., etc., all create a texture of stifling dishonesty within which Helene Alving is brought, struggling, out of her own massive self-deception. Keeping in mind the wider perspectives of the play, these multiple internal and external deceits suggest a huge falsification of cultural reality, an experience Ibsen commented on when trying to find trustworthy accounts of Julian the Apostate. This work of falsification is one in which we all have a share and the movement to truth and freedom, which must be experienced in the intimate reality of our daily life as in the larger rhythm of universal reality, requires that the whole substance of our idea of reality be ruthlessly exposed as false—a task requiring the whole Cycle, for *Ghosts* is only one of its moments.

If the action of *Ghosts* reveals what is spiritually bankrupt in the traditions of Europe, in both its pagan and Christian inheritance, it also clears the way for the recovery of what is essential to the future, by separating the false from the true. Such a process is the sustaining principle of the Cycle, which always has as its goal that "Resurrection Day" that is the masterpiece of Ibsen's last artist. Ibsen's demolition work is so ruthlessly thorough because he has building plans to justify the devastation. For this reason, his return to the past is totally different from the more sentimental revivalisms of the Celtic, Classical, Viking, or medieval twilights so typical among artists and writers of Ibsen's times.

Ghosts, then, ends its dialectical movement on an image of recovery and collapse: Osvald, collapsed in the armchair with the sun streaming behind him; Helene clutching the "twelve white tablets," uncertain whether or not to finish him off, and the rising sun, flooding the stage as this long journey into light ends by dispelling the specters of the past.[26] The arrival of the sun, connected as it is, in Osvald's description of his own art, with *livsglede*, surrounds the little human tragedy with the invincible creative power of the universe: of great life-renewing energies beyond human power, which terribly and ironically reproach Helene's lifelong battle against this cosmic Dionysos. The human moral order had shown itself to be *contra natura* and, whether the crime was conscious or unconscious, it must be punished, for it cannot be suffered by Nature. The final, terrible conjunction of these two dimensions, that of aberrant little human order with that of the suprahuman cosmic order, and the inevitable de-

---

[26] "The mounting sun dispels all magic and bids the spirits back to their subterranean abodes" (Grimm, III, 720).

struction of the former for its hubris, closely resembles the conclusions of many Greek tragedies in which the gods uphold a natural order that the human protagonists have offended. Thus the "small" dimension of Oedipus' personal history is brought up against the cosmic order his history has offended; and the house of Atreus, convulsed and suffering through its generations, affirms the eternal structure of reality against which it had rashly set itself.

In *Ghosts* the intersection of these two dimensions is imperceptibly created in the gradually increasing light, in which Mrs. Alving's little lamplight is absorbed by the greater light of the sun—an effect more apparent in the theater, of course, where the greater light is itself stage-managed. The light of the little lamp is analogous to Helene's lonely, questing intellect, the individual reason absorbed in the universal, "Absolute" Reason, which is the driving force of the whole Cycle. Thus the horrible human drama is seen as only a particular moment of the total Concept: a moment that, to be sure, requires courage to be comprehended and endured, but that must be endured if the human spirit is to attain to truth and freedom.

The ironic *structure* of *Ghosts* is as important to its total meaning as the particular events dramatized within that structure. The play is a massive mythopoeic reaction to an unexpiated offense. Mrs. Alving had tried to reconstruct reality and the identity of her husband, from her own one-sided vision but, as she acts, so reality and the identity of Alving are being reconstructed inevitably and in opposition to her endeavor, revealing the reality behind the false construct she both consciously and unconsciously erected and whose emblem is the asylum, destroyed before it can function. The Hellenic archetypes that the dialectic of the play discovers within the events of the Alving family's history are as fictional as Mrs. Alving's fiction of her husband, but they are truer, because more adequate, fictions: they find a place for values that must not be excluded from our humanity.

Much of the power of *Ghosts* derives from this convergence of archetypal patterns with everyday events: a form of *redemption* of everyday reality occurs through *epiphanies* or "showings forth" of the divine. As with *Oedipus Tyrannos*, *Ghosts* is not a tragedy of painful but avoidable actions—a ghastly mistake or accident—but of painful and unavoidable *knowledge*. Helene Alving is tragic because, like Oedipus, she stubbornly pushes forward to inevitable tragic insight, because she possesses the qualities of courageous intellect that make her capable of tragic—that is, meaningful—suffering. The sunrise that concludes the tragedy is, from one perspective, pure indifferent materialism and cosmic mechanism merely signifying the relative positions of planet and star within an indifferent cosmos. From another perspective, however, it is just as much meaning-filled Spirit, the huge emblem of *livsglede*—joy-of-life—that had been so intensely and painfully localized in the little drawing room and now is extended into the cosmos itself.

For all the complexity of analysis Ibsen is conducting in *Ghosts*, the play moves faultlessly to the fully unfolded horror of Osvald's last dialogue with his mother, and it is here that the distinguished *reticence* of Ibsen's method is most striking. An inferior writer would not have been able to resist the opportunity for fine writing, or for pathos: but Ibsen's eye is not upon the "effects" but upon the adequate revelation of his subject, which he allows to emerge with Sophoclean severity. He wishes the audience to face the same heart of darkness that the Athenian audience was tough enough to contemplate, and he interposes nothing between the audience and that confrontation that will prevent them from attaining that Greek toughness. It is for this reason, and not for its lurid subject matter, that the play retains its power today—and also retains its value. Ibsen has a long-[meditated] vision of reality: of human history and destiny that impels him to view the structure of contemporary reality in a certain way. He wishes us to see this vision, too, and his dramatic art is created, not because he has happened to have found a good subject that can be given effective treatment, but, in his own words, to make us "*see.*"

Just what the nature of this seeing is, Ibsen's own description of Greek tragedy may help to define. Writing to Bjørnson while he was in Rome, Ibsen asked:

> Do you remember "The Tragic Muse" that stands in the room outside the Rotunda in the Vatican? No statue that I have yet seen in Italy has taught me so much. I would say that it has revealed the essence of Greek tragedy to me. That indescribably sublime, calm joy in the expression of the face, that laurel-crowned head with something supernaturally exuberant and bacchantic about it, those eyes that look both inward and yet through and far beyond the outward object they are fixed on—that is Greek tragedy.[27]

As in Greek tragedy (e.g., *Oedipus Tyrannos*) the conscious, rational and ethical decisions and actions have resulted in unconscious, irrational, and appalling actions and consequences, which, however, lead to the truth and to spiritual growth as conscious activity alone could not have done. It is by a terrible "cunning of Reason" that the protagonists finally are led to "see," so that, as in the best Greek tragedy, there is a dark, unconscious action counterpointing the conscious action, the intentional action bring-

---

[27] Letter to Bjørnson, Rome, 28 January 1865 (*Letters and Speeches*, 39).

ing about the more adequate, unintended result. The "little" rhythm of individual and conscious reason is lured, by the structure of reality, to a better comprehension of the universal Reason in reality. It is this ironic movement toward an unwelcome but necessary heart of darkness, revealing the rationality of reality *in spite of* the individual's own confident rationality, that signals the recovery of the tragic dimension, the tragic vision, in *Ghosts*.

Lou Andreas-Salomé

Ibsen's Heroines

This piece is part of Chapter II: Mrs. Alving/ *Ghosts,* from *Lou Andreas-Salomé, Ibsen's Heroines,* edited, translated and with an introduction by Siegfried Mandel, copyright Siegfried Mandel, 1985, published by Black Swan Books.

I have not written roles for actors and actresses.
I have written to portray human beings.

—Ibsen

II MRS. ALVING

"Now I see what happened.... And now I can speak out.
And yet, no ideals will collapse."

If the unattainable and the uncertain is implied by the idea of "wondrous," it also contains unlimited possibilities and perspectives. If it is a battle and no victory that Nora [from *A Doll House*] is about to encounter, she is ready with a youthful, strong, and golden armor. If she parts in pain, it is not mere sorrowful and patient acceptance of a pain that comes from the loss of ideals but a contention and striving for a new ideal. She is imbued with refreshing boldness which bodes promise and beginning—the ending remains open. She only crosses the threshold where life—the chosen path of life—first begins. For that reason the drama of her development and her protest against every suppression of her growth are only the prelude to the tragedy that engulfs her successor—Helene Alving.

Like Nora, Helene steps from a limiting girlhood and immaturity into marriage. But instead of a gay doll house, she finds herself growing up in a school of rigid habits and religious indoctrination, and instead of titillating play that robs Nora of seriousness and truth, dreary demands of responsibility act as bars to her unfolding as a personality in the freedom and joy of authentic life.

These impressions during adolescence explain why Helene's first, innocent enthusiasm is directed to a clergyman; she needs a minister in order to fuse her dark, life-yearning drive with his studied, earnest discipline. Yet it appears equally and emphatically significant that this Pastor Manders is a naïve idealist, replete with harmless pretensions and untainted spirituality, upon whom she bestows the first, free stirrings of her heart. This sheds a touching light on the transition from girlhood to the tragedy of a marriage through which she is victimized by coarseness and degradation.

The shy dream of her first love has no power to protect her from the tragedies ahead. It is the same reverence for what is held sacred and pure, represented by Pastor Manders, that impels Helene in her choice of a husband and presses her to bow to the God-willed authority of her family. And so, she agrees to marry the young, wealthy army officer Alving, who is considered a "good catch," despite his loose living that is in such marked contrast to the austerity of his environment.

Wherever Alving appeared, "it was like Spring weather. And then, his tireless strength and liveliness.... And now, this hedonistic child, for at that time he acted like one, had to wander around a middle-sized city that could offer only pleasantries rather than heady pleasures. Here he had to stay in a minor occupation, without purpose in life. He saw no prospects for work which would engage his energies. He had no friend who could share the joy of life; he had only drinking companions and consorted only with idlers."

Perhaps he dreamed of a wife and house, a lovely homestead to satisfy his needs. And perhaps the contentment and beauty of such living would have stirred her like the pealing of a pure bell. But Helene could not have known this. She says of herself, "I was taught something about duties and the like, in which I had believed until the present; everything terminates in duties, mine and his."

Despite her obedient consent, Helene does not face her husband with Nora's childlike naïveté. One thing has fully developed within the limitations of her dogmatic upbringing, namely, the inner compulsion to judge everything strictly from the standpoint of the ideal and the religious. She is far from seeing, as Nora did, that marriage is a blessed and humbly received gift. Helene sees in marriage a challenge for herself and her husband. As a girl with an unripe mind, she is unable to assess and understand things correctly. And yet, she judges him instantly by comparing him with a preconceived idealized picture against which, in any case, his natural youthful strength must appear coarse and dissolute. Instead of freely drawing from his vitality and releasing herself from a bleak upbringing, she raises a barrier between them from the start, with all the acquired strength and coldness of her own schooling.

From the start, her husband becomes estranged and disappointed; then rejected, he flees the house and takes up again the pleasures and distractions of his earlier days. To the same degree that Helene's indignation and contempt rise, he sinks deeper and deeper in the choice of his pleasures, until after a year of marriage she is justified in calling him an absolute libertine.

A wild and overwhelming disgust seizes her, which breaks through all the preconceptions and schooling she had brought into the marriage. She takes refuge with the spiritual friend of her home, Pastor Manders. Although the tender effusion of her dreamlike girlishness prevents self-assertion, there occurs the first unconscious expression of her indignant nature, a sudden and abrupt outcry, a cry she takes up instantaneously and ruthlessly. She had permitted the marriage knot to be tied because she had been taught to believe in the sacramental union of marriage; stronger, however, than obedience is her dark inner sense that justifies the tearing of a knot which she recognizes to be neither unifying nor sacramental.

In the passionate power of this awareness, her enthusiasm for a man of purity, who is the object of her childlike imaginings, gains heightened importance: he must appear to her almost as the incarnation of all her strict and sensitive ideals; moreover, the effective desacralising of her ideals drives Helene away from her husband. Only in this sense is it possible for her to come to her friend Manders, with the cry, "I am here. Take me!"

This cry does not wrest itself from an irresponsible woman but from a horrified child whose eyes are opened to the hateful and gross in life; it is no demand for the delights of love but a flight from her defilement. All the injured and angered stirrings of her nature burst into a passionate self-offering that stems from inner purity and innocence.

During the course of her later life, for that reason, the personal impulse that drove her to Manders, and that initially gave her the strength to break with accustomed obedience, becomes increasingly pronounced until it dominates and changes her existence: she is determined to shake off what she has perceived as untruth and to pursue and bow only to truth.

The wild arousal of her nature could have, indeed, meant her emancipation if only the husband toward whom her admiration and trust had been directed were not the eager representative of all the ossified and disciplined doctrines of her own upbringing. Distraught and displeased with the sacrilege of her flight, Manders resists every offered temptation and directs her return, as a matter of duty, to her husband, however dissolute he may be. She is obliged to maintain the marriage, sealed before God, and devote herself to it in the future as the only goal and ideal.

As yet, her personality has not developed sufficiently to decline obedience to tradition; once again, she bows to it. What she had pursued half-thinkingly in a passive acquiescence grounded in her education, she now consciously fashions into the content and goal of her life. She shuns no struggle nor sacrifice to set obstacles in the path of her husband's philanderings; these obstacles remain useless because they can serve only the same rigid measures that had driven him away from her into isolation. She cannot now heal his pleasure-seeking because earlier she had neither understood nor entered into it. And so, despite every struggle for a true marriage, she is unable to merge seriousness and the joy of life, moodiness and frivolity; she can only preserve the outer appearance of marriage. So that no one may perceive the sad secret within her marriage and know of her husband's life, she keeps him securely in her home by yielding to his voluptuary tastes; she offers herself as partner to his despicable orgies, drinks and laughs with him until she is sure of his secure tranquillity. As with her body, she cloaks the sacrament of her marriage from external view.

Even this remains without success because her husband pursues intimate relations with the domestic maid, a relationship that has fateful consequences. From that point on, Helene determinedly wrests from him both his authority and freedom. She becomes as much his tyrant as earlier she had been his near-whore. And while he slowly and passively sickens under the impact of a disease incurred by corruption, she takes firm measures to put all suspicions to rest by linking his name and resources to charitable enterprises, preserving his name and reputation. Thanks to her resoluteness, he was held in esteem as a gentleman up to the time of his death. Her self-imposed task is bolstered by her concern for her only child, Oswald, who represented her sole source of happiness. And yet, she sent him abroad for his education so that he would not breathe the poisoned atmosphere of the home; when he returns after his father's death, he would at least retain untainted ideals.

That is the external appearance of her life's course: the pursuit of a traditional goal, without inner conflict or doubts. But her adaptation to conventions was not without struggle, and this lonely and desperate struggle eventually developed her total energies and independence. In this respect, her personality is steeled and it breaks the bondage of submission to piety. It becomes clear to her that the goals for which she continues to battle, and for which she had suffered, had been imposed from without and that they do not stem from her own convictions.

The idealized motto inscribed over the entrance to her life was not written by her; she was under the devotional delusion that a divine hand had indelibly inscribed it in gold. Her first instinctive decision was different; it was spontaneous rejection and flight. Then she had to develop according to imposed criteria and to battle for what she neither stood for nor wanted. And so it was that her actions belonged to her inherited conventions, while their implications put her in doubt. With every victory over herself, she clearly realized the tragic subversion of her own interests and disposition. With that, her first instinctive flight from imposed duty culminates slowly and terribly in a tragic division of her inner life; after sacrifice and victimization, she finally realizes that she has fought a false war and that the gods under whose banner she had fought were ghosts and disembodied shadow-pictures.

In this battle and dividedness, her inner being is in turmoil, so that she could not raise against her own marriage Nora's reproach that marriage had kept her as tightly closed as an unripe bud. Forcefully and ruthlessly Helene's buds are torn open, not by the natural light rays of the sun, but through the disgusting influence of a repulsive and unnerving power that resembles a crawling, devouring worm which opens up buds only to defoliate them.

If, however, she must in this fashion buy knowledge with a leaf from her blossoming life, she must also take the detour that marks a mutilated and sacrificed—instead of a naturally unfolding—life, in order to reach the truth: for all that, one must reach it!

Her deepest instincts tell her that this is both possible and necessary, despite everything. The cast of her mind justifies completely and retrospectively the passionate outcry with which she hurled herself into the arms of Manders, who personified in her childish eyes the true and the pure. It is the same cry that wrenches loose from her after pain and struggle when she faces the most painful import of the truth. Like a battle-weary hero in an untenable position, with no lament, she had seen everything around her decimated, one thing after another, without retreating in defeat. Then on the eve of battle, she sinks to her knees, overwhelmed by shame and longing, with words that declare her youth humbly and honestly: "I am here. Take me!"

For Pastor Manders her cry, at any rate, retains, even in the light of truth, the same frivolous, sinful meaning as it previously had—as he himself was judged by it. When he visits Mrs. Alving after Oswald's return to his mother and for the first time learns about the latter course of her marriage, he is quite naturally upset, but he is also indignant about the turn of her attitudes. And precisely as in the years earlier, he only has this reaction: " ... and what will become of ideals?"

And in her reply also, grounded in painfully matured clarity, is that which once moved her in passion and confusion, as she simply poses a counterquestion: "And what about the truth?"

Without a trace, life has passed the goodhearted and goodnatured Pastor Manders by. Life had revealed nothing to him, and in his guilelessness and naïveté, there exists neither untruth nor impurity—no matter how obvious their presence. It is easy for him to be deceived and exploited. Mrs. Alving soon is witness to that when the carpenter Engstrand, lame in body and mind, pulls the wool over Manders' eyes; nevertheless, the Pastor, proud of his knowledge of humans, triumphantly exclaims, "What do you say now, Mrs. Alving?"

What does she say? She allows him his triumph. And as she approaches him, her soul is diffused with an indescribably deep grace toward Manders whose advice and persuasion led to the destruction of her fortunes: "I do believe, Pastor Manders, that you are a big infant, and will ever be one!—And, I also think that it would give me pleasure to put my arms around your neck."

Lovely words! And doubly nice because in them is expressed the contrast between her mature control and the conquered, old ideals of youth. From the vantage point of her lonely, steep, and stony heights she looks down—but, with warmth, compassion, and nostalgia, as a strong and tested man looks down upon a beloved child one has outgrown. No recrimination, and no ridicule, no sharpness or bitterness—not even one accusation; nothing except a silent gazing that transcends by far everything personal. There is something grand in her prim bearing with which she manages her suffering and fate. It is the superlative trait of her expansive womanly nature to gather all personal agony and experience into silent understanding and perception.

This trait is nothing more than her longing for truth, which emanates from all the confusion and the striving to shape her own personality. This longing pushes her life into a tragic direction, divided by action directed against her own longings; she converted pain into perception and lament into generosity.

Her earliest actions had set a decisive course, and therefore she could not be saved from the ensuing tragic events. Her ultimate, human delusion is the belief that she can escape the consequences of her past, with the burial of her husband, and could be able to chart a new life with Oswald. For once, there is happiness in such delusion. She is happy to be able to love, with all her accumulated and suppressed tenderness, another being, and to bring unreserved mother love and sacrifice to bear, instead of being sacrificed to the demands of despised duties. And as part of this new and great happiness, she makes one concession to her duties inherited from the past, an honoring that does no honor to truth, namely, the retention of reverence for the image of the father in the son's memory, a final and gentle prevention of hurt for the dead as well as the living.

And Oswald seems to justify the unbounded pride of this mother; in alien surroundings, he had grown beautiful and industrious as a talented painter. All his paintings breathed sunshine and a passion for life, all "centered on a joyousness of life."

In that manner, the philandering pleasure-seeking of his father had become transformed in Oswald into the artistic sense; it was as if the spiritual inheritance from his mother contributed something dignified and silent to the transformation. But that mother's blessing could not eradicate the curse of the father which lay upon Oswald. In the monotonous village and homelife, and with a despondency fostered by the grayness of the rains that hindered his out-of-doors pleasures, Oswald begins to favor wine and an intimacy with the domestic maid Regina. He has not the slightest suspicion that she, the daughter of a previous maid, is his half-sister. But Mrs. Alving sees arising from all this the first ghost out of the past; others will soon follow rapidly and inexorably.

Tearfully Oswald confesses that the cause of his alleged travel weariness lies in some malady of the brain that had already led to a spell of madness. His fear of its recurrence had brought him back home; the doctor's diagnosis pointed to his eventual decline into incurable idiocy. Bitter self-reproaches merge with his deadly terror; he feared that he himself had incurred the terrible malady through what seemed to be simple, youthful diversions, and he indignantly brushed away the doctor's surmises that the cause could be found in the philandering life of his father. With Oswald's confession, Mrs. Alving's hope about being able to free herself from the past collapses. At the same time, the inferno that engulfs the orphanage built in the memory of her husband is like the fire that sweeps into her life, and with one cascading glow levels everything to the ground in ashes.

Yet even here the deep drive, which has triggered her tragic experiences and pains, does not disavow its aim to recognize and heed the call of truth. Along with her last happiness sinks her last veil. Not only does a conflagration scorch and destroy; it throws a wide circle of brilliant light around itself and high into the sky. And so, the red-glowing flame that with finality destroyed her life's happiness also brings her clear revelations and illuminations.

It is through Oswald that she is consumed. He complains that he has fled back to their home because of fear, but that now the melancholy monotony of their home overwhelms him with dismal thoughts. And the gray cloud of melancholy and depression, like the rain cloud outside that obliterates everything sunny, awakens an involuntary propensity for indecent and forbidden pleasures, and brings a harvest of perverse desires out of youthful yearnings that had lain fallow.

Mrs. Alving listens to him silently, and in her inner vision, the past unfolds in a new light. It seems to her as if her husband had reappeared as she had known him in his first youthful and unquenchable vitality; it seems to her as if he points to Oswald as his advocate. It is not, above all, the brooding atmosphere at home and the lack of activity and joyousness which drives Oswald into his father's tracks? Would he not have to become what his father was? It becomes clear to her that what Oswald never tires of glorifying in his sunlit, joy-breathing paintings is merely the artistic expression of the same longing that impelled his father to look for the sun in a life darkened by an overcast sky.

At the same time that the tragedy of her past fulfills itself through Oswald and mercilessly repeats itself like a returning ghost, the tragedy reveals itself in all its causative dimensions. And therefore, the tragedy becomes transformed in him. That ghost no longer appears in Mrs. Alving's eyes like a despised and discarded figure which awakens shudders and disgust; it blossoms in Oswald's youthful beauty and drives, not with a lecherous and coarse outlook, but with ardent pining. The ugliest truth has been removed from Mrs. Alving, like a repugnant burden that has weighted her down. Her judgment of the past is no longer condemnatory; it is only an immeasurable lament and commiseration. She is able to forgive, without disturbing the truth, because she is able to understand.

And with it, she gains courage to deal truthfully with Oswald by taking away his self-reproaches when she shows him what his father was really like. She does this with almost delighted confidence, despite Pastor Manders' indignation at her declaration: "Now I see what happened! And now I can speak out! ... And yet, no ideals will collapse!"

In that declaration rejoicingly rings the possibility of a reconciliation of the split in her life. What the enforced upholding of the sacrament of tradition was unable to accomplish, was achieved by an objective realization: she was not able to match lovingly the spirit and essence of her husband, nor to open her gentle soul to him. Up until now, the truth had mercilessly stalked her life and had destroyed her ideals, but she pursued it unafraid with passionate intensity. Now the truth with its all-encompassing glow finally enveloped her, so that she could now view and revere the ideal and the truth as a new and triumphant unity.

In this brief scene, the drama peaks, completing its inner development. It is like the aftermath of the burning orphanage; the glow of the subsiding conflagration drives ghostly clouds of smoke against a dark evening sky. And yet, the glare of the destruction has turned into a soft glow that hovers over Mrs. Alving as she bravely attends to her stricken and tortured child. And in the softness of his illuminating glow, her totally destroyed life stands in noble transformation—tragic though conciliated.

What then follows is the last, inevitable course of outer fate: Oswald's outbreak of madness and Mrs. Alving's oath that she will give him the liberating poison. She will give it to him, she will do it with a symbolic gesture: she will be compelled to destroy with her own hand what she has built up on a false foundation, just as she had to disavow and recant what she had bred and defended in her involuntary mistakes.

With the poison in her hesitating hand, hunched over Oswald during this last night, she struggles through her last earthly battle amid total isolation, in the overwhelming anguish of a mother. And the day breaks above the mountains. Ghostly veils still rest in the depths, and ghostly shadow pictures rise from the valleys. Above them at the highest peak, the quivering, purplish morning is revealed to the eye.

That vision floats before Oswald's dusky consciousness and the inhabitants of the valley—like a dream vision of happiness and blessing which he longingly and dreamily greets with a stammer, "The sun!" Mrs. Alving's clear vision sees things differently. She knows that she must remain until the last in the depths and under the shadows, never to scale those sunny heights; yet, the sun will rise for her and she will be granted a flash of clarity—and with it her release.

For Mrs. Alving, the perceived ideal no longer is the same as that for which Nora, who was ready for the struggle with youthful confidence, searched: a future wondrous happening that lay hidden beyond the distant horizon. For Mrs. Alving, there is no future, no line of the horizon where heaven and earth seem to merge harmoniously; she can only cast a glance upward and backwards upon an abandoned battlefield, strewn with the sacrifices that marked her life. Instead of Nora's wobbling search for insight and development, instead of her painful, first parting from accepted and beloved ideals, Helene Alving has already been immersed in the truth, has experienced it, and has grasped it with capable and firm hands. And so, in place of Nora's hopeful and contentious battle for ideals and truth, tranquility and peace come to Helene Alving. She does not, like Nora, wander into the unforeseeable, dark distance; she may rest quietly under a sky which has been illuminated. She lifts her face and hands toward the great transformation that breaks into her life, toward the truth—toward the sun.

Emma Goldman   *Ghosts*

This piece is from Emma Goldman's book *The Social Significance of Modern Drama* (Copyright 1914 by Richard G. Badger and Copyright 1987 by Applause Theatre Book Publishers).

The social and revolutionary significance of Henrik Ibsen is brought out with even greater force in "Ghosts" than in his preceding works.

Not only does this pioneer of modern dramatic art undermine in "Ghosts" the Social Lie and the paralyzing effect of Duty, but the uselessness and evil of Sacrifice, the dreary Lack of Joy and of Purpose in Work are brought to light as most pernicious and destructive elements in life.

Mrs. Alving, having made what her family called a most admirable match, discovers shortly after her marriage that her husband is a drunkard and a *roué*. In her despair she flees to her young friend, the divinity student *Manders*. But he, preparing to save souls, even though they be encased in rotten bodies, sends *Mrs. Alving* back to her husband and her duties toward her home.

Helen Alving is young and immature. Besides, she loves young *Manders*; his command is law to her. She returns home, and for twenty-five years suffers all the misery and torture of the damned. That she survives is due mainly to her passionate love for the child born of that horrible relationship—her boy *Oswald*, her all in life. He must be saved at any cost. To do that, she had sacrificed her great yearning for him and sent him away from the poisonous atmosphere of her home.

And now he has returned, fine and free, much to the disgust of *Pastor Manders*, whose limited vision cannot conceive that out in the large world free men and women can live a decent and creative life.

> *Manders*. But how is it possible that a—a young man or young woman with any decent principles can endure to live in that way?—in the eyes of all the world!
> *Oswald*. What are they to do? A poor young artist—a poor girl. It costs a lot of money to get married. What are they to do?
> *Manders*. What are they to do? Let me tell you, Mr. Alving, what they ought to do. They ought to exercise self-restraint from the first; that's what they ought to do.
> *Oswald*. Such talk as that won't go far with warm-blooded young people, over head and ears in love.
> *Mrs. Alving*. No, it wouldn't go far.

Manders. How can the authorities tolerate such things? Allow it to go on in the light of day? *(To Mrs. Alving.)* Had I not cause to be deeply concerned about your son? In circles where open immorality prevails, and has even a sort of prestige—!

Oswald. Let me tell you, sir, that I have been a constant Sunday-guest in one or two such irregular homes—

Manders. On Sunday of all days!

Oswald. Isn't that the day to enjoy one's self? Well, never have I heard an offensive word, and still less have I ever witnessed anything that could be called immoral. No; do you know when and where I have found immorality in artistic circles?

Manders. No! Thank heaven, I don't!

Oswald. Well, then, allow me to inform you. I have met with it when one or other of our pattern husbands and fathers has come to Paris to have a look around on his own account, and has done the artists the honor of visiting their humble haunts. *They* knew what was what. These gentlemen could tell us all about places and things we had never dreamt of.

Manders. What? Do you mean to say that respectable men from home here would—?

Oswald. Have you never heard these respectable men, when they got home again, talking about the way in which immorality was running rampant abroad?

Manders. Yes, of course.

Mrs. Alving. I have, too.

Oswald. Well, you may take their word for it. They know what they are talking about! Oh! that that great, free, glorious life out there should be defiled in such a way!

Pastor Manders is outraged, and when *Oswald* leaves, he delivers himself of a tirade against Mrs. Alving for her "irresponsible proclivities to shirk her duty."

Manders. It is only the spirit of rebellion that craves for happiness in this life. What right have we human beings to happiness? No, we have to do our duty! And your duty was to hold firmly to the man you had once chosen and to whom you were bound by a holy tie.... It was your duty to bear with humility the cross which a Higher Power had, for your own good, laid upon you. But instead of that you rebelliously cast away the cross.... I was but a poor instrument in a Higher Hand. And what a blessing has it not been to you all the days of your life, that I got you to resume the yoke of duty and obedience!

Emma Goldman: GHOSTS

The price *Mrs. Alving* had to pay for her yoke, her duty and obedience, staggers even *Dr. Manders,* when she reveals to him the martyrdom she had endured those long years.

Mrs. Alving. You have now spoken out, Pastor Manders; and tomorrow you are to speak publicly in memory of my husband. I shall not speak tomorrow. But now I will speak out a little to you, as you have spoken to me.... I want you to know that after nineteen years of marriage my husband remained as dissolute in his desires as he was when you married us. After Oswald's birth, I thought Alving seemed to be a little better. But it did not last long. And then I had to struggle twice as hard, fighting for life or death, so that nobody should know what sort of a man my child's father was. I had my little son to bear it for. But when the last insult was added; when my own servant-maid—Then I swore to myself: This shall come to an end. And so I took the upper hand in the house—the whole control over him and over everything else. For now I had a weapon against him, you see; he dared not oppose me. It was then that Oswald was sent from home. He was in his seventh year, and was beginning to observe and ask questions, as children do. That I could not bear. I thought the child must get poisoned by merely breathing the air in this polluted home. That was why I placed him out. And now you can see, too, why he was never allowed to set foot inside his home so long as his father lived. No one knows what it has cost me.... From the day after tomorrow it shall be for me as though he who is dead had never lived in this house. No one shall be here but my boy and his mother. *(From within the dining-room comes the noise of a chair overturned, and at the same moment is heard:)*

Regina *(sharply, but whispering).* Oswald! take care! are you mad? Let me go!

Mrs. Alving *(starts in terror).* Ah! *(She stares wildly toward the half-opened door. Oswald is heard coughing and humming inside).*

Manders *(excited).* What in the world is the matter? What is it, Mrs. Alving?

Mrs. Alving *(hoarsely).* Ghosts! The couple from the conservatory has risen again!

Ghosts, indeed! *Mrs. Alving* sees this but too clearly when she discovers that though she did not want *Oswald* to inherit a single penny from the purchase money *Captain Alving* had paid for her, all her sacrifice did not save *Oswald* from the poisoned heritage of his father. She learns soon enough that her beloved boy had inherited a terrible disease from his father, as a result of which he will never again be able to work. She also finds out that, for all her freedom, she has remained in the clutches of

Ghosts, and that she has fostered in *Oswald's* mind an ideal of his father, the more terrible because of her own loathing for the man. Too late she realizes her fatal mistake:

> *Mrs. Alving.* I ought never to have concealed the facts of Alving's life. But ... in my superstitious awe for Duty and Decency I lied to my boy, year after year. Oh! what a coward, what a coward I have been! ... Ghosts! When I heard Regina and Oswald in there, it was as though I saw the Ghosts before me. But I almost think we are all of us Ghosts, Pastor Manders. It is not only what we have inherited from our father and mother that "walks" in us. It is all sorts of dead ideas, and lifeless old beliefs, and so forth. They have no vitality, but they cling to us all the same, and we can't get rid of them.... There must be Ghosts all the country over, as thick as the sand of the sea. And then we are, one and all, so pitifully afraid of the light.... When you forced me under the yoke you called Duty and Obligation; when you praised as right and proper what my whole soul rebelled against, as something loathsome. It was then that I began to look into the seams of your doctrine. I only wished to pick at a single knot; but when I had got that undone, the whole thing ravelled out. And then I understood that it was all machine-sewn.... It was a crime against us both.

Indeed, a crime on which the sacred institution is built, and for which thousands of innocent children must pay with their happiness and life, while their mothers continue to the very end without ever learning how hideously criminal their life is.

Not so *Mrs. Alving* who, though at a terrible price, works herself out to the truth; aye, even to the height of understanding the dissolute life of the father of her child, who had lived in cramped provincial surroundings, and could find no purpose in life, no outlet for his exuberance. It is through her child, through *Oswald,* that all this becomes illumed to her.

> *Oswald.* Ah, the joy of life, mother; that's a thing you don't know much about in these parts. I have never felt it here.... And then, too, the joy of work. At bottom, it's the same thing. But that too you know nothing about.... Here people are brought up to believe that work is a curse and a punishment for sin, and that life is something miserable, something we want to be done with, the sooner the better.... Have you noticed that everything I have painted has turned upon the joy of life? always, always upon the joy of life?— light and sunshine and glorious air, and faces radiant with happiness? That is why I am afraid of remaining at home with you.

Mrs. Alving. Oswald, you spoke of the joy of life; and at that word a new light burst for me over my life and all it has contained.... You ought to have known your father when he was a young lieutenant. He was brimming over with the joy of life! ... He had no object in life, but only an official position. He had no work into which he could throw himself heart and soul; he had only business. He had not a single comrade that knew what the joy of life meant— only loafers and boon companions— ... So that happened which was sure to happen.... Oswald, my dear boy; has it shaken you very much?

Oswald. Of course it came upon me as a great surprise, but, after all, it can't matter much to me.

Mrs. Alving. Can't matter! That your father was so infinitely miserable!

Oswald. Of course I can pity him as I would anybody else; but—

Mrs. Alving. Nothing more? Your own father!

Oswald. Oh, there! "Father," "father"! I never knew anything of father. I don't remember anything about him except—that he once made me sick.

Mrs. Alving. That's a terrible way to speak! Should not a son love his father, all the same?

Oswald. When a son has nothing to thank his father for? has never known him? Do you really cling to the old superstition?—you who are so enlightened in other ways?

Mrs. Alving. Is that only a superstition?

In truth, a superstition—one that is kept like the sword of Damocles over the child who does not ask to be given life, and is yet tied with a thousand chains to those who bring him into a cheerless, joyless, and wretched world.

The voice of Henrik Ibsen in "Ghosts" sounds like the trumpets before the walls of Jericho. Into the remotest nooks and corners reaches his voice, with its thundering indictment of our moral cancers, our social poisons, our hideous crimes against unborn and born victims. Verily a more revolutionary condemnation has never been uttered in dramatic form before or since the great Henrik Ibsen.

We need, therefore, not be surprised at the vile abuse and denunciation heaped upon Ibsen's head by the Church, the State, and other moral eunuchs. But the spirit of Henrik Ibsen could not be daunted. It asserted itself with even greater defiance in "An Enemy of the People,"—a powerful arraignment of the political and economic Lie,—Ibsen's own confession of faith.

Henrik Ibsen *Letters*

The following letters were originally translated by either John Nilsen Laurvik and Mary Morison in *Letters of Henrik Ibsen* (New York, 1908) (published in England as the *Correspondence of Henrik Ibsen*, London, 1905) or by Arne Kildal in *Speeches and New Letters* (Boston, 1910; London, 1911). All translations were revised by Brian Johnston and checked against the text of the letters as given in the Norwegian Centennial Edition.

To Georg Brandes, Rome, January 3, 1882
(Trans. by Laurvik and Morison)

Dear Brandes, Yesterday I had the great pleasure of receiving from Hegel your brilliant, perspicuous, and very flattering review of *Ghosts*. Accept my warmest and heartiest thanks for the invaluable service you have again rendered me. Anyone who reads your article must, it seems to me, get to understand what I intended in my new book—that is to say, if they have any desire to understand. For I cannot get rid of the impression that a very large number of the false interpretations that have appeared in the newspapers are the work of people who know better. In Norway, however, I do believe that the blundering has in most cases been unintentional; and the reason is not far to seek. In that country a great many of the professional reviewers are theologians, more or less disguised; and these gentlemen are as a rule quite unable to criticize literature in a rational way. That enfeeblement of the judgment which, at least in the case of the average man, is an inevitable consequence of protracted occupation with theological studies betrays itself more especially in judging human character, human actions, and human motives. Practical business judgment, on the other hand, does not suffer so much from theological studies. Hence the reverend gentlemen are often very excellent members of local boards; but they are, unquestionably, our worst critics.

And what can be said of the attitude assumed by the so-called liberal press—of these leaders of the people who speak and write of freedom of action and thought but who at the same time make themselves the slaves of the supposed opinions of their subscribers? I receive more and more corroboration of my conviction that there is something demoralizing in engaging in politics and in joining parties. It will never, in any case, be possible to me to join a party that has the majority on its side. Bjørnson says, "The majority is always right."

And as a practical politician he is bound, I suppose, to say so.[1] I, on the contrary, must of necessity say, "The minority is always right." Naturally I am not thinking of that minority of stagnationists who are left behind by the great middle party that we call liberal; I mean that minority which leads the vanguard and pushes on to points the majority has not yet reached. I mean: that man is right who has allied himself most closely with the future.

I have written this as a kind of apologia, if such should prove necessary.

I was prepared for the storm of protest against *Ghosts*. But I did not feel that I could take any notice of it; that would have been cowardice.

I have to thank you not only for the article in *Morgenbladet*, but also, and quite as much, for your lecture on me and my work, and your intention of having the said lecture printed. Hegel writes that you wish to make use of some passages in my letters to you. I have, of course, no objection to your doing so. I have perfect confidence in you in this matter as in every other. If you wish to quote from the present letter also, you are at liberty to do so.

When I think how slow and heavy and dull the general intelligence is at home, when I notice the low standard by which everything is judged, a deep despondency comes over me, and it often seems to me that I might just as well end my literary activity at once. They really do not need poetry at home; they get along so well with the *Parliamentary News* and the *Lutheran Weekly*. And they also have their party papers. I have not the gifts that go to make a satisfactory citizen, nor yet the gift of orthodoxy; and I prefer to keep out of what I have no gift for. Liberty is the first and highest condition of life for me. At home they do not trouble much about liberty, but only about liberties—a few more or a few less, according to the position their party adopts. I feel, too, most painfully affected by the crudity, the plebian element in all our public discussion. The very praiseworthy attempt to make our nation a democratic community has inadvertently gone a good way toward making us a plebeian community. The aristocracy of mind and spirit seems to be decaying at home.

I must break off here today. Please give our very kindest regards to your wife, and assure her that we do not forget her. Thank you once more, dear Brandes, for everything that you have done and are still doing for me.

Yours always,
Henrik Ibsen

---

[1] Ibsen's allusion to Bjørnson as a practical politician was quite obviously written before he had seen the December 22 issue of the Norwegian *Dagblad* wherein Bjørnson defends *Ghosts* vigorously.

Henrik Ibsen: Letters

To Sophus Schandorph, Rome, January 6, 1882
(Trans. by Laurvik and Morison)

> Sophus Schandorph, (1837–1901) a writer, was an intimate friend of Georg Brandes.

Dear Sir: Accept my sincere thanks for the letter that you were good enough to write me, and excuse my not having found time to answer it until today. It came as a very welcome Christmas greeting at the time when my new play was being misrepresented at home and subjected to all kinds of foolish criticism.

I was quite prepared for the hubbub. If certain of our Scandinavian reviewers have no talent for anything else, they have an unquestionable talent for thoroughly misunderstanding and misinterpreting the authors of the books they undertake to judge.

Is it, however, really nothing but misunderstanding? Have not many of these misrepresentations and distorted interpretations been presented to the public by writers fully aware of what they were doing? I can hardly think otherwise.

They endeavor to make me responsible for the opinions expressed by some of the characters in my play. And yet there is not in the whole book a single opinion, a single utterance, that can be laid to the account of the author. I took good care to avoid this. The method in itself, the technique which determined the form of the work, entirely precluded the author's appearing in the speeches. My intention was to produce the impression in the mind of the reader that he was experiencing something real. Now, nothing would more effectively prevent such an impression than the insertion of the author's private opinions in the dialogue. Do they imagine at home that I have not enough dramatic instinct to be aware of this? Of course I was aware of it, and I acted accordingly. And in none of my other plays is the author such an outsider, so entirely absent, as in this one.

And then they say that the book preaches nihilism. It does not. It preaches nothing at all. It merely points out that there is a ferment of nihilism under the surface, at home as elsewhere. And this is inevitable. A Pastor Manders will always provoke some Mrs. Alving into rebelling. And just because she is a woman, she will, once she has begun, go to great extremes.

I hope that Georg Brandes' article in *Morgenbladet* will be of great assistance in producing a more correct impression of the play. *Morgenbladet* has on several occasions shown good will towards me; and I trust you will be good enough to convey my deep gratitude to the editors.

Your letter was both a pleasure and an honour; and it has begun an acquaintance which I have long desired. Your writings have given much enjoyment to me and my more immediate circle; and I have followed you on your different literary and critical campaigns, with great pleasure and interest.

I hope that a meeting, somewhere or other, is in store for us.—Believe me,

> Yours very respectfully and sincerely.
> Henrik Ibsen

P.S. If any part of the above letter is likely to be of interest to readers of *Morgenbladet*, I have no objection to its publication.

To Olaf Skavlan, Rome, January 24, 1882
(Trans. by Laurvik and Morison)

Olaf Skavlan was editor of a new periodical, *Nyt Tidsskrift.*

... These last weeks have brought me a wealth of experiences, lessons, and discoveries. I was quite prepared that my new play would provoke a howl from the camp of the stagnationists; and that bothers me about as much as a pack of chained dogs barking at my heels. But the alarm which I have observed among the so-called liberals has given me cause for reflection. The very day after my play was published, the [Norwegian] *Dagblad* rushed a hurriedly written article into print with the evident purpose of removing itself from any suspicion that it approved of my play. This was entirely unnecessary. I myself am responsible for what I write. I and no one else. I cannot possibly embarrass any party, for I do not belong to any. I stand like a solitary sharpshooter at the outpost, acting entirely on my own.

The only man in Norway who has stood up frankly, boldly, and courageously for me is Bjørnson. It is just like him: he has, in truth, a great and noble soul; and I shall never forget what he has done just now.

But how about all these champions of liberty who have been frightened out of their wits? Is it only in the field of politics that the work of emancipation shall be permitted to go on? Must not men's minds be emancipated first of all? Men with such slave souls as ours cannot make use even of the liberties they already possess. Norway is a free country peopled by unfree men and women.

I sincerely trust that I may find I have been mistaken in the discoveries I have been making these last weeks as to the nature of Norwegian liberalism. I cannot but believe that there must be explanatory circumstances of which I am unaware.

Henrik Ibsen: Letters

I am sure you will understand me when I tell you that I must refrain from any kind of collaboration. No one contributor to a magazine ought to take a position totally different from the others. In the present case could I avoid doing so? I cannot say at this moment. I am very much confused as regards the situation at home and need time to get my bearings. Remember me to all those who are silently my friends.

Yours most sincerely,
Henrik Ibsen

To Otto Borchsenius, Rome, January 28, 1882
(Trans. by Laurvik and Morison)

> Otto Borchsenius was from 1880–1884 one of the editors of *Ude og hjemme (Home and Abroad)*, a Danish weekly paper of liberal tendencies.

Dear Sir, Although I see that the [Norwegian] *Dagblad* is annoyed with me because I write letters to Copenhagen, I shall no longer delay answering the letter that I had the honor of receiving from you last autumn at Sorrento.

You desired at the time some little poem in my handwriting, to be published in *Ude og hjemme* [*At Home and Abroad*] with marginal illustrations; and you referred me to the weekly in question for guidance in the matter of size of page, etc. I have looked in it in vain for similar contributions from other authors that could give me the hints required, and, concluding that the editors' plan has for some reason or other been given up, I have not sent you a contribution. However, if you still desire one, be good enough to let me know, and it shall be sent at once. Only please remember that I have nothing to offer you except what is already in print. It will simply be a copy of one of the small poems in my collection—either the last poem, or any other which your artist might propose as more suitable for illustration.

Allow me to avail myself of this opportunity to offer you my best and warmest thanks for your favorable and instructive review of my latest play. By writing of it as you have done, you have rendered me a service for which I shall always feel indebted to you. It was a great consolation to me in the midst of the storm of excitement that has been raging both in Denmark and Norway, to read your temperate judgment of the work, unaffected as it is by any party considerations.

It may well be that the play is in several respects rather daring. But it seemed to me that now was the time when some boundary posts had to be moved. And for that undertaking an older writer like myself was more fitted than the many younger authors who might desire to do something of the same nature.

I was prepared that a storm of protest would break over me. But a man cannot alter his course because of that; that would be cowardice.

It is not the attacks that have depressed me most, but the fear and trembling manifested by the so-called liberals in Norway. They would be poor fellows to man barricades with. The Norwegian *Dagblad* has refused to print any more articles by Bjørnson. And if one looks carefully, there is much that indicates how isolated both he and I are in our own country. If we did not have Denmark, it would be a bad lookout for us and for the work of intellectual emancipation in Scandinavia generally. Once more my best thanks.

Yours most sincerely,
Henrik Ibsen

To Bjørnstjerne Bjørnson, Rome, March 8, 1882
(Trans. by Kildal)

Dear Bjørnson: For a long time I have been thinking about writing to thank you for having so forthrightly and honestly come to my defense at a time when I was attacked on so many sides [after the publication of *Ghosts*]. It was really no more than I might have expected from a man possessing a great and courageous spirit of leadership. But still, there was no compelling reason for you to step forward and express yourself as you did. And the thought that you did not hesitate to throw yourself into the conflict will always stay with me, I can assure you of that.

I am also aware that during your tour of America you wrote about me in kind and complimentary terms. For this I also thank you, and let me say at the same time that you were scarcely ever out of my thoughts the whole time you were away. I was extremely uneasy just at that time, and an American trip has always seemed an uncomfortably daring venture to me. On top of that, I heard that you were ill over there, and then, just when you were expected to return, I read about the storms on the ocean. It became vividly clear to me how infinitely much you mean to me—and to all of us. I felt that if anything should happen to you, if such a great calamity should befall our country, then all the pleasure would be taken from my work.

Next summer it will be twenty-five years since *Synnøve Solbakken* [Bjørnson's first novel] appeared. I traveled up through Valders and read it on the way. I hope this memorable year will be celebrated as it deserves to be. If things turn out as I wish, I too would like to go home for the celebration.

Henrik Ibsen: Letters

There is one matter I ought to mention. Through *Dagbladet,* or in some other way, you have probably become acquainted with the contents of the letter that I wrote to State Comptroller Berner about a year ago [March 27, 1881]. I did not have the opportunity to confer with you then, but I did not imagine that you would have any fundamental objection either to the contents of the letter or to the application itself. It seems a searing injustice to me that we should remain so long without legal protection for our literary property. I have now written to Berner again and given him a survey of the income that I, for one, have lost. Considering only the two royal theaters at Stockholm and Copenhagen, this amounts to about 25,000 kroner [$6,700]. *A Doll's House,* which was paid for according to the new convention, yielded 9,000 kroner [$2,412] in Copenhagen. Each one of your plays that was performed there would have yielded you at least as much if the convention had been in force. Count up what that amounts to! And then Germany!

In order to work with full force and undivided attention in the cause of spiritual emancipation, one must have a certain degree of economic independence. The standpat party obviously opposes the spread of our writings, and there are theaters that refuse to perform our plays. It would only be for the best of the people themselves if we did not have to pay any attention to this in our future writings.

That is why I hope you will not disapprove of the measures I have taken. I have simply asked for justice, nothing more.

Give your wife our best wishes. And please accept my repeated thanks.

Yours sincerely and gratefully,
Henrik Ibsen

To Frederik Hegel, Rome, March 16, 1882
(Trans. by Laurvik and Morison)

Dear Mr. Hegel, I ought to have replied long ago to your kind letter of February 16. Of course, I have not the slightest doubt that it was written out of sincere regard for me, but I must entreat you not to lend an ear to advisers in my affairs, especially when they are persons who have no proper understanding of all the really new elements in the literature of the last twenty years.

I know quite well how greedy the gossips of our little provincial towns are for all kinds of information regarding the private affairs of authors and artists, but it seems to me that I am as cautious as anyone can possibly be. Indeed, some of my friends feel that I injure myself by being too reserved. Mr. Otto Borchsenius writes on the ninth of February that almost all my Copenhagen friends are agreed that this would be the right time for me to give a distinct and complete explanation of my position. He adds (I quote directly from his letter): "Your publisher, too, asked me explicitly if there was anybody who could make you (me) speak." I only quote this to show you the variety of opinions on the matter. Your last letter makes it clear beyond any doubt that he must have misinterpreted your words.

I long ago abandoned the literary plan [for an autobiography] that I once mentioned to you, and I am now completely occupied with the preparations for a new play [*An Enemy of the People*].

It will be a very peaceable play this time, one which may safely be read by the state councilors and the rich merchants and their ladies; and the theaters will not have to recoil in horror from it. It will be easy to write and I shall try to have it ready early in the autumn.

As regards *Ghosts*, I feel certain that in due time, and not very long at that, the real meaning of the play will penetrate the minds of the good people at home. All the decrepit old fossils who jumped in to attack my play will have a shattering sentence pronounced on them in future histories of literature. And the anonymous poachers and highwaymen who have showered me with abuse from their ambush in Professor Goos's[2] shopkeepers' newspaper and other such places are certain to be found out sooner or later. My book belongs to the future. Those fellows who have bellowed so about it have no real connection with the living spirit of their own times.

Consequently, I have been very cold-blooded about this part of the affair. I have made many studies and observations during the storm—which I shall find very useful in my future works.

And now I have a favor to ask of you. Will you kindly again lend me 1,000 kroner [$268]? I expressly say "lend"; for I wish to pay interest on any advance payments I receive from you. It would make no sense for me to put my own money in securities and then take advance payments from you gratis. Since I only require the money for a few months, I do not wish to part with any of my bonds. I hope you will see the matter from my point of view.

With kindest regards to you and your family, I remain, dear Mr. Hegel,

Yours most sincerely,
Henrik Ibsen

---

[2]Carl Goos was at this time professor of jurisprudence at the University of Copenhagen, conservative member of the lower house of the Danish parliament, and publisher of the Danish right-wing paper *Dagbladet*.

James Joyce *Selected Letters*

From William Archer, manuscript at Cornell University

23 April 1900   *2 Vernon Chambers, Southamptom Row, W.C.*

Dear Sir

I think it will interest you to know that in a letter I had from Henrik Ibsen a day or two ago he says 'I have read, or rather spelt out, a review by Mr James Joyce in the *Fortnightly Review*[1] which is very benevolent ("velvillig") and for which I should greatly like to thank the author if only I had sufficient knowledge of the language.'

Yours truly
William Archer

To William Archer, manuscript at British Museum

28 April 1900   *13 Richmond Avenue, Fairview, Dublin*

Dear Sir

I wish to thank you for your kindness in writing to me. I am a young Irishman, eighteen years old, and the words of Ibsen I shall keep in my heart all my life.

Faithfully yours,
Jas A. Joyce

To Henrik Ibsen, manuscript at Cornell University

March 1901   *8 Royal Terrace, Fairfield, Dublin*

Honoured Sir:

I write to you to give you greeting on your seventy-third birthday and to join my voice to those of your well-wishers in all lands. You may remember that shortly after the publication of your latest play, *When We Dead Awaken,* an appreciation of it appeared in one of the English reviews—*The Fortnightly Review*—over my name. I know that you have seen it because some short time afterwards Mr William

IBSEN'S GHOSTS: *A DRAMATURGICAL SOURCEBOOK*

Archer wrote to me and told me that in a letter he had had from you some days before, you had written, 'I have read or rather spelled out a review in *The Fortnightly Review* by Mr James Joyce which is very benevolent and for which I should greatly like to thank the author if only I had sufficient knowledge of the language.' (My own knowledge of your language is not, as you see, great but I trust you will be able to decipher my meaning.) I can hardly tell you how moved I was by your message. I am a young, a very young man, and perhaps the telling of such tricks of the nerves will make you smile. But I am sure if you go back along your own life to the time when you were an undergraduate at the University as I am, and if you think what it would have meant to you to have earned a word from one who held as high a place in your esteem as you hold in mine, you will understand my feeling. One thing only I regret, namely, that an immature and hasty article should have met your eye rather than something better and worthier of your praise. There may not have been any wilful stupidity in it, but truly I can say no more. It may annoy you to have your works at the mercy of striplings but I am sure you would prefer hotheadedness to nerveless and 'cultured' paradoxes.

    What shall I say more? I have sounded your name defiantly through the college where it was either unknown or known faintly and darkly. I have claimed for you your rightful place in the history of drama. I have shown what, as it seemed to me, was your highest excellence—your lofty impersonal power. Your minor claims—your satire, your technique and orchestral harmony—these, too, I advanced. Do not think me a hero-worshipper—I am not so. And when I spoke of you in debating societies and so forth, I enforced attention by no futile ranting.

    But we always keep the dearest things to ourselves. I did not tell them what bound me closest to you. I did not say how what I could discern dimly of your life was my pride to see, how your battles inspired me—not the obvious material battles but those that were fought and won behind your forehead, how your wilful resolution to wrest the secret from life gave me heart and how in your absolute indifference to public canons of art, friends and shibboleths you walked in the light of your inward heroism. And this is what I write to you of now. Your work on earth draws to a close and you are near the silence. It is growing dark for you. Many write of such things, but they do not know. You have opened the way—though you have gone

---

[1] Joyce's first published article 'Ibsen's New Drama', appeared in the *Fortnightly Review*, n.s. v. 67 (1 April 1900), 575–90.

as far as you could upon it—to the end of *John Gabriel Borkman* and its spiritual truth—for your last play stands, I take it, apart. But I am sure that higher and holier enlightenment lies—onward.

As one of the young generation for whom you have spoken I give you greeting—not humbly, because I am obscure and you in the glare, not sadly, because you are an old man and I a young man, not presumptuously, nor sentimentally—but joyfully, with hope and with love, I give you greeting.

Faithfully yours,
James A. Joyce

James Joyce

Epilogue to Ibsen's Ghosts *April 1934*

Dear quick, whose conscience buried deep
The grim old grouser has been salving,
Permit one spectre more to peep.
I am the ghost of Captain Alving.

Silenced and smothered by my past
Like the lewd knight in dirty linen
I struggle forth to swell the cast
And air a long-suppressed opinion.

For muddling weddings into wakes
No fool could vie with Pastor Manders.
I, though a dab at ducks and drakes,
Let gooseys serve or sauce their ganders.

My spouse bore me a blighted boy,
Our slavey pupped a bouncing bitch.
Paternity thy name is joy
When the wise sire knows which is which.

Both swear I am that self-same man
By whom their infants were begotten.
Explain fate, if you care or can,
Why one is sound and one is rotten.

Olaf may plod his stony path
And live as chastely as Susanna
Yet pick up in some Turkish bath
His *quantum est* of *Pox Romana*.

IBSEN'S GHOSTS: *A DRAMATURGICAL SOURCEBOOK*

While Haakon hikes up primrose way,
Spreeing and gleeing while he goes,
To smirk upon his latter day
Without a pimple on his nose.

I give it up I am afraid
But if I loafed and found it fun
Remember how a coyclad maid
Knows how to take it out of one.

The more I dither on and drink
My midnight bowl of spirit punch
The firmlier I feel and think
Friend Manders came too oft to lunch.

Since scuttling ship Vikings like me
Reck not to whom the blame is laid,
Y.M.C.A., V.D., T.B.,
Or Harbourmaster of Port Said.

Blame all and none and take to task
The harlot's lure, the swain's desire.
Heal by all means but hardly ask
Did this man sin or did his sire.

The shack's ablaze. That canting scamp,
The carpenter, has dished the parson.
Now had they kept their powder damp
Like me there would have been no arson.

Nay more, were I not all I was,
Weak, wanton, waster out and out,
There would have been no world's applause
And damn all to write home about.

George Bernard Shaw

Ghosts at the Jubilee

Ghosts. By Henrik Ibsen. The Independent Theatre, Queen's Gate Hall, South Kensington, 24, 25, and 26 June, 1897.

The Jubilee and Ibsen's "Ghosts"! On the one hand the Queen and the Archbishop of Canterbury: on the other, Mrs. Alving and Pastor Manders. Stupendous contrast! how far reflected in the private consciousness of those two august persons there is no means of ascertaining. For though of all the millions for the nourishment of whose loyalty the Queen must submit to be carried through the streets from time to time, not a man but is firmly persuaded that her opinions and convictions are exact facsimiles of his own, none the less she, having seen much of men and affairs, may quite possibly be a wise woman and worthy successor of Canute, and no mere butt for impertinent and senseless Jubilee odes such as their perpetrators dare not, for fear of intolerable domestic scorn and ridicule, address to their own wives or mothers. I am myself cut off by my own profession from Jubilees; for loyalty in a critic is corruption. But if I am to avoid idolizing kings and queens in the ordinary human way, I must carefully realize them as fellow-creatures. And so, whilst the nation was burning war incense in a thousand cannons before the throne at Spithead, I was wondering, on my way home from "Ghosts," how far life had brought to the Queen the lessons it brought to Mrs. Alving. For Mrs. Alving is not anybody in particular: she is a typical figure of the experienced, intelligent woman who, in passing from the first to the last quarter of the hour of history called the nineteenth century, has discovered how appallingly opportunities were wasted, morals perverted, and instincts corrupted, not only—sometimes not at all—by the vices she was taught to abhor in her youth, but by the virtues it was her pride and uprightness to maintain.

Suppose, then, the Queen were to turn upon us in the midst of our jubilation, and say, "My Lords and Gentlemen: You have been good enough to describe at great length the changes made during the last sixty years in science, art, politics, dress, sport, locomotion, newspapers, and everything else that men chatter about. But have you not a word to say about the change that comes home most closely to me? I mean the change in the number, the character, and the intensity of the lies a woman must either believe or pretend to believe before she can graduate in polite society as a well brought-up lady." If Her Majesty could be persuaded to give a list of these lies, what a document it would be! Think of the young lady of seventy years ago, systematically and piously lied to by parents, governesses, clergymen, servants, everybody; and slapped, sent to bed, or locked up in the bedevilled and beghosted dark at every rebellion of her common sense and natural instinct against sham religion, sham propriety, sham decency, sham knowledge, and sham ignorance. Surely every shop-window picture of "the girl Queen" of 1837 must tempt the Queen of 1897 to jump out of her carriage and write up under it, "Please remember that there is not a woman earning twenty-four shillings a week as a clerk to-day who is not ten times better educated than this unfortunate girl was when the crown dropped on her head, and left her to reign by her mother wit and the advice of a parcel of men who to this day have not sense enough to manage a Jubilee, let alone an Empire, without offending everybody." Depend on it, seventy-eight years cannot be lived through without finding out things that queens do not mention in Adelphi melodramas. Granted that the Queen's consort was not a Chamberlain Alving, and that the gaps made in a wide, numerous and robust posterity are too few for even Ibsen to see in the dissoluteness of the ancestors of the First Gentleman in Europe any great menace to the longevity of their descendants; still nineteenth-century life, however it may stage-manage itself tragically and sensationally here, or settle itself happily and domestically there, is yet all of one piece; and it is possible to have better luck than Mrs. Alving without missing all her conclusions.

Let us therefore guard ourselves against the gratuitous, but just now very common, assumption that the Queen, in her garnered wisdom and sorrow, is as silly as the noisiest of her subjects, who see in their ideal Queen the polar opposite of Mrs. Alving, and who are so far right that the spirit of "Ghosts" is unquestionably the polar opposite of the spirit of the Jubilee. The Jubilee represents the nineteenth century proud of itself. "Ghosts" represents it loathing itself. And how it *can* loathe itself when it gets tired of its money! Think of Schopenhauer and Shelley, Lassalle and Karl Marx, Ruskin and Carlyle, Morris and Wagner and Ibsen. How fiercely they rent the bosom that bore them! How they detested all the orthodoxies, and respectabilities, and ideals we have just been bejubilating! Of all their attacks, none is rasher or fiercer than "Ghosts." And yet, like them all, it is perfectly unanswerable. Many generations have laughed at comedies like "L'Etourdi," and repeated that hell is paved with good intentions; but never before have we had the well-brought-up, high-minded nineteenth-century lady and her excellent clergyman as the mischiefmakers. With them the theme, though still in its essence comic, requires a god to laugh at it. To mortals who may die of such blundering it is tragic and ghastly.

George Bernard Shaw: GHOSTS *at the Jubilee*

The performance of "Ghosts" by the Independent Theatre Society left the two previous productions by the same society far behind. As in the case of "The Wild Duck," all obscurity vanished; and Ibsen's clearness, his grip of his theme, and the rapidity, directness and intensity of the action of the piece produced the effect they can always be depended on to produce in capable hands, such as Mr. Charrington's, so far alone among those of Ibsenite stage-managers, have proved to be. Mrs. Theodore Wright's Mrs. Alving, originally an achievement quite beyond the culture of any other actress of her generation, is still hardly less peculiar to her. Mrs. Wright's technique is not in the least that of the Ibsen school. Never for a moment would you suspect her of having seen Miss Janet Achurch or any one remotely resembling her. She is unmistakably a contemporary of Miss Ellen Terry. When I first saw her act she was playing Beatrice in "Much Ado About Nothing," with a charm and intuition that I have not seen surpassed, and should not have seen equalled if I had never seen Miss Terry wasting her gifts on Shakespeare. As it happened, Mrs. Theodore Wright, perhaps because she was so fond of acting that the stage, where there is less opportunity for it than anywhere else in England, bored her intolerably, found her way behind the scenes of the revolutionary drama of the century at a time when the happy ending now in progress had not been reached, and played Shakespeare and recited Shelley, Hood and George Eliot before Karl Marx, Morris, Bradlaugh and other volcanic makers of the difference between 1837 and 1897, as proudly as Talma played to his pit of kings. Her authors, it will be seen, were not so advanced as her audiences; but that could not be helped, as the progressive movement in England had not produced a dramatist; and nobody then dreamt of Norway, or knew that Ibsen had begun the drama of struggle and emancipation, and had declared that the really effective progressive forces of the moment were the revolt of the working classes against economic, and of the women against idealistic, slavery. Such a drama, of course, immediately found out that weak spot in the theatrical profession which Duse put her finger on the other day in Paris—the so-called stupidity of the actors and actresses. Stupidity, however, is hardly the word. Actors and actresses are clever enough on the side on which their profession cultivates them. What is the matter with them is the characteristic narrowness and ignorance of their newly conquered conventional respectability. They are now neither above the commonplaces of middle-class idealism, like the aristocrat and poet, nor below them, like the vagabond and Bohemian. The theatre has become very much what the Dissenting chapel used to be: there is not a manager in London who, in respect of liberality and enlightenment of opinion, familiarity and sympathy with current social questions, can be compared with the leaders of Nonconformity. Take Sir Henry Irving and Dr. Clifford for example. The "Dissenter" is a couple of centuries ahead of the actor: indeed, the comparison seems absurd, so grotesquely is it to the disadvantage of the institution which still imagines itself the more cultured and less prejudiced of the two. And, but for Mr. Henry Arthur Jones, the authors would cut as poor a figure from this point of view as the actors. Duse advises actors to read; but of what use is that? They *do* read—more than is good for them. They read the drama, and are eager students of criticism, though they would die rather than confess as much to a critic. (Whenever an actor tells me, as he invariably does, that he has not seen any notices of his performance, I always know that he has the "Saturday Review" in his pocket; but I respect the delicacy of an evasion which is as instinctive and involuntary as blushing.) When the drama loses its hold on life, and criticism is dragged down with it, the actor's main point of intellectual contact with the world is cut off; for he reads nothing else with serious attention. He then has to spin his culture out of his own imagination or that of the dramatist and critics, a facile but delusive process which leaves nothing real to fall back on but his technical craft, which may make him a good workman, but nothing else.

If even technical craft became impossible at such a period—say through the long run and the still longer tour destroying the old training without replacing it by a new one—then the gaps in the actor's cultivation and the corresponding atrophied patches in his brain would call almost for a Mission for his Intellectual Reclamation. Something of this kind might have happened in our own time—I am not sure that a few cases of it did not actually happen—if Ibsen had not come to the rescue. At all events, things had gone so far that the reigning generation of actor-managers were totally incapable of understanding Ibsen: his plays were not even grammar and spelling to them, much less drama. That what they found there was the life of their own time; that its ideas had been seething round their theatres for years past; that they themselves, chivalrously "holding up the banner of the ideal" in the fool's paradise of theatrical romance and sentiment, had served Ibsen, as they formerly served Goethe, as reductions-to-absurdity of that divorce of the imagined life from the real which is the main peril of an age in which everybody is provided with the means of substituting reading and romancing for real living: all this was quite outside their comprehension. To them the new phenomenon was literally "the Ibsen craze," a thing bound to disappear whilst they were rubbing their eyes to make sure that they saw the absurd monster clearly. But that was exactly Mrs. Theodore Wright's opportunity. A lady who had talked over matters with Karl Marx was not to be frightened by Pastor Manders. She created Mrs. Alving as easily, sympathetically, and intelligently as Miss Winifred Emery or Miss Kate Rorke will create the heroine of the next adaptation from the French drama of 1840 by Mr. Grundy; and by that one step she walked over the heads of the whole profession, I cannot say into the first

George Bernard Shaw: GHOSTS *at the Jubilee*

intellectual rank as an English actress, because no such rank then existed, but into a niche in the history of the English stage the prominence of which would, if they could foresee it, very considerably astonish those who think that making history is as easy as making knights. (The point of this venomous allusion will not be missed. It is nothing to be a knight-actor now that there are two of them. When will Sir Henry Irving bid for at least a tiny memorial inscription in the neighborhood of Mrs. Theodore Wright's niche?)

The remarkable success of Mr. Courtenay Thorpe in Ibsen parts in London lately, and the rumors as to the sensation created by his Oswald Alving in America, gave a good deal of interest to his first appearance here in that part. He has certainly succeeded in it to his heart's content, though this time his very large share of the original sin of picturesqueness and romanticism broke out so strongly that he borrowed little from realism except its pathologic horrors. Since Miss Robins's memorable exploit in "Alan's Wife" we have had nothing so harrowing on the stage; and it should be noted, for guidance in future experiments in audience torture, that in both instances the limit of the victims' susceptibility was reached before the end of the second act, at which exhaustion produced callousness. Mrs. Alving, who spared us by making the best of her sorrows instead of the worst of them, preserved our sympathy up to the last; but Oswald, who showed no mercy, might have been burnt alive in the orphanage without a throb of compassion. Mr. Leonard Outram improved prodigiously on his old impersonation of Pastor Manders. In 1891 he was still comparatively fresh from the apprenticeship as a heroic rhetorical actor which served him so well when he played Valence to Miss Alma Murray's Colombe for the Browning Society; and his stiff and cautious performance probably meant nothing but cleverly concealed bewilderment. This time Mr. Outram really achieved the character, though he would probably please a popular audience better by making more of that babyish side of him which excites the indulgent affection of Mrs. Alving, and less of the moral cowardice and futility posing as virtue and optimism which brings down on him the contemptuous judgment of Ibsen himself. Miss Kingsley's attractions, made as familiar to us by the pencil of Mr. Rothenstein as Miss Dorothy Dene's by that of Leighton, were excellently fitted to Regina; and Mr. Norreys Connell, after a somewhat unpromising beginning, played Engstrand with much zest and humor.

Other Reviews

Other Reviews

**"An Articulate 'Ghosts'."
By Sylvie Drake**

March 15, 1993, Copyright, 1993, *Los Angeles Times*. Reprinted by permission.

SAN DIEGO—One thing Norway and the United States have in common is a puritanical heritage. It usually plays havoc with our protestations of freedom and equality, and especially with freedom of speech. We see contradiction at work on a daily basis in the endless debate over such items as art, abortion, homosexuality, pornography and civil rights.

The analogy between this state of affairs and the dark world of Victorian Norway comes into sharp focus in director Jack O'Brien's lucid revival of Henrik Ibsen's "Ghosts," which opened Saturday at the Old Globe Theatre's Cassius Carter Centre Stage.

You know. The play about syphilis and the sins of the fathers being visited upon the sons.

In this case, it is the return of the afflicted son Osvald (Christopher Collet) to the home of his supposedly emancipated mother, Mrs. Alving (Patricia Conolly). It is a bitter irony for this powerful woman, who has made a life's work of suffering her husband's depravities while concealing them from the world, to find them so vengefully brought home. Pivotal to the dialectic is the mentor role of rigid Pastor Manders (Richard Easton), a lethal pillar of propriety.

Lace the plot with the complication of Capt. Alving's illegitimate daughter Regina—or Regine, as she is called here—and her designs on Osvald, and you have the classic well-made play, driven by shock and discourse.

It's fire and brimstone time about sin and retribution that has more echoes in our modern world than even Ibsen dreamed of. Take AIDS, and the high cost of denial. The production at the Carter doesn't miss a temblor. And its aftershocks constitute a powerful rebuke to lingering intolerance and persistent narrow thinking.

Lucky the young person who has never seen "Ghosts" before and can therefore be struck by its reverberations at the Carter. Luckier still the older person who *has* seen "Ghosts," and should find renewed admiration for Ibsen's modernity—a modernity not always so apparent in his plays, though certainly in "A Doll's House," "Hedda Gabler" and "Ghosts." Especially "Ghosts."

Perhaps the analogy in the case of "Ghosts" is enhanced by the presence next door of "Falsettos," the William Finn and James Lapine musical about tolerance and AIDS. ("Falsettos," in previews at the Globe, opens officially Thursday.) The aptness of the association did not escape O'Brien who noted the merit of presenting these two "plague plays" side by side.

All that separates them is a century—a long, tormented century in which we appear to have made almost no progress at all.

There is a dreaded tendency in American theater to play Ibsen solemnly and two-dimensionally; in other words, to play the obvious, which almost always spells theatrical suicide. So a great deal of credit goes to O'Brien for delivering a production of "Ghosts" that is dramatically palatable without minimizing the seriousness of its subject, and easy on the ear thanks to a richly current translation by Nicholas Rudall.

What makes this revival captivating, aside from the flow of the language, is O'Brien's focus on the actor as motivational force. This enlarges the written word and makes it flesh, giving the play subtlety and dimension.

This enhancement is exemplified by Easton's masterful portrayal of Manders, a role whose centrality is all too frequently undervalued. Not here. His Manders is a well-meaning menace, a fearful fool with a head full of the wrong ideas, who is virtually caged by his views. Without Easton, the production might have been far less than it is.

Conolly's Mrs. Alving is almost as major an undertaking. In the disdainful curl of her lip or the habit she has of staring off into the distance, as if looking at her surroundings would be too painful, Conolly provides a clue to this controlling woman's downfall, the arrogant edge of overconfidence that turns drama to tragedy. Even her tendency to posture and attitudinize works to the role's advantage.

Emily Bly's insolent Regina is a thorn in all their sides, a dangerous presence that symbolizes the futility of lies (of which she is a walking example). She is a sharp contrast to the transparently deceitful—and thereby neutralized—Engstrand, played with his usual muted flourish by Jonathan McMurtry.

Collet's Osvald is slightly more problematic, not in his performance as the injured innocent baffled by the turn of events, which is on target, but because his verbal delivery, in contrast to the others, is too casually contemporary.

Dona Granata has dressed everyone in autumnal clothes, as if in mourning for the "ghosts of dead ideas," making sure nonetheless that the women are endowed with the sensuous hour-glass figures of the period. Ralph Funicello's simple setting of tables and chairs is given atmosphere by Ashley York Kennedy's surreptitious lights.

The effect is eloquently dirgeful, in an articulate production strongly rooted in the present.

Other Reviews

CAST:

Emily Bly	Regine
Jonathan McMurty	Engstrand
Richard Easton	Pastor Manders
Patricia Conolly	Mrs. Alving
Christopher Collet	Oswald

Director: Jack O'Brien. Playwright: Henrik Ibsen. Translator: Nicholas Rudall. Sets: Ralph Funicello. Lights: Ashley York Kennedy. Costumes: Dona Granata. Sound: Jeff Ladman. Dramaturg: Anne Charlotte-Harvey. Production stage manager: Douglas Pagliotti.

**"AIT Stages Haunting 'Ghosts'."
By Christopher Rawson**

June 27, 1985. *The Pittsburgh Post-Gazette.*

All the ghosts sifting through Henrik Ibsen's text are present and accounted for in the American Ibsen Theater's "Ghosts"—the heritage of spiritual and physical decay, the sins of the parents, the folly of the children, skeletons, remorse and dead ideals.

But in this opening production of the AIT's third season, there is nothing in the least ghostly. In performance Ibsen can seem musty, swathed in Victorian bric-a-brac. Not here. Director Travis Preston's production keeps coming after you with a meat cleaver in one hand and a glint in its eye for 110 minutes uninterrupted by intermission.

The AIT has lost none of its nerve. Its work is part of the eclectic, nonrealist theatricalism abroad in today's American theater. Like Preston's "Doll House" in 1983, "Ghosts" explores its subtexts, often illuminating them with expressionistic flashes.

Knowing what we do of Ibsen's iconoclasm and quest for new theatrical technique, I'm convinced he would have approved of Preston's unconventional mix of modern and 19th-century elements. But the true test is *our* response. Mine was to be progressively intrigued, impressed, fascinated and finally moved.

Rolf Fjelde's translation is faithful. The austere plot retains the iron inevitability of Greek tragedy as Mrs. Alving, a wealthy widow, gradually uncovers the truths about herself, her son, a young woman named Regina, her dead husband and her clergyman, Pastor Manders.

Preston's and dramaturg Royston Coppenger's central stylistic idea is to heighten and shape the text with gestures and motifs from horror films. But these are just the lurid peaks. Look closely and you'll see a careful control of ideas and themes.

As before, Preston is supported by designer Christopher Barreca, who has turned the Chatham College Eddy Theater inside-out. The audience sits on the stage, looking toward the actors on the forestage and beyond them to the bank of empty seats. Necessarily, no one is admitted after the start of the play.

The auditorium is briefly used for action, but primarily it is empty, dominated by a huge golden astrolabe—an elegant but coldly mathematical "sun," the clockwork God of a culture that has lost its traditional faith.

On the set are statues of the five characters—their ghosts, or the externals by which we often judge others? A packed dirt floor provides extra intimacy, softening sounds and facilitating some carefully planned dramatic moments. The statues' placement implies a great deal about relationships, and soon they seem additional actors as characters move them, assault them and sometimes talk to them in preference to their human counterparts.

Barreca's design is continuously suggestive. One payoff comes when the handsome red curtain closes at just the necessary moment, wrapping the audience and the Alving living room in the claustrophobia of the gathering tragedy, while Osvald speaks of the "cherry red velvet draperies" of his fevered brain.

Preston devises a telling entrance for each character. Even the most casual gestures are calibrated for precise effect. Unfortunately, the most *florid* gestures sometimes are not. This is the defect of the production's vigorous virtues. And our surprise or laughter at some of the flashes of melodrama help relieve the tension, before it screws itself up to a tighter pitch.

Jennifer Harmon's Mrs. Alving is as good as any performance I've seen in Pittsburgh. It would be worth a second visit just to feast on all that goes on in her eyes. Steven McHattie's passionate Manders gives her a far fitter adversary than the reactionary fool you usually see.

Often played for laughs is the reprobate Engstrand, but Robert Toperzer makes him a robust scourge sent to these people for their sins. Corliss Preston is a plausible Regina, carrying off difficult business with aplomb.

Only John Rubin's Osvald is disappointing. Osvald is a whiny poseur to start with, and Rubin lacks the necessary precision to keep the melodrama from getting out of hand. But his final moment, like McHattie's, is very fine.

Compared to this "Ghosts," most of the theater we normally see is only television—passive and pallid.

Other Reviews

"Liv Ullmann Is the Star of 'Ghosts'."
By Mel Gussow

August 31, 1982, *The New York Times.*

New York: Ibsen's "Ghosts" is a symbolic ghost story as well as a tragedy of classic proportions, gradually yielding up its secrets as characters realize the sham of their illusions. Mystery is one of several important elements missing from the production starring Liv Ullmann that opened last night at the Brooks Atkinson Theater.

John Neville gives the evening's most persuasive performance in the role of the pietistic Pastor Manders, but as director—replacing John Madden before the play opened in New York—he has averted the darker recesses of the play. Rarely do we feel the intensity and the metaphorical mist of unforgiving memory that pervade this blighted Nordic household. Too much of the acting is single-edged. Furthermore, the setting (by Kevin Rupnik) is bright and cheerful. There is no sense of the interminable inclement weather outside, and there is an insufficient indication of the demons within. This version of "Ghosts" is not chilling.

It has been said that the play, written directly after "A Doll's House," represents the reverse side of the Ibsenian coin, posing the question: What would have happened if Nora had not slammed the door, but had remained victimized within her oppressive marriage? The author's answer is that she would have turned into Mrs. Alving, a woman who has dedicated herself to a false ideal—and wasted her life. To preserve the sanctity of her marriage, and to assure the purity of her son, she has created a fiction, making the world believe that her dissolute husband was a paragon of virtue. It is Mrs. Alving's awakening to the hollowness of blind duty that provides the main dramatic thrust.

Temperamentally, the role of Mrs. Alving suits Miss Ullmann better than her previous New York stage ventures, with the definite exception of her virtuoso one-woman performance of Cocteau's "The Human Voice." Although she is more youthful than many who have previously played Mrs. Alving, she can convey the necessary maturity and dignity. In contrast, it was difficult to believe her on stage as a doll-wife and as a down-and-out "Anna Christie."

In "Ghosts," the picture she presents is of a formidable keeper of the flame—with a determination that one can read in her erect bearing. As an actress, she rises to her most demanding scenes. Her face flushes as she attacks society for its sins, "its dead ideals and lifeless old beliefs."

IBSEN'S GHOSTS: A DRAMATURGICAL SOURCEBOOK

Sympathetically she marshals herself to the needs of her diseased son in the play's climax.

However, at other moments she is a figure of placidity. For example, when Manders and the unscrupulous carpenter, Engstrand, have a first-act colloquy, Mrs. Alving has to remain silent on stage for a long period. Miss Ullmann is not only silent, but almost immobile. Other times, when she is speaking, her voice is expressionless. She may have the emotional range to encompass the role, but at least in English, she appears to lack the vocal dexterity. For obvious reasons, one never noticed this disparity in her superb acting in films by Ingmar Bergman.

On the other hand, there is Mr. Neville, with his classically tuned voice and theatrical ease, as he keeps Manders from becoming a bore. He is so sincere about his sanctimony and his devotion to duty that he is amusing. Just before the pastor is to dedicate an orphanage in honor of Mrs. Alving's husband, she offers shocking revelations about her marital sufferings. He is aghast, and wonders, "How am I going to deliver my sermon?" Mr. Neville makes the question plaintive. The actor also has an urbane manner and look; one can believe, as one should, that there was once a promise of romance between him and Mrs. Alving.

The other three in the cast seem to have stepped in from a different, melodramatic production. Edward Binns neglects the Dickensian richness of Engstrand, and makes him simply a scoundrel. As his daughter, Mrs. Alving's maid, Jane Murray is transparent about her motivations. With flirtatious smiles, she lets us know far too easily that she has set her cap for the young master of the house and is pleased as punch about her possibilities. As the son, Kevin Spacey also accents one note, youthful ardor, and never convinces us that he has artistic inclinations or a terminal illness.

On the credit side, Arthur Kopit's translation is both colloquial and faithful to its source, and Theoni V. Aldredge's costumes are stylishly in character. The evening has its isolated moments of effectiveness, but it does not illuminate Ibsen. In direct contrast, there is the brilliant ensemble production of "A Doll's House," currently at the Royal Shakespeare Company in London.

GHOSTS, by Henrik Ibsen; adaptation by Arthur Kopit; directed by John Neville; scenery designed by Kevin Rupnik; costumes designed by Theoni V. Aldredge; lighting designed by Martin Aronstein. Presented by the John F. Kennedy Center, the CBS Broadcast Group and James M. Nederlander. At the Brooks Atkinson Theater, 256 West 47th Street.

Other Reviews

The Cast:

Regina Engstrand	Jane Murray
Jacob Engstrand	Edward Binns
Pastor Manders	John Neville
Mrs. Helen Alving	Liv Ullmann
Oswald Alving	Kevin Spacey

**"A Great Landmark Is Weakly Revived."
By Louis Kronenberger**

February 18, 1948 *PM Exclusive*.

Time, in taking from *Ghosts* much of its original purpose, has taken, too, something of its original power. Nor did the play ever, perhaps, represent Ibsen at his *artistic* best. Yet anybody with a spark of historical imagination must see that no mightier hammer-blow was struck in all of 19th-century drama; and that few fiercer blasts against an existing social morality are to be found anywhere in literature. Certainly in some ways the play is terrific still. As the masterly first act begins uncoiling; as Mrs. Alving, having been brutally rebuked by Pastor Manders, turns round and brutally rebuts him, we feel that a whole era, so to speak, has shifted its weight. And while Ibsen with one hand turns a highly respectable dwelling into an all-glass house, with the other hand he is already busy throwing stones. And what stones, thrown at what statues! Half the moral statuary of the age ends by being toppled from its pedestals. The role of woman, the rights of a wife, the responsibilites of a moral adviser; the dangers of concealment, the concept of duty, the bugbear of respectability–all these loom as large in *Ghosts* as the more vivid of sins of the fathers or mercy-killing of the children.

* * * *

If they all do not loom as large in our age as they did in Ibsen's dramatically at least (thanks to Ibsen's own sense of drama) there is still life in them. In the right hands, as Nazimova proved a dozen years ago, *Ghosts* is still powerful. In the wrong hands, as the current production makes all too plain, *Ghosts* grows pretty ponderous, exhibiting its period weaknesses much more than its permanent strength. At the Cort Monday night, the battle *Ghosts* was waging seemed over long ago; whereas we could have been made to feel that the *kind* of battle is never over. For Pastor Manders, at any rate, is an eternal type, an eternal menace:

the discreet cough and deprecating voice of respectability-at-any-cost; the homage, one might almost say, that virtue renders to vice. It is unfortunate that Ibsen over-did Manders; but that's as nothing compared with how Herbert Berghof over-does Ibsen. His Manders plays up everything it should try to play down, and almost belongs in one of those bad Victorian melodramas that are revived for laughs.

* * * *

And if Mr. Berghof's Manders is much too much, Miss LeGallienne's Mrs. Alving is somewhat too little. It is well enough spoken at times, but never sharply or movingly enough acted: it has rather a deadening effect on a play that must somehow acquire new life. Jean Hagen's Regina seems over-simplified; Robert Emhardt's Engstrand, effective only on character-part terms. As Oswald, Alfred Ryder has the toughest assignment in the play: he is far from notable in it, but he makes it the most satisfactory performance of the evening. His Oswald, for one thing, avoids a touch of the metallic that gets into most of the other roles, and that I think must be charged against Miss Webster's direction.

"At the Theater."
By Brooks Atkinson

February 17, 1948, *The New York Times*.

Let's consider that Eva Le Gallienne has done her duty by Ibsen's drama about duty. She plays the leading character in "Ghosts' as intelligently as Ibsen wrote the part. With the assistance of Margaret Webster, who directed the performance, she has mounted the play respectfully at the Cort, where it opened last evening. But nearly seventy years have slipped away since "Ghosts" shocked and outraged respectable people in Europe, although the British were not shocked and enraged until a little later. For critical judgments worse than those you are getting today, see the collection of noisome abuse William Archer put together and Shaw included in "The Quintessence of Ibsenism."

* * * *

Since "Ghosts" is planned and written by a master craftsman of the old school, it can still be made exciting by great acting or by a novel point of view. Nazimova gave it size and the aura of malevolence in her revival in 1935. Long ago Mrs. Fiske, overburdened with mischief, made a comedy out of it, which was obviously incorrect, though rather ingratiating.

Miss Le Gallienne is an honest actress with a lucid style. She knows Ibsen as thoroughly as she knows Chekhov, and the Mrs. Alving she plays is no doubt Ibsen's character. But his ponderous assault upon duty seems more like history now than a criticism of life. With the help of Shaw a couple of decades later Ibsen won that revolution. No one has ever done anything from a sense of duty since Ibsen and Shaw destroyed middle-class culture.

* * * *

As the chief prioress of intelligence in our theatre, Miss Le Gallienne gives us a liberated Mrs. Alving, who is no longer humbugged by polite superstition. Working in a small compass, as becomes her, she makes a carefully wrought design out of the character. A nod, a gleam, a fleeting gesture, a hurried step or two, a limp manner of sitting on the divan while the parson roars virtuous bombast—she designs a full-length character out of these and other bits of eloquence. She also speaks uncommonly well. But for a play that needs so much drive and strength to compensate for hardened arteries, Miss Le Gallienne's performance is weak. She leaves it well inside the grounds of the old folks' home.

And isn't the pace unnecessarily torpid? Everything else about the performance seems excellent. Alfred Ryder does a particularly good job with young Oswald, describing the whole progress of the character from filial affability through mounting terror to madness. As the pious stuffed shirt, Herbert Berghof gives a forceful performance that catches the sanctimonious stupidity of the part. Jean Hagen's scheming servant-girl is well played also—the commonness harshly breaking out of the demure reserve in the last scene. And Robert Emhart's obsequious knavery is amusing.

In designing and lighting the setting Watson Barratt has achieved complete illusion without crowding the stage with manufacturing and construction. His nineteenth-century drawing-room, stuffy without being dull, is one of his best pieces of work. There is a lot of good work in this revival of "Ghosts." But it does not conjure the dullness out of the script. Respectability can be as pernicious as duty. After a violent birth in 1881, "Ghosts" is respectable now.

Ibsen's Ghosts: A Dramaturgical Sourcebook

"Outdated Situations Haunt 'Ghosts' Revival."
By William Hawkins

February 17, 1948. *New York World-Telegram*.

There is no denying that Ibsen's "Ghosts" is potent drama. There is less denying that it concerns a mode of life and problems that no longer exist. They are not old enough to have historical interest in themselves. They are simply old-fashioned enough to breed impatience.

There is much about the play as a work of art that merits revival. But it must have vitality and sharpness, as well as archaic authenticity, or a lot of it is likely to seem silly.

Any wide exaggeration in the playing makes a mockery of the play. In this production there is no sustained tone, no subdued strength that can bring alive its very real horror. The cast's attack is varied to a point where it seems that no two actors agree on style.

This causes a constant shift of mood, until it is impossible to know what is expected of an onlooker. His only hope is to dissociate the performance from the play, which is quite a trick and not the pleasantest form of theater going.

The most remarkable asset of the play is the way Ibsen in a few consecutive hours reveals the entire life story of his characters. One learns of some three decades in Mrs. Alving's existence, from the time she was first urged into marriage, through her long bout with lies, to the devastation of her final summoning of truth.

She has hated the false legend she preserved about her dissolute husband. But when she steels herself to be honest with her son, the truth sends him into the insanity he dreaded.

Stimulated to Truth

The superficial standards and hypocrisy of Manders, whom she has loved, stimulate her to truthfulness.

Engstrand, the carpenter, has been a slovenly pawn who saved Alving's name when he fathered a serving maid's child. Regina has the willful greed of the dead Alving, and young Oswald has inherited his eagerness for excitement, but more importantly his fatal disease.

Mrs. Alving's desire to meet life on honest terms, and the sacrifices she makes for her son are timeless. The life she has had to lead, and the boy's inheritance of disease are presently unthinkable for people of even much less means.

Only a slight false note, or the substitution of pedestrian awe for dignity in admitting passe conventions, makes the play a tiresome relic. In this case it barely survives.

Inner Intensity

Miss Le Gallienne is usually more successful than the rest. She has an inner intensity that can hold interest through long conversational scenes, and except for emphasizing manual tricks, brings power to emotional moments.

In marking the intellectual facets of Mrs. Alving she conveys the stubborn exhaustion of her deceptive life, but never wholly reveals the steel will or the capacity for elaborate wiles such a woman must have had.

The bare lines written for the Rev. Manders reveal all that is necessary to know about him. Herbert Berghof stylizes the role with indignant postures, until the man becomes a travesty rather than a tragically deluded figure.

Robert Emhardt is successful at depicting the devious Engstrand, and Jean Hagan has temper and assurance in what always seems the thankless role of Regina. Alfred Ryder is an adequate Oswald, though he seems more like a well-mannered young salesman than a hypersensitive artist.

"Bleak Night at Mrs. Alving's."
By Ward Morehouse

February 17, 1948. *The Sun.*

The woes of Mrs. Alving and her tortured household were brought back to the New York stage last night, Eva LeGallienne coming forth at the Cort in her own translation of the Ibsen tragedy. It's a plodding and unimpressive revival of a play that has belonged to the theater for more than half a century.

You must know, by now, the substance of Ibsen's tale of suffering in western Norway—the story of Oswald, the young painter, who is a victim of a disease inherited from a dissolute father, and who finally becomes a hopeless imbecile, with his terrified mother bound by her promise to administer poison.

"Ghosts," which is Ibsen's bitter indictment of hypocritical conventions and the acceptance of duty in marriage regardless of the circumstances, can often be powerful and vibrant drama. It was when Nazimova played it at the Empire thirteen years ago. But there is listlessness instead of sustained intensity in this new LeGallienne-Margaret Webster production.

Miss LeGallienne, in her playing as Mrs. Alving, has some effective moments, but she projects coldness rather than anguish; it is a jerky, straining peformance, and one that offers only occasional excitement. Herbert Berghof is quite miscast as the futile and pious Pastor Manders, an advocate of fundamentalism. He contributes materially to the clumsiness of the production with his broad and declamatory performance. Alfred Ryder does well enough as Oswald, whose agonies are attributed to the sins of the father, and so does Jean Hagen as the earthy, human, buxom Regina, who wants nothing to do with the care of an invalid. Robert Emhardt gets a good deal of a characterization into the role of the sly blackguard, Engstrand.

'Ghosts" is strong-meat drama that comes to a hideous conclusion. It loses something of its theatrical excitement in Miss LeGallienne's translation and it is not helped along by last night's uninspired performance at the Cort.

Contributors

LOU ANDREAS-SALOMÉ— Described by Anaïs Nin as a woman who "symbolizes the struggle to transcend conventions and traditions in ideas and in living," Lou Andreas-Salomé's book *Henrik Ibsens Frauen-Gestalten (Ibsen's Heroines)* first appeared in 1892 and was enthusiastically hailed by Ibsen himself. A contemporary Norwegian critic, Arne Garborg, acclaimed: "The book is a poetically interpretative representation through which Ibsen's characters are reborn." Born in 1861, Lou Andreas-Salomé was on intimate terms with such men as Rainer Maria Rilke, Sigmund Freud, and Friedrich Nietzsche, who called her "the most intelligent of all women." Possessing charismatic beauty coupled with a strong will, Andreas-Salomé wrote a book about those prototypes of women struggling to overcome the confines imposed by the social *milieu* of the day. In *Ibsen's Heroines*, Andreas-Salomé's psychological, impressionistic approach uncovers the essential crisis of will and spirit within her analysis of the interconnected nature of tragedy and exultation in Ibsen's work. Lou Andreas-Salomé died in 1937.

WILLIAM ARCHER—Born in 1856, William Archer was a British critic, dramatist, and translator of Henrik Ibsen. Archer began his career as a journalist on the *Edinburgh Evening News*, moved to London in 1878, and was drama critic successively for the *London Figaro*, the *World*, the *Tribune*, and the *Nation*. Among his critical works were *English Dramatists of Today* (1882), *Masks or Faces* (1888), and *The Old Drama and the New* (1923). He was a friend of George Bernard Shaw and joined with Shaw in enthusiastic praise and support of Henrik Ibsen. Ibsen was Archer's model playwright, and his translations of Ibsen (collected 1906–8) did as much as his own writings on Ibsen to spread the Norwegian playwright's ideas and fame. William Archer died in 1924.

RICK DAVIS—Co-translator of *Ghosts*, Rick Davis collaborated with Brian Johnston on the volume *Ibsen: Four Major Plays* (1995), published by Smith & Kraus. Their Ibsen texts have been performed at Center Stage, Baltimore; the Alliance Theatre, Atlanta; Alabama Shakespeare Festival; Perseverance Theatre in Alaska; Critical Mass Theater in Austin, Texas, and a variety of other professional and academic theaters. Rick is currently Artistic Director of Theater of the First Amendment, the resident professional theater at George Mason University in Fairfax, Virginia. He has directed theater and opera in regional companies across the U.S., including Center Stage, Opera Idaho, Players Theater Columbus, Lake George Opera Festival, Delaware Theatre Company, and the American Ibsen Theater, which he co-founded. Rick was educated at Lawrence University and the Yale School of Drama, and has taught at Washington University, Goucher College, the Johns Hopkins University, and George Mason University.

FRANCIS FERGUSSON—The late Francis Fergusson was a widely influential critic and analyst of the forms of drama, who was, until his retirement in 1969, University Professor of Comparative Literature at Rutgers University in New Brunswick, New Jersey. He was also a noted lecturer at many colleges and universities across the country. His book, *The Idea of a Theatre,* published by Princeton University Press, is considered a seminal work in understanding the development of modern drama. Besides a study of Dante's *Purgatorio,* he was also the author of *The Human Image in Dramatic Literature.* Professor Fergusson taught previously at Bennington College in Bennington, Vermont, and was a member of J. Robert Oppenheimer's Institute for Advanced Study at Princeton University.

ROLF FJELDE—Rolf Fjelde was born in New York City of Scandinavian ancestry. He was educated at Yale University, including the Yale School of Drama, and at Columbia University. His poetry and criticism has appeared in many leading periodicals, as well as in two collections of verse; and his original plays and Ibsen translations have been staged in England, Norway, Canada, and throughout the United States. He has edited *Ibsen: A Collection of Critical Essays* in the Twentieth Century Views Series and translated the final twelve-play realistic cycle in the volume *Ibsen: The Complete Major Prose Plays.* Mr. Fjelde is founding president of the Ibsen Society of America. He currently teaches drama and film at Pratt Institute in New York City. He is a recipient of the Royal Medal of St. Olav from the King of Norway, as well as the Academy Award in Literature from the American Academy of Arts and Letters.

EMMA GOLDMAN—Activist, feminist, philosopher, and professed anarchist, Emma Goldman's pioneering 1914 work *Social Significance in Modern Drama* was one of the first to bridge modern drama and political philosophy, pointing out the ways in which 'modern' drama can become a theatre of social empowerment. In 1887, Ms. Goldman's radicalization commenced with the Haymarket affair in Chicago, wherein a group of anarchists were charged in a bomb-throwing incident and executed after a trial that even at the time was recognized as unjust. Emma Goldman became notorious in 1892 when she was involved in an unsuccessful assassination attempt on Henry Clay Frick, a Pittsburgh steel magnate. True infamy took hold in 1901 when newspapers ran banner headlines claiming that the assassin of President William McKinley, Leon Czolgosz, confessed

Contributors

to having been incited to assassinate President McKinley by Emma Goldman. Although a fabrication, the accusation severed her ties to all but the extreme far left fringes of American society. The one political ideology that Emma Goldman held most dear was that of anarchism, which she defined as "the philosophy of a new social order based on liberty unrestricted by man-made law; the theory that all forms of government rest on violence, and are therefore wrong and harmful, as well as unnecessary." So radical was her political thought that the American government had "Red Emma" declared an enemy of the state and deported to Russia in 1919. By 1921 Emma had become greatly disillusioned with communism. When she began to openly criticize the Soviet regime they too asked her to leave the country. Emma Goldman died in Canada, in political exile, in 1940.

BRIAN JOHNSTON—Brian Johnston graduated from Cambridge University, England and has taught at the Norges Laererhogskolen, Trondheim, Norway; at Cambridge University; at Northwestern University, the University of California (Berkeley and Santa Barbara); at the University of Washington, Seattle, Washington; at Yarmouk University, Irbid, Jordan; and at the American University of Beirut, Beirut, Lebanon. From 1983 through 1986, Professor Johnston was the Resident Dramaturg of the American Ibsen Theatre in Pittsburgh, Pennsylvania, the first attempt to found a theatre in the United States devoted openly to Henrik Ibsen's dramatic and social ideals. He currently teaches Dramatic Literature at Carnegie Mellon University in Pittsburgh, Pennsylvania. He is the author of three highly acclaimed studies of Ibsen's drama: *To the Third Empire: Ibsen's Early Drama* (University of Minnesota Press, 1980), *Text and Supertext in Ibsen's Drama* (1989) and *The Ibsen Cycle* (Revised Edition 1992), both published by the Pennsylvania State University Press in University Park, Pennsylvania. The Brian Johnston/Rick Davis translation of *Ghosts*, first appeared in *Ibsen: Four Major Plays* (1995) published by Smith and Kraus, Inc., of Lyme, New Hampshire. Smith and Kraus, Inc., published a second volume of translations, *Ibsen: Four Major Plays, Volume II*, containing Professor Johnston's translations of *Pillars of Society, The Wild Duck, Rosmersholm*, and *The Master Builder*, in 1996.

JAMES JOYCE—Born in Dublin, Ireland in 1882, James Joyce was a novelist noted for his experimental use of language and exploration of new literary methods in such large works of fiction as *Ulysses* (1922) and *Finnegan's Wake* (1939). Joyce was educated at University College, Dublin, where he studied languages and immersed himself in extracurricular activities, reading widely - particularly books not recommended by the Jesuits who staffed the college. He also took an active part in the college's Literary and

Historical Society. Greatly admiring Henrik Ibsen, Joyce learned Dano-Norwegian to read Ibsen's work in their original language, and had an article, "Ibsen's New Drama"—a review of *When We Dead Awaken*—published in the *London Fortnightly Review* in 1899 just after his 18th birthday. This early success confirmed Joyce in his resolution to become a writer and persuaded his family, friends, and teachers that the resolution was justified. Joyce died in Zurich in 1941.

DONALD MARINELLI—Editor of the *Dramaturgical Sourcebook Series* published by Carnegie Mellon University Press, Dr. Marinelli was for many years managing director of the scholarly theatre journal, *Theatre Three*, published by the Carnegie Mellon University College of Fine Arts. Dr. Marinelli is an Associate Professor of Drama & Arts Management at Carnegie Mellon and also serves as Co-Director of the *Entertainment Technology Center* (a joint initiative between the College of Fine Arts and the School of Computer Science). Dr. Marinelli is an affiliated faculty member in the H.J. Heinz III School of Public Policy and Management teaching in the Master of Arts Management program, and is a Fellow in the Studio for Creative Inquiry in Carnegie Mellon's College of Fine Arts. From 1981 until 1995 Professor Marinelli served as first Assistant and then Associate Head of Carnegie Mellon University's Drama Department. He is past president of the Theatre Association of Pennsylvania, which honored him with the *William T. Gardner Award for Contributions to Theatre in Pennsylvania* in 1994. Dr. Marinelli received his undergraduate education at the University of Tampa; a master's degree in clinical psychology from Duquesne University in Pittsburgh, Pennsylvania, and a doctorate in theatre from the University of Pittsburgh in 1987.

GEORGE BERNARD SHAW—Considered by many to be the pre-eminent theatre practitioner of the twentieth century, this Anglo-Irish dramatist, literary critic, and recipient of the Nobel Prize for Literature in 1925, was born in Dublin, Ireland in 1856 and died in England in 1950. He began his literary career as an unpublished novelist and speaker on a variety of topical subjects, mainly for the Fabian Society. His early critical writings spanned the spectrum of cultural topics, from music to art to literature and, most especially, drama. Shaw's interest in drama was fueled by his devotion to the work of Henrik Ibsen. Together with his close friend William Archer, Shaw championed Ibsen's work in Britain. In 1885, Shaw started work on his first play, *Widowers' Houses*, which was staged finally in 1892. This was followed by *Arms and the Man* (1894) which saw considerable success. His subsequent play, *Mrs. Warren's Profession* was written in 1893 but fell afoul of the Lord Chamberlain who banned the play because it concerned prostitution. The ban on the play wasn't lifted until

Contributors

1925. Shaw's run-in with the Lord Chamberlain reflected Shaw's desire to broach subjects previously taboo in the theatre, and to do so in a realistic manner. Thus began a prolific career as a dramatist that would see Shaw pen *Candida* (1895), *The Devil's Disciple* (1897), *Caesar and Cleopatra* (1898), *Man and Superman* (1903), *John Bull's Other Island* (1904), *Major Barbara* (1905), *The Doctor's Dilemma* (1906), *Misalliance* (1910), *Androcles and the Lion* (1912), *Pygmalion* (1913), *Heartbreak House* (1913-19), *Back to Methuselah* (1918-20) *Saint Joan* (1921) *The Apple Cart* (1930), *The Millionaress* (1935), *In Good King Charles' Golden Days* (1939), *Buoyant Billions* (1948), and *Far-Fetched Fables* (1950). Shaw's legacy is in the development of a drama of moral passion and of intellectual conflict and debate. His finely tuned comedy of manners, his ventures into symbolic farce and into a theatre of disbelief helped shape the theater of his era. So broad were his interests and critical intelligence that he helped mold the political, economic, and sociological thought of three generations.

Bibliography

Abrams, M. H. *Natural Supernaturalism: Tradition and Revolution in Nineteenth Century Literature,* New York: W. W. Norton, 1971.
Aeschylus. *The Libation Bearers.* In *Aeschylus I: Oresteia,* translated by Richmond Lattimore, 91–131. *The Complete Greek Tragedies,* edited by David Grene and Richmond Lattimore. Chicago: University of Chicago Press, 1953.
———. *The Oresteia.* Translated by Richmond Lattimore. Chicago: University of Chicago Press, 1951.
Anderson, A. R. "Ibsen and the Classical World." *The Classical Journal* XI (1916): 216–25.
Andreas-Salomé, Lou. *Ibsen's Heroines.* Edited, translated, and with an introduction by Siegfried Mandel. Redding, Conn.: Black Swan Books, 1985.
Archer, William. *The Old Drama and the New.* London: Heinemann, 1923.
———. *Playmaking.* New York: Dover Publications, 1960.
———. ed. *The Collected Works of Henrik Ibsen.* 13 vols. New York: Scribner, 1917.
Arestad, Sverre. "Ibsen's Concept of Tragedy." *PMLA* LXXIV (June, 1959): 285–97.
Atkinson, Brooks. "At the Theatre." *New York Times,* February 17, 1948.
Auerbach, Erich. *Mimesis: The Representation of Reality in Western Literature.* Translated by Willard R. Trask. Princeton: Princeton University Press, 1968 [1946].
Barnes, Howard. "LeGallienne's 'Ghosts.'" *New York Herald Tribune,* February 17, 1948 in *New York Theatre Critic's Reviews 1948.* New York: N.Y., 1948, pp. 343–344.
Barthes, Roland. "Theory of the Text." In *Untying the Text,* edited by Robert Young. London: Routledge and Kegan Paul, 1981.
Bennett, Benjamin. *Modern Drama and German Classicism: Renaissance from Lessing to Brecht.* Ithaca: Cornell University Press, 1979.
Bentley, Eric. *In Search of Theater.* New York: Alfred A. Knopf, 1953.
———. *The Life of the Drama.* New York: Atheneum, 1967.
———. *The Playwright as Thinker.* New York: Reynal and Hitchcock, 1946. Revised ed. San Diego, Cal.: Harcourt, Brace, Jovanovich, 1987.
———. ed. *The Theory of the Modern Stage.* New York: Penguin, 1968.
Beyer, Edvard. *Ibsen: The Man and His Work.* Translated by Marie Wells. New York: Taplinger Publishing Co., 1980.

Brandes, Georg. *Henrik Ibsen, Bjørnstjerne Bjørnson: Critical Studies.* London: William Heinemann, 1899.

——. *Main Currents in 19th Century Literature.* New York: Boni & Liveright, 1923.

Brustein, Robert: *The Theater of Revolt.* Boston: Little Brown, 1964.

Buchanan, Robert. "The Fleshly School of Poetry: Mr. D. G. Rossetti." *Contemporary Review,* no. 20 (London, 1871): 334–50.

Campbell, T. M. *Hebbel, Ibsen and the Analytical Exposition.* Heidelberg: C. Winter, 1922.

Cardullo, Bert. "Ghosts and Oedipus Rex." *Language Quarterly* 26.3–4 (1988): 47–48.

Carlson, Marvin. *Theories of the Drama.* Ithaca: Cornell University Press, 1984.

Clurman, Harold. *Ibsen.* New York: Macmillan, 1977.

Collins, R. G., ed. *From an Ancient to a Modern Theater.* Winnipeg: University of Manitoba Press, 1972.

Davis, Derek Russell. "A Reappraisal of Ibsen's *Ghosts.*" In *Henrik Ibsen.* Ed. James McFarlane. Middlesex, England, 1970, pp. 369–383.

Downs, Brian. *Ibsen: The Intellectual Background.* Cambridge: Cambridge University Press, 1948.

——. *Modern Norwegian Literature: 1860–1918.* Cambridge: Cambridge University Press, 1966.

——. *A Study of Six Plays by Ibsen.* Cambridge: Cambridge University Press, 1950.

Drake, Sylvie. "An Articulate 'Ghosts.'" *Los Angeles Times,* March 15, 1993.

Dukes, Ashley. *Modern Dramatists.* London: F. Palmer, 1911.

Durbach, Errol. *"Ibsen the Romantic": Analogues of Paradise in the Later Plays.* Athens: University of Georgia Press, 1982.

——. ed. *Ibsen and the Theatre: Essays in Celebration of the 150th Anniversary of Henrik Ibsen's Birth.* London: Macmillan, 1980.

Eagleton, Terry. *Literary Theory: An Introduction.* Minneapolis: University of Minnesota Press, 1983.

——. "Text, Ideology, Realism." In *Literature and Society,* edited by Edward Said, 149–73. Baltimore: John Hopkins University Press, 1980.

Edwards, Herbert. "Henry James and Ibsen." *American Literature,* 54, no. 2 (May 1952): 208–23.

Egan, Micheal, ed. *Ibsen: The Critical Heritage.* London: Routledge and Kegan Paul, 1972.

Eliade, Mircea. *Cosmos and History.* Translated by Willard R. Trask. New York: Harper, 1959.

Euripides. *The Bacchae.* Translated by William Arrowsmith. Chicago: University of Chicago Press, 1959.
———. *The Bakkhai.* Translated by Robert Bagg. Amherst: University of Massachusetts Press, 1978.
Ewbank, Inga-Stina. "Ibsen's Dramatic Language." In *Contemporary Approaches to Ibsen.* Oslo: Universitetsforlaget (Norwegian Research Council for Science and Humanities), 1966.
Faaland, Josef. *Henrik Ibsen og antikken* (Henrik Ibsen and the Ancients). Oslo: Johan Grundt Tanum, 1943.
Fergusson, Francis. *The Idea of a Theater.* Princeton: Princeton University Press, 1949.
Findlay, J. N. *Hegel: A Re-Examination.* New York: Macmillan, 1958.
Fjelde, Rolf. "The Dimensions of Ibsen's Realism." In *Contemporary Approaches to Ibsen,* vol. 2. Oslo: Universitetsforlaget (Norwegian Research Council for Science and Humanities), 1971. 161–80.
———. ed. *Ibsen: A Collection of Essays.* Englewood Cliffs, N. J.: Prentice Hall, 1965.
———. trans. and ed. *Ibsen: Four Major Plays, Vol II.* New York: New American Library, 1970.
Flores, Angel, ed. *Ibsen.* New York: Haskell House, 1966.
Freud, Sigmund. *Civilization and Its Discontents.* Translated and edited by James Strachey. New York: W. W. Norton, 1962.
———. Preface to his *Three Essays on the Theory of Sexuality.* 4th ed, edited by John Strachey. New York: Avon Books, 1965. (Originally published 1920).
Frye, Northrup. *Anatomy of Criticism: Four Essays.* Princeton: Princeton University Press, 1953.
Garton, Janet. *Facets of European Modernism: Essays in Honour of James McFarlane.* Norwich: University of East Anglia Press, 1985.
Gassner, John, and Edward Quinn, eds. *The Reader's Encyclopedia of World Drama.* New York: Crowell, 1969.
George, David, *Henrik Ibsen in Deutschland: Rezeption und Revision* Götlingen: Vandenhoeck & Ruprecht, 1968.
Goldman, Emma. *The Social Significance of Modern Drama.* New York: Applause Books, 1987.
Gosse, Edmund. *Henrik Ibsen.* New York: Scribner's, 1915.
Gray, Ronald. *Ibsen: A Dissenting View.* London: Cambridge University Press, 1977.
Grene, David. *Reality and the Heroic Pattern: Last Plays of Ibsen, Shakespear, and Sophocles.* Chicago: University of Chicago Press, 1967.

Grimm, Jacob. *Teutonic Mythology.* Translated by James Steven Stallybrass. 4 vols. London: George Bell and Sons, 1883–88. Reprint. New York: Dover Publications, 1966.

Gussow, Mel. "Liv Ullman is the Star of 'Ghosts'." *New York Times,* August 31, 1982.

Haakenson, Daniel, ed. *Contemporary Approaches to Ibsen,* Oslo: Unviersitetsforlaget, 1966.

———. *Contemporary Approaches to Ibsen* 2. Ibsen Yearbook 11. Oslo, 1971.

———. *Contemporary Approaches to Ibsen* 4. Reports from the Fourth International Ibsen Seminar, Oslo: 1978.

Haugen, Einar. *Ibsen's Drama: Author to Audience.* Minneapolis: University of Minnesota Press, 1979.

Hawkins, William. "Outdated Situations Haunt 'Ghosts' Revival." *New York World-Telegram,* February 17, 1948 in *New York Theatre Critic's Reviews 1948.* New York: N.Y., 1948, p. 346.

Hegel, Georg Wilhelm Friedrich. *Hegel on Tragedy.* Edited by Anne and Henry Paolucci. New York: Doubleday, 1962.

———. *Phänomenologie des Geistes.* Hamburg: Felix Meiner, 1952.

———. *The Philosophy of Hegel.* Edited by Carl Friedrich. New York: Modern Library, 1953.

———. *The Philosophy of History.* Translated by J. Sibree. New York: Dover, 1956.

———. *The Phenomenology of Mind.* 2d ed., rev., translated by J. B. Baillie. London: Allen and Unwin, 1949.

———. *The Phenomenology of Spirit.* Translated by A. V. Miller, with analysis of the text and foreword by J. N. Findlay. Oxford: Clarendon Press, 1977.

———. *The Philosophy of History.* Translated by J. Sibrée, with preface by Charles Hegel and J. Sibrée, and a new introduction by C. J. Friedrich. New York: Dover Publications, 1956.

———. *The Philosophy of Mind.* Translated by William Wallace and A. V. Miller. Oxford: Clarendon Press.

———. *Reason in History: A General Introduction to the Philosophy of History.* Translated with an introduction by Robert S. Hartman. Library of Liberal Arts Series. Indianapolis and New York: Bobbs-Merrill, 1953.

Heiberg, Hans. *Ibsen: A Portrait of the Artist.* Translated by John Tate. Coral Gables: University of Miami Press, 1969.

Heller, Otto. *Henrik Ibsen: Plays and Problems.* Boston: Houghton Mifflin, 1912.

Hemmer, Bjørn. "Italy in Ibsen's Art." *Contemporary Approaches to Ibsen* VI, 9–26. London: Norwegian University Press, 1988.

Highet, Gilbert. *The Classical Tradition.* New York: Oxford University Press, 1957.

Holtan, Orley I. *Mythic Patterns in Ibsen's Last Plays.* Minneapolis: University of Minnesota Press, 1970.

Homer. *The Iliad of Homer.* Translated by Richmond Lattimore. Chicago: University of Chicago Press, 1951.

———. *The Odyssey of Homer.* Translated by Richmond Lattimore. New York: Harper & Row, 1967.

Hornby, Richard. *Patterns in Ibsen's Middle Plays.* Lewisburg, PA.: Bucknell University Press, 1981.

Hyppolite, Jean. *Studies on Marx and Hegel.* New York: Basic Books, 1969.

Ibsen, Bergliot. *The Three Ibsens: Memories of Henrik, Suzannah and Sigurd.* Translated by Gerik Schjelderup. London: Hutchinson & Co., Ltd., 1951.

Ibsen, Henrik. *The Collected Works of Henrik Ibsen.* Edited by William Archer. 13 vols. New York: Scribner's, 1917.

———. *The Complete Major Prose Plays.* Translated and introduced by Rolf Fjelde. New York: NAL, 1978.

———. *Letters of Henrik Ibsen.* Translated and edited by J. N. Laurvik & M. Morison. New York: Duffield, 1908.

———. *Letters and Speeches.* Edited by Evert Sprinchorn. New York: Hill and Wang, 1964.

———. *The Oxford Ibsen.* 8 vols. Edited by James W. MacFarlane. Oxford: Oxford University Press, 1970–77.

———. *Samlede Verker. Hundreårsutgaven.* Edited by Francis Bull, Halvdan Koht, and Didrik Arup Seip. 21 vols. Oslo: Gyldendal, 1928–58.

Ibsen, Sigurd. *Human Quintessence.* New York: B. W. Huebsch, 1912.

Jacobsen, Per Schelde and Leavey, Barbara Fass. *Ibsen's Forsaken Mermen.* New York: New York University Press, 1988.

James, Henry. *The Scenic Art.* New York: Hill and Wang, 1948.

———. *The Scenic Art.* New Brunswick, NJ: Rutgers University Press, 1948.

Johnston, Brian. *To the Third Empire: Ibsen's Early Drama.* Minneapolis: University of Minnesota Press, 1980.

———. *Text and Supertext in Ibsen's Drama.* University Park: Pennsylvania State University Press, 1989.

———. *The Ibsen Cycle.* University Park: Pennsylvania State University Press, 1992.

———. "The 'Abstractions' of *Emperor and Galilean.*" *Ibsen News and Comment* 6 (1985): 11–18.

Jorgenson, Theodore. *Henrik Ibsen: A Study in Art and Personality.* Northfield, Minn.: St. Olaf Norwegian Institute, 1945.
———. *History of Norwegian Literature.* New York: Macmillan, 1933.
Joyce, James. "Epilogue to Ibsen's *Ghosts.* " In *Henrik Ibsen.* Ed. James McFarlane. Middlesex, England, 1970, pp. 383–385.
Kenner, Hugh. "Joyce and Ibsen's Naturalism." In *Critical Essays on Henrik Ibsen,* edited by Charles R. Lyons, 53–66. Boston: G. K. Hall, 1987.
Kierkegaard, Soren. *The Concept of Irony: With Constant Reference to Socrates.* New York: Harper & Row, 1966.
———. *Either/Or,* Vols. I and II. Princeton: Princeton University Press, 1971.
———. *For Self-Examination and Judge For Yourselves and Three Discourses.* Princeton: Princeton University Press, 1944.
———. *A Kierkegaard Anthology.* Edited by Robert Bretall. Princeton: Princeton University Press, 1973.
Kissel, Howard. "Ghosts." *Women's Wear Daily,* August 31, 1982 in *New York Theatre Critic's Reviews 1982.* New York: N.Y., 1982, pp. 238–239.
Knight, G. Wilson. *Henrik Ibsen.* Edinburgh: Oliver and Boyd, 1962; and New York: Grove, 1962.
Koht, Halvdan. *Henrik Ibsen.* Rev. ed. 2 vols. Oslo: Aschehaug, 1954.
Kronenberger, Louis. "A Great Landmark is Weakly Revived." *PM Exclusive,* February 18, 1948 in *New York Theatre Critic's Reviews 1948.* New York: N.Y., 1948, p. 341.
———. *Life of Ibsen.* New York: B. Blom, 1971.
Lavrin, Janko. *Ibsen: An Approach.* New York: Russell and Russell, Inc. 1969 [1950].
Lee, Jeanette. *The Ibsen Secret: A Key to the Prose Dramas of Henrik Ibsen.* New York: Putnam's 1907.
Levenson, Michael H. *A Genealogy of Modernism.* Cambridge: Cambridge University Press, 1986.
Levin, Harry. "The Wages of Satire." In *Literature and Society,* edited by Edward Said, 1–14. Baltimore: John Hopkins University Press, 1980.
Lyons, Charles. *Henrik Ibsen: The Divided Consciousness.* Carbondale: Southern Illinois University Press, 1972.
———. ed. *Critical Essays on Henrik Ibsen.* Boston: G. K. Hall & Co., 1987.
McFarlane, James W. *Ibsen and the Temper of Norwegian Literature,* London: 1960.
———. ed. *Discussions of Henrik Ibsen.* Boston: D. C. Heath & Co., 1962.
———. ed. *Ibsen: A Critical Anthology.* Harmondsworth: Penguin Books Ltd., 1970.
———. *Ibsen and Meaning: Studies, Essays and Prefaces 1953–87.* Norwich: Norvik, 1989.

McCarthey, Justin Huntley. *Impressions and Opinions.* London: 1914.
Marcuse, Herbert, *Eros and Civilization.* Boston: Beacon, 1955.
May, Keith M. *Ibsen and Shaw.* London: The Macmillan Press, 1985.
Meyer, Michael. *Henrik Ibsen.* New York: Ungar, 1972.
——. *Ibsen: A Biography.* 3 vols. London: Rupert Hart-Davis, 1967.
Morehouse, Ward. "Bleak Night at Mrs. Alving's." *The Sun,* February 17, 1948 in *New York Theatre Critic's Reviews 1948,* New York: N.Y., 1948, p. 346.
Moses, Montrose J. *Henrik Ibsen: The Man and His Plays.* New York: M. Kennerly, 1908.
Nelson, Don. "Liv Ullman in Colloquial 'Ghosts.'" *New York Daily News,* August 31, 1982 in *New York Theatre Critic's Reviews 1982.* New York: N.Y. 1982, pp. 240–241.
Nietzsche, Friedrich. *Beyond Good and Evil.* Translated by Walter Kaufmann. New York: Vintage, 1966.
——. *The Birth of Tragedy.* Translated by Francis Golffing. New York: Doubleday, 1954.
——. *The Birth of Tragedy and the Case of Wagner.* Translated by Walter Kaufmann. New York: Vintage Books, 1967.
——. *The Birth of Tragedy and the Geneology of Morals.* New York: Doubleday, 1956.
——. *The Portable Nietzsche.* Edited and translated by Walter Kaufmann. New York: Penguin, 1976.
Northam, John. *Ibsen: A Critical Study.* Cambridge: Cambridge University Press, 1973.
——. *Ibsen's Dramatic Method: A Study of the Prose Dramas.* London: Faber & Faber, Ltd., 1953.
Orme, Michael. *J. T. Grein.* London: John Murray, 1936.
Paludan-Müller, Frederik. *Adam Homo.* New York: The Twickenham Press, 1981 [1841–1848].
Peacock, Ronald. *The Poet in the Theatre.* New York: Hill and Wang, 1960
Pearce, John C. "Hegelian Ideas in Three Tragedies by Ibsen." *Scandinavian Studies* 34 (1962): 245–57.
Postlewait, Thomas, ed. *William Archer on Ibsen.* Westport, Conn: Greenwood Press, 1984.
Quigley, Austin. *The Modern Stage and Other Worlds.* New York: Methuen, 1985.
Rawson, Christopher. "AIT stages Haunting 'Ghosts.'" *Pittsburgh Post-Gazette,* June 27, 1985, Sec. A, p. 18.
Reich, John. "The Rebirth of Tragedy." In *From an Ancient to a Modern Theater,* edited by R. G. Collins, 1–12. Winnipeg: University of Manitoba Press, 1972.

Rhodes, Norman. *Ibsen and the Greeks*. Bucknell University Press, Lewisburg, Pa., Associated University Press, 1995.
Rilke, Rainer Maria. *Selected Letters, 1902–1926*. London: Quartet Books, 1988.
Rydberg, Viktor. *Teutonic Mythology*. Translated by Rasmus B. Anderson. London, Norronea Society, 1889.
Said, Edward, ed. *Literature and Society*. Baltimore: Johns Hopkins University Press, 1980.
Salomé, Lou. *Ibsen's Heroines*. Edited, translated, and with an introduction by Siegfried Mandel. Redding, Conn.: Black Swan Books, 1985.
Schánke, Robert A. *Ibsen in America*. Metuchen, N.J.: The Scarecrow Press, 1988.
Schiller, Friedrich von. *Friedrich Schiller: An Anthology for Our Time*. Translated and selected by Frederick Ungar. New York: Frederick Ungar, 1959.
——. *Naive and Sentimental Poetry/On the Sublime*. With introduction and notes by Julias A. Elias. New York: Frederick Ungar, 1966.
Selenick, Laurence, ed. *National Theater in Northern and Eastern Europe*. Cambridge: Cambridge University Press, 1991.
Seznec, Jean. *The Survival of the Pagan Gods*. New York: Harper, 1962.
Shaw, George Bernard. *The Quintessence of Ibsenism: Now Completed to the Death of Ibsen*. New York: Hill and Wang, 1957, 1964.
——. *Dramatic Opinion*, Vol II. New York: Brentano's, 1928.
Simonson, Robert. "The Literary Guy: Defining the Dramaturge." *Backstage*, December 8, 1995, pp. 21–23.
Soll, Ivan. *An Introduction to Hegel's Metaphysics*. Chicago: University of Chicago Press, 1969.
Sophocles. *Sophocles I: Oedipus the King*, translated by David Grene; *Antigone*, translated by Elizabeth Wyckoff; *Oedipus at Colonus*, translated by Robert Fitzgerald. Chicago: University of Chicago Press, 1954.
Sprinchorn, Evert, ed. *The Genius of the Scandinavian Theatre*. New York: NAL, Mentor, 1964.
——. *Ibsen: Letters and Speeches*. New York: Hill & Wang, 1964.
Steegmuller, Francis, ed. *The Letters of Gustave Flaubert 1857–1880*. London: Faber & Faber, 1982.
Steiner, George. *Antigones*. New York: Oxford University Press, 1974.
——. *The Death of Tragedy*. New York: Oxford University Press, 1980.
Tennant, P. F. D. *Ibsen's Dramatic Technique*. London: Cambridge University Press, 1948.
Theoharis, Theoharis, C. *Ibsen's Drama: Right Action and Tragic Joy*. New York: St. Martin's Press, 1996.
Törnqvist, Egil. *Transposing Drama: Studies in Representation*. New York: St. Martin's, 1991.

Valency, Maurice. *The Flower and the Castle: Introduction to Modern Drama.* New York: Macmillan, 1963.
Van Laan, Thomas F. "Ibsen's Beginnings." *Journal of Dramatic Theory and Criticism* 3.ii (1989): 19–36.
Weigand, Hermann J. *The Modern Ibsen: A Reconsideration.* New York: 1960 [1925].
Wicksteed, Phillip H., *Four Lectures on Henrik Ibsen.* Port Washington, NY: Kennikat Press, 1969 [1892].
Williams, Raymond. "Ibsen's Non-Theatrical Plays," In *Discussions of Henrik Ibsen,* edited by James W. McFarlane. Boston: D. C. Heath & Co., 1962.
Woerner, R., *Henrik Ibsen,* 2 vols. Munich: Becksche, 1910, [1900].
———. *Henrik Ibsens Jugenddramen.* Munich: Becksche, 1895.
Young, Robert, ed., *Untying the Text: a Poststructuralist Reader.* London: Routledge and Kegan Paul, 1987 [1981].
Ystad, Vigdis. "Tragedy in Ibsen's Art." *Contemporary Approaches to Ibsen* VI, 69–80. London: Norwegian University Press, 1988.